CAMPUS PROGRESS

Supporting the Scholarship of

Teaching and Learning

Barbara L. Cambridge, volume editor

Marcia Babb, Constance E. Cook, Richard Gale, Devorah Lieberman, Duane Roen, and Ellen L. Wert, section editors

Stephanie Cole, editorial assistant

AAHE
AMERICAN ASSOCIATION
for HIGHER EDUCATION™

AAHE is an independent, membership-based, nonprofit organization dedicated to building human capital for higher education. AAHE is the source of choice for information about higher education on issues that matter in a democratic multi-racial society; AAHE promotes and disseminates examples of effective educational practices that address those issues.

AAHE members are a national talent pool willing and ready to share their expertise with colleagues in higher education, policymakers, media professionals, and the public at large.

American Association for Higher Education
One Dupont Circle, Suite 360
Washington, DC 20036-1143
(202) 293-6440
www.aahe.org

The American Association for Higher Education, as a partner in the Carnegie Academy for the Scholarship of Teaching and Learning (CASTL), has worked with more than 200 campuses to foster the scholarship of teaching and learning at the institutional level. The experience and commitment of colleges and universities in the CASTL Campus Program have yielded the extensive and useful knowledge in this book.

For more information about the Campus Program, go to http://chef.aahe.org/chef/portal. At the time of this writing, 12 national clusters are providing leadership into the future with the active support of AAHE and The Carnegie Foundation for the Advancement of Teaching.

The centrality of collaboration, one theme of this book, is epitomized in AAHE's and Carnegie's work together on the scholarship of teaching and learning. Carnegie's Marcia Babb, Richard Gale, Pat Hutchings, Mary Huber, and Lee Shulman exhibit the kind of collegiality that makes learning and even doing hard work worthwhile.

Recommended bibliographic listing:
Cambridge, B. L. (Ed.). (2004). *Campus progress: Supporting the scholarship of teaching and learning.* Washington, DC: American Association for Higher Education.

Any opinions expressed in this publication are the contributors' and do not necessarily represent the views of the American Association for Higher Education or its members.

To order additional copies of this publication, call the American Association for Higher Education's fulfillment office at (301) 645-6051 or visit www.aahe.org/pubs. AAHE members receive special pricing. Bulk orders are offered at a discount.

10 9 8 7 6 5 4 3 2 1

ISBN: 1-56377-066-0

TABLE OF CONTENTS

Transforming Campus Cultures Through the Scholarship of Teaching and Learning

Barbara L. Cambridge
American Association for Higher Education

Passion has a lot to do with knowledge. When a group of people feels strongly about something, investigates and develops it, and shares results of inquiries and actions, it becomes a community of practice. The scholarship of teaching and learning constitutes multiple communities of practice that are generating energy, increasing knowledge, influencing teaching and learning locally and nationally, and changing the culture of institutions of higher education.

"Communities of practice are groups of people who share a concern, a set of problems, or a passion about a topic, and who deepen their knowledge and expertise in this area by interacting on an ongoing basis" (Wenger, McDermott, & Snyder, 2002, p. 4). *Campus Progress: Supporting the Scholarship of Teaching and Learning* examines features of communities of practice focused on the scholarship of teaching and learning, developed within and across disciplines, and situated at both national and local levels. What emerges is a picture of significant, increasingly transformational change.

Two frameworks are helpful in surveying the reports from campuses in this book. First, in their research about communities of practice in multiple settings, Etienne Wenger (2002) and colleagues identified five stages of a com-

munity of practice: potential, coalescing, maturing, stewardship, and transformation. Our hope is that this volume will provide a window into structures, collaborations, policies, and means of assessment that emerge as campuses move through these stages. Second, the American Council on Education, through a major project with multiple campuses, identified four stages of change at the campus level: adjustment, isolated change, pervasive change, and transformational change. This volume aims to help readers place the scholarship of teaching and learning movement in this framework of institutional change.

Potential

My AAHE colleague Gene Rice recently wrote in the *Campus Compact Reader,* "The way issues are framed and key words defined can fundamentally shape public understanding and the future of movements aimed at making a difference in higher education" (Rice, 2003, p. 1). The potential for development of a community or a movement rests on collectively defining the issues and learning how to talk about them. For campuses featured in this book, issues about the scholarship of teaching and learning were framed in part through a national project, the Carnegie Academy for the Scholarship of Teaching and Learning

(CASTL). As authors examine initiatives on their own campuses, some refer to this national project that involved individual scholars, scholarly societies, and colleges and universities. Campuses in this book were not operating in isolation; they were part of a developing community that welcomed campuses committed to the scholarship of teaching and learning.

As Gene Rice points out, key terms are also crucial in the way that change comes about. CASTL's design assumed that *scholarship of teaching and learning* was a term that would encompass various kinds of work. In order to start conversations about this operative term, CASTL furnished a draft definition that was modified, sometimes slightly and often significantly, by campuses making their way to a term that could undergird their work. The draft read, "The scholarship of teaching is problem posing about an issue of teaching or learning, study of the problem through methods appropriate to disciplinary epistemologies, application of results to practice, communication of results, self-reflection, and peer review."

As you can imagine, local definitions varied greatly. For example, after a series of departmental and college meetings and discussions on an interactive Web page, Abilene Christian University decided that the definition overemphasized the process of doing scholarship of teaching and learning while excluding some research methodologies appropriately classified as the scholarship of teaching. Its succinct definition became, "The scholarship of teaching is public discourse conceptualizing teaching." On the other hand, Indiana University-Purdue University Indianapolis chose more words to express its definition:

The scholarship of teaching and learning addresses the intellectual work of the classroom, especially teaching and learning, as the focus of disciplinary-based inquiry, captures that work in appropriate formats for self-reflection or presentation to peers, and applies the results to practice. The scholarship of teaching and learning regards teaching as part of the collaborative inquiry undertaken by faculty and students that drives the intellectual work of an academic community.

Many other campuses in this book rewrote the draft definition based on their own understanding and beliefs about scholarship, teaching, and learning.

Coalescing

At the same time that individual campuses were generating their ideas about what constitutes the scholarship of teaching and learning, national project conversations continued and were augmented by other national initiatives. Over the course of many years, language regarding the scholarship of teaching and learning has been refined. For example, in an article in *Change* magazine, Pat Hutchings and Lee Shulman (1999) make important distinctions among teaching, scholarly teaching, and the scholarship of teaching and learning. All faculty, they note, have an obligation to teach well, to engage students, and to foster important forms of student learning. Faculty who do scholarly teaching add classroom assessment, the latest ideas about teaching within a field, and peer collaboration and review. Faculty who engage in the *scholarship of teaching and learning* design and carry out inquiry into issues of student learning that is distinguished by "being public, open to critique and evaluation, and in a form that others can build on." In the scholarship of teaching and learning, "faculty frame and systematically investigate questions related to student learning — the conditions under which it occurs, what it looks like, how to deepen it, and so forth — and do so with an eye not only to improving their own classroom but to advancing practice beyond it" (p. 13).

The combination of local definitions and synthetic national definitions has moved the discourse of the scholarship of teaching and learning from the potential to the coalescing stage. As such, more and more people can use terms across contexts with understanding and continued scrutiny and refinement.

Maturing and Stewardship

A community of practice matures through shared learning. Throughout the CASTL project, campuses reported successes, failures, and plans for the future. In 2001, more than 55 of the involved campuses undertook an extensive self-examination in 10 areas identified collectively as important for encouraging institutional change regarding the scholarship of teaching and learning. The degree of maturation of campus communities became apparent in their self-studies as campuses described for themselves and for others where they were in building infrastructure, expanding collaboration, instituting policies, and assessing impact. The sections of this book mirror these four crucial marks of emerging maturity.

Building Infrastructure
When CASTL was conceived, project leaders spent time imagining what structures would best support the scholarship of teaching and learning. Would having a teaching academy

honor the work? Would forming or expanding a teaching and learning center add value to the campus? Could a campus achieve the aim of doing and applying this scholarly work with no structure at all?

Section One of this book illustrates a range of infrastructures that campuses have in place to support the scholarship of teaching and learning. Configurations described there include a systemwide teaching–learning center partnering with campus teaching–learning centers; a teaching–learning center partnering with a teaching academy; a teaching academy; a systemwide teaching–learning center; a teaching–learning center serving faculty, staff, and students; a teaching–learning center that includes the scholarship of teaching and learning; a teaching–learning center devoted specifically to the scholarship of teaching and learning; and a freestanding scholarship of teaching and learning initiative.

Individual institutions advocate for different strategies. Berea College, for example, makes use of existing infrastructure by working with extant programs, creating infrastructure that coordinates, rather than competes, with other campus initiatives and programs. The University of Georgia contends that its freestanding teaching academy, which exists outside the governing structure of the university, offers forums for deliberation rather than for advancing certain positions. The Maricopa Community Colleges' Institute for Learning enables the building of what the author calls "a community of scholars that will engage in classroom-based inquiry, reflective practice, and conversations about the scholarship of teaching and learning." The University of Wisconsin realigned its systemwide faculty development office to make more visible and effective connections with campuses through the scholarship of teaching and learning. This included adding a Leadership Site to study how realignment works across the system and to connect scholarship of teaching and learning work with existing or newly formed initiatives on individual campuses. Just as definitions need to emerge from the discourse community that uses them, structures are built to serve the needs of individual campuses or systems.

The same principle holds for the larger scale CASTL infrastructure. From a project with central leadership of all campuses, CASTL has evolved into a distributed leadership model with 12 clusters of campuses, with one or two institutions serving as leader and others as members. Fourteen campuses that are mature in various aspects of the scholarship of teaching and learning have moved into the stewardship phase of this community work. In his book, *Stewardship: Choosing Service Over Self-Interest,* Peter Block writes, "stewardship begins with the willingness to be accountable for some larger body than ourselves — an organization, a community" (Block, 1993, p. 6). Each cluster leader has assumed responsibility for facilitating the work of member campuses in a specific topic area.

The cluster campuses have selected topics that fit their current interests and needs. These topics include building networked community practice, examining achievement and success in the first year, pooling education resources, creating a multicultural framework, mentoring new scholars of teaching and learning, organizing to foster the scholarship of teaching and learning, developing research university consortial work, exploring the cognitive-affective relationship in teaching and learning, identifying active pedagogies, and supporting scholarly work at learning-centered universities.

Cluster representatives meet regularly through the AAHE WebCenter and twice a year in person to coordinate work across clusters.

Expanding Collaboration

Mature communities are characterized by strong collaborations. Because changing a campus culture is so complex, multiple constituents must be part of the equation. Section Two of this book establishes the relationship between collaboration and the sustainability of a campus change agenda.

Institutions describe and advocate different configurations of participants. At Buffalo State College, early administrator–faculty collaboration was "pivotal" — changes viewed as the initiative of any *one* campus group would have been stonewalled. At Middlesex Community College, participation by all academic divisions serves as an "antidote to the isolation of our professions and the lack of time for pedagogical discussions within departments and divisions." At The Citadel, collaboration has helped faculty members to integrate perspectives, pool resources, enhance visibility, and provide mutual support. Through its faculty development program, Rider University promotes cross-disciplinary projects in which, as the University of Georgia states in Section One, Chapter Four, collaboration "creates comfort zones outside of established departmental cultures." The University of Montana-Missoula describes strategies that represent what it labels vertical and horizontal collaboration. Vertical strategies include selecting a mix of faculty, students, and administrators for the AAHE Summer Academy team that planned the University's next steps for fostering the scholarship of teaching and learning. Horizontal strategies include discussing change among those of similar status on campus so that people could be more candid and engage in less

> Integration of related work supports mutuality among multiple constituents who influence teaching, learning, and the scholarship of both.

politicized communication. At the University of Maryland College Park, an interdisciplinary team oversees the funding of local initiatives, which contributes multiple perspectives on what is most valuable to support. As evidenced by these examples, campuses have developed, over time, appropriate collaborations for their contexts and needs — collaborations that persist or evolve as circumstances warrant.

Strong collaborations do not necessarily focus exclusively on the scholarship of teaching and learning. Change is transformative when it becomes institutionwide, often through linking initiatives so that the whole is greater than the sum of the parts. For example, early in the Campus Program work, when Augustana College chose to revisit its general education program, it decided to treat the analysis as a scholarly project. It designed its inquiry through faculty research groups that reviewed literature about general education, created hypotheses about what the college might do, designed a model, decided on appropriate components of the model, implemented it, and reported nationally on its process and outcomes. Augustana practiced the scholarship of teaching and learning through doing what

most institutions do periodically — revising curricula. In another example, the University of Michigan is building on its excellent record of interdisciplinary curriculum development by incorporating the scholarship of teaching and learning. These networked initiatives are another form of collaboration important to the maturation and sustainability of work on the scholarship of teaching and learning.

A 2004 CASTL brochure, "Leadership for the Scholarship of Teaching and Learning," identifies ways that educational leaders can support the scholarship of teaching and learning through related activities and collaborative ventures. The brochure suggests campus conversations, allied initiatives, graduate education, undergraduate research, processes for defining excellence, ongoing support, peer review, departmental criteria, annual reporting, and teaching awards as opportunities for connecting the scholarship of teaching and learning with other initiatives. This integration of related work supports mutuality among multiple constituents who influence teaching, learning, and the scholarship about both.

Transformation

Instituting Policies
Good practice can lead to sound policy decisions, and sound policy decisions can lead to good practice. These two processes must be inextricably linked if transformation is to occur. The American Council on Education typology of four quadrants of change — adjustments, isolated change, far-reaching change, and transformational change — has as axes depth and pervasiveness. Adjustment is the modification of existing practice and is neither widespread nor deep. Isolated change is deep, but only in a particular case, whereas per-

vasive change is extensive but shallow. Transformational change occurs when the change "exhibits dimensions of *both* depth and pervasiveness" (Eckel, Green, & Hill, 2001, p. 16). An example of transformational change would be when a college or university decides in its mission (a prominent policy statement) that learning for students and faculty is central, determines that scholarship that contributes to this learning is valuable and worthy of reward, and develops practices that support improved student learning through both scholarly teaching and the scholarship of teaching and learning. Both attributes of pervasive policy and deep learning would signal a transformation in either the ACE or the Wenger framework.

Are we there yet with regard to the scholarship of teaching and learning? No college or university in this book would claim that it has reached Wenger's fifth stage of development of a community of practice or ACE's fourth quadrant of transformation. Still, a valid claim can be made that many campuses are on the way to transformation. Whether this work is on the front or the back burner, to use a metaphor found in the book's conclusion, policies and practices are at very different places at different institutions, but they are being considered and developed.

Fortunately, some institutions have pioneered shifts in policy that make possible the use of effective practices discovered through scholarly work on teaching and learning. Section Three's introduction points out four particularly significant elements that lead to policy change:

1. "Institutional initiatives have resulted from wide-ranging, prolonged conversations." The result is shared authority for policy changes.

2. "Committed leaders can make a difference." This point reappears throughout this volume.

3. "External support can make a difference." That support includes the kinds of collaboration described in this book as well as financial support.

4. "Faculty roles and rewards are inextricably linked."

The final point about faculty roles and rewards is common across institutional types. North Carolina State University decided that informed peer review would influence the reward system. Through a Teaching Effectiveness and Evaluation Committee and its teaching and learning center, North Carolina State set conditions for effective peer review: administrative and faculty buy-in; reviewer and department head training; recognition for reviewing, including modified faculty activity reports; and periodic college review of departmental peer review progress. Rockhurst University and Keystone College, very different kinds of institutions, have also focused on their reward systems, developing numerous strategies for influencing those systems. Iowa State University has important data to show the effects of changing reward criteria on who attains promotion and tenure.

A valid claim can be made that many campuses are on the way to transformation.

Yet, those policies are part of a larger set. The University of Georgia System has instituted a "complementary, comprehensive package of policy directions focused on the need to recruit and retain top quality faculty and staff who would provide the best education and services possible to students of the University of Georgia System." Each college and university in the system must have written institutional policies, criteria, and procedures regarding recruitment and hiring; annual evaluation of faculty; pre-tenure, promotion and tenure, and post-tenure review; rewards and recognition of outstanding performance; and opportunities for continuing development. One can see from these examples how mutually supportive policies are essential for transformational change.

A central problem in changing policy, whether on the campus, system, state, or national level, however, is lack of understanding about the issues involved in supporting teaching and learning. In his book *Clueless in Academe: How Schooling Obscures the Life of the Mind,* Gerald Graff "looks at academia from the perspective of those who don't get it" (Graff, 2003, p. 1). His subject is "cluelessness, the bafflement…felt by students, the general public, and even many academics in the face of the impenetrability of the academic world." Graff's argument is "that academia reinforces cluelessness by making its ideas, problems, and ways of thinking *look* more opaque, narrowly specialized, and beyond normal learning capacities than they are or need to be" (p. 1).

Section Two, Chapter Six describes the ways in which technology can help us become more effective in making scholarly work on teaching and learning transparent and accessible. For example, on the AAHE WebCenter, campus groups can first "make campus- and discipline-based scholarship visible to key decision makers and argue for change in policies that further support their work." Clusters as well as campuses have "protopublic spaces in which to hatch and mature ideas, strategies, and representations in dialogue with like-minded others" before publicly addressing audiences "who may be unfamiliar or resistant." Scholars and policy makers alike need not remain clueless.

Assessing Impact

To influence policies and encourage continued scholarship and application of scholarly knowledge, we need evidence of results. No single indicator is, of course, sufficient. ACE notes that explicit and implicit indicators of change are useful in determining a stage of change. "Compounded evidence signals changes leading to transformation" (Eckel, Green, & Hill, 2001, p. 8). This compounded evidence includes explicit indicators, such as changes in curriculum, pedagogy, student learning outcomes, policies, budget priorities, organizational structures, and decision-making structures, along with implicit indicators such as interactions, self-image, rationales, and relationships between institutions and stakeholders.

The Campus Program's Mapping Progress process, which identified features of change and provided questions for self-examination, enabled campuses to determine what evidence they had or would like to have about key dimensions of change regarding the scholarship of teaching and learning. Section Four, Chapter One maintains that:

> The mapping process creates the possibility of bringing coherence to what could otherwise be isolated pieces, intentionality to what might otherwise seem random, collaboration and community without requiring everyone to occupy the same space and time; and a sense of importance to an effort

time; and a sense of importance to an effort that otherwise might be seen as just one more initiative.

Some institutions represented in Section Four home in on particular aspects of the whole picture. For example, Oxford College of Emory University uncovered campus constituent attitudes toward the scholarship of teaching and learning, while Western Washington University focused on learning that emerges from undertaking, and studying, this scholarship. Oxford College found that documenting progress served as an incentive to maintain enthusiasm, an issue identified as crucial by several institutions in this book. In addition, Oxford found that self-assessment provided leverage for additional funding, a baseline for measuring future impact, and a basis for sharing best practices with other institutions. By tracking resources, involvement, and attitudes, Oxford learned what it needed to do in these areas in the future. For instance, although Oxford's self assessment revealed an increase in familiarity with the scholarship of teaching and learning and an increase in positive attitudes, leaders decided to showcase the impact of this scholarly work on campus so that more people could understand how individuals doing the work were effecting institutional change.

Western Washington University discovered that new voices needed to be heard in the assessment process. Assessment of the impact of an innovative course in Adult and Higher Education leadership, which included faculty and students, led to changes in the content and format of the course. Moving from an interview to a case study methodology, faculty members reported:

It is not so much about having a fixed set of outcomes in place. Rather, it is about the ongoing discussion and reinvention of

those outcomes over time — the staying power. The only way we can continue to stay in touch with this evolving learning is to invite students into those ongoing conversations.

Other colleges and universities have begun the difficult task of generating longitudinal data that show impact over time. Illinois State University, for example, examined thesis and dissertation titles, annual reports from their Research and Sponsored Programs office, grant reports from the Center for Advancement of Teaching, faculty productivity reports, promotion and tenure guidelines, and information on formal scholarship of teaching and learning positions. Illinois State also used a self-administered questionnaire to gather additional information. Examination of results provided a baseline against which Illinois State can examine its progress over time.

Nationally, CASTL did an analysis of 58 Mapping Progress reports. Ninety-five percent of campuses reported having sponsored campuswide and departmental events, conferences, workshops, and retreats for faculty interested in the scholarship of teaching and learning, and they reported regular increases in the percentage of faculty attending such events. Seventy-two percent reported grants, stipends, or release time for faculty or departments for the scholarship of teaching and learning. Seventy-one percent reported new infrastructures, such as a teaching and learning center, office, committee, or positions. Although many policies were newly written or adopted, 60 percent of campuses had included the scholarship of teaching and learning in promotion and tenure systems. Other statistics indicate additional impact of systematic attention to the scholarship of teaching and learning.

At the same time, a difficult aspect of assessing impact remains on the horizon. How does the scholarship of teaching and learning contribute to student learning? Regional and specialized accrediting associations are now quite rightly focusing on student learning outcomes. What will colleges and universities be able to say about the relationship of their faculty and student scholarly work on teaching and learning and student learning on their campuses or elsewhere? This is a question for further investigation as the movement evolves, and it is clearly one that will have different answers in different contexts.

In an early video describing CASTL, Carnegie Foundation president Lee Shulman answered the question, "How will you know when the scholarship of teaching and learning is successful?" He said that he would know this work is successful when faculty members who meet each other in the halls naturally and often talk about their teaching and their students' learning as logical and important concerns. How will we measure the degree to which this scholarship permeates the minds and actions of faculty, administrators, students, and all educators on our campuses?

As you read this volume, I encourage you to ask questions like the ones I've just posed. You'll find that many authors report that answering one set of questions generates another set, the very essence of scholarly inquiry. You'll also find that the conclusion of this book synthesizes some responses to these questions by viewing them through three important lenses. I began with an assertion about the relationship of passion and knowledge. In Section Five of this book, you will read about "Learning Along the Way." The section's journey motif unites the chapters, each of which describes milestones in a campus's journey in institu-

tionalizing the scholarship of teaching and learning. Yet, as Eckel, Green, and Hill (2001) note, change can look "like a failure from the middle. The work not yet accomplished often is more visible than the changes made. Taking stock is helpful not only because it provides useful feedback for mid-course corrections, but because it also affirms accomplishment and nourishes future work" (p. 27). The passion of the authors in Section Five verifies that, even with potholes and rocky terrain, examining progress yields affirmations, places for new strategies, and hopes for future steps. One hope of all authors of this volume is that you will join us on the road to transformational change in higher education led by the scholarship of teaching and learning.

References

Block, P. (1993). *Stewardship: Choosing service over self-interest.* San Francisco: Berrett-Koehler.

Eckel, P., Green, M., & Hill, B. (2001). *On change V. Riding the waves of change: Insights from transforming institutions.* Washington, DC: American Council on Education.

Graff, G. (2003). *Clueless in academe: How schooling obscures the life of the mind.* New Haven, CT: Yale University Press.

Hutchings, P., & Shulman, L. (1999, September/October). The scholarship of teaching and learning: New elaborations, new developments. *Change, 31*(5), 10-15.

Leadership for the scholarship of teaching and learning. (2004). Menlo Park, CA: The Carnegie Foundation for the Advancement of Teaching.

Rice, E. (2003, Fall). Rethinking scholarship and engagement: The struggle for new meanings. *Campus Compact Reader,* 1-9.

Wenger, E., McDermott, R., & Snyder, W. M. (2002). *Cultivating communities of practice.* Boston: Harvard University Business School Press.

INTRODUCTION TO SECTION ONE
Developing Infrastructure

Constance E. Cook
University of Michigan

The beginning of the 21st century may well be remembered as an era when higher education devoted sustained attention to student learning. Campuses are improving student learning in a myriad of ways — from integrative courses to learning communities, from undergraduate research projects to community service learning, from interdisciplinary courses to civic engagement. Each of these tried-and-true initiatives for improving the educational experience involves a curricular or cocurricular program for students. Initiatives to promote the scholarship of teaching and learning are another well-established approach to improving student learning, but these initiatives do so through faculty inquiry projects. As a result, projects in the scholarship of teaching and learning lead to not only greater student learning, but also faculty learning.

For many years, AAHE and the Carnegie Foundation have recognized the value of the scholarship of teaching and learning and have worked to establish and maintain its momentum. They have created a national infrastructure to provide its intellectual underpinnings and promote its dissemination. The dissemination methods are varied and include selection and training of faculty leaders and offers of speakers, books, grants, and summer academy support to campuses. Faculty can "go public" nationally with their projects in the scholarship of teaching and learning through AAHE and Carnegie conferences, websites, and publications like this one. Thanks to the leadership of the two organizations, institutions that create local infrastructures to support this work are, at the same time, involving their faculty in a national infrastructure that connects them productively to colleagues across the country. Eight institutions are represented in this section, each of which has a robust set of programs in the scholarship of teaching and learning. The authors from each institution describe their campus infrastructures and the ways these infrastructures support the programs. Though the local models are very different, one common element is their reliance on the national infrastructure. Each chapter provides testimony of the value of the national framework in serving as catalyst for development of a local set of supports.

Role of Infrastructure in Institutional Transformation

Common wisdom says that the development of infrastructure is a key element in the process of institutional transformation, but structure alone is not the answer. An over-emphasis on the importance of structure can imply a rigid, causal determinism that simply does not hold true in real life. Structures change over time, and human agency, that is, the efficacy of human actions, plays a major role in determining outcomes, no matter what the structure may be (see Sewell, 1992, for an extensive treatment of the role of structure). As established in other sections of this book, it is the people involved, both leaders and those with whom they work, who ultimately shape a structure to fit an institution.

Even with capable leadership, no single form of infrastructure facilitates change in every setting. Structures play out differently in different environments and cultures. What works well in one setting may be completely unworkable in another. That is especially true in the diverse world of higher education, with so many institutional types and so many unique institutional personalities.

Nonetheless, each chapter in this section shows that infrastructure is a key element, first in making institutional transformation possible, and second, in sustaining it. The premise of this section is that, in spite of the unique characteristics of individual institutions, higher education leaders can learn from each other by exploring institutional similarities and examining their differences (Eckel, Hill, Green, & Mallon, 1999). Faculty members and administrators who understand the value of the scholarship of teaching and learning can use these campus models to decide how best to craft or augment their own campus infrastructures around this work.

Eight Institutions, Eight Different Approaches

The eight institutions whose stories appear in this section range from a community college system to a state university system, and from baccalaureate colleges to master's institutions and doctorate-granting universities. These institutions were selected because they have made the scholarship of teaching and learning a priority and have developed infrastructures to support this work.

Table 1 categorizes the infrastructure on each of the eight campuses. One campus houses a systemwide teaching–learning center, and another has a systemwide center that works in concert with a campus center. Two institutions have both centers and teaching academies, with differing degrees of collaboration between them. Three institutions depend only on a campus teaching–learning center to facilitate activity in the scholarship of teaching and learning. The remaining institution has a freestanding initiative overseen by a faculty committee, with no center or academy at all. The table shows a continuum of the extent of infrastructure represented by the eight institutions, and they appear in the approximate order of most- to least-developed infrastructure.

Initiatives in the scholarship of teaching and learning work best when built on existing faculty development infrastructure.

Table 1

Infrastructure for Campus Coordination of Scholarship of Teaching and Learning Initiatives

Institution	System teaching–learning center	Campus teaching–learning center	Teaching academy	Initiatives without an office or academy structure
University of Wisconsin-Milwaukee and the University of Wisconsin System	X	X		
Texas Tech University		X	X	
University of Georgia*		X	X	
Maricopa Community Colleges	X			
Berea College		X		
University of Wyoming		X		
Youngstown State University		X		
Elon University		(X)**		X

* The teaching academy and the teaching–learning center at the University of Georgia are in the process of developing more of a connection than they have had in the past.

** Elon University is in the process of developing a teaching–learning center.

A brief overview of the infrastructure of each of the eight institutions demonstrates eight models that meet the needs of individual campuses or systems of campuses in supporting their initiatives in the scholarship of teaching and learning.

System-wide Teaching–Learning Center Partnering with a Campus Teaching–Learning Center

The University of Wisconsin System's Office of Professional and Instructional Development partners with the UW-Milwaukee's Center for Instructional and Professional Development on a variety of initiatives in the scholarship of teaching and learning. UW-Milwaukee is the Leadership Site for the scholarship of teaching and learning for the whole UW System.

Teaching Academy in Collaboration with a Teaching–Learning Center

Texas Tech University has a faculty-led Teaching Academy that works in close coordination with the Teaching, Learning, and Technology Center. The Center funds the programs and operating expenses of the Academy and the two collaborate closely, with Academy faculty serving on Center advisory boards and presenting at Center programs.

Freestanding Teaching Academy

The University of Georgia Teaching Academy, which is composed of faculty, is not a formal part of the university's administrative structure or faculty governance system. The Academy currently has no clear connection to the Office of Instructional Support and Development, the university's teaching–learning center, but a connection is starting to develop. The Academy's principal role is to offer advice to the administration on teaching-related matters, and its funds come from a private foundation.

Systemwide Teaching–Learning Center in Collaboration with a Major Program

Maricopa Community Colleges' Center for Learning and Instruction is a comprehensive faculty development and support center for all 10 of the Maricopa colleges. Its programs include the Maricopa Institute for Learning, an annual fellowship program for faculty who are engaged in initiatives related to the scholarship of teaching and learning.

Teaching–Learning Center Serving Faculty, Staff, and Students

Berea College's Center for Learning, Teaching, Communication, and Research differs from other teaching–learning center models in that it takes a holistic approach to professional development and the scholarship of teaching and learning, and it serves the entire college community — faculty, staff and students.

Campus Teaching–Learning Center in Collaboration with a Major Program

The University of Wyoming's Ellbogen Center for Teaching and Learning coordinates the inVISIBLEcollege, a initiative in the scholarship of teaching and learning that involves a new cohort of faculty each year. The Center often funds and features faculty who participate in the inVISIBLEcollege.

Teaching–Learning Center Devoted Specifically to the Scholarship of Teaching and Learning

Youngstown State University developed its Center for the Advancement of Teaching and Learning (CATALYST) to provide leadership for activities related to the scholarship of teaching and learning. Youngstown State is a unionized campus where the faculty contract provides some reassigned time to carry out initiatives related to this scholarship.

Freestanding Initiative in the Scholarship of Teaching and Learning

Project Interweave at Elon University funds faculty–student teams annually to engage in projects related to the scholarship of teaching and learning for a two-year period. The Elon Carnegie Committee, composed of faculty members who have been on one of the funded teams, oversees the Project. The University currently is developing a teaching–learning center to house the scholarship of teaching and learning and other faculty development activities.

Centrality of Teaching–Learning Centers in the Infrastructure

What the eight models in this section make clear is the centrality of teaching–learning centers to the development and implementation of initiatives in the scholarship of teaching and learning. Most universities now have a campuswide teaching–learning center for faculty development, and many colleges have them as well. Of the eight institutions featured here for their robust programs in this scholarship, seven have a center. The exception is Elon University, which is in the process of developing one. The institutions have recognized that initiatives in the scholarship of teaching and learning work best if they build on extant faculty development infrastructures. A well-developed faculty development program in a teaching–learning center seems to facilitate a well-developed program in the scholarship of teaching and learning.

Veteran faculty developers, who wrote many of the chapters in this section, discuss the relationship between the scholarship of teaching and learning and the other work they do. For example, Nelson and Kleinsasser refer to this scholarship as a particularly powerful form of faculty development at the University of Wyoming, and Ciccone describes it as a good organizing principle for faculty development work at the University of Wisconsin. Faculty development is a term that often is used synonymously with instructional development, that is, activities designed to enhance college teaching and, thereby, improve student learning (Cook, 2002), which is what the scholarship of teaching and learning accomplishes.

There are many reasons for housing initiatives in the scholarship of teaching and learning in teaching–learning centers, as part of a faculty development infrastructure, rather than creating a separate infrastructure. Such collaborations, as noted in the chapter on Berea College, allow initiatives in the scholarship of teaching and learning to take root without engendering the resentment that comes from new expenditures in a zero-sum budget. In these tight budget times, it does not make sense for institutions already strapped for funds to build new and possibly redundant structures. Instead, most institutions take small steps, on a trial-and-error basis, as they implement changes in policy and programs. This approach to policy change, known as disjointed incrementalism (Lindblom, 1959), seems to be the guiding principle not only for public policymaking (which is the sense in which the term was first used), but also for development of new infrastructure. Consequently, infrastructures established for the scholarship of teaching and learning are rarely freestanding.

The section authors enumerate other reasons for the usual connection between the scholarship of teaching and learning and teaching–learning centers. Jones notes the value at Berea College of placing new initiatives in traditionally successful offices — offices that faculty already count on for useful support. By definition, center staff members are experts in pedagogy, and they can suggest readings for gatherings and consult with faculty about their inquiry projects. Harper-Marinick says that placing Maricopa Community Colleges' programs in the scholarship of teaching and learning in an existing center provides a sense of permanence and continuity within the institution; it institutionalizes what otherwise could be a short-term campus project. As both the Wyoming and Berea chapters mention, centers give faculty easy access to publicity so they can showcase their work in the scholarship of teaching and learning more readily through the centers' programs and publications. Similarly, most centers have grant competitions and can allocate grants to faculty engaged in this scholarship. For example, the teaching–learning center at UW-Milwaukee funds five Center Scholars each year to do systematic inquiry projects.

Most centers, including all of those featured in this section, are part of the office of the vice president for academic affairs. That reporting relationship allows the programs to connect easily to current priorities on the institutional agenda as well as draw resources from the chief academic officer. It also allows the center staff to serve prominently as campus advocates for teaching and learning improvements (Sorcinelli, 2002; Wright, 2000). Over the last two decades, most faculty development initiatives have moved from a peripheral institutional position to a central one (Chism, 1998; Gaff & Simpson, 1994), as is the evolving case with initiatives in the scholarship of teaching and learning.

The Challenge of Maintaining Faculty Ownership of Infrastructure

For faculty, the scholarship of teaching and learning has multiple attractions. One is the opportunity to use years of doctoral training on research methods and critical analysis in the service of the daily activity of teaching students. Since faculty members on most campuses face increasing expectations for teaching, research, and service, the scholarship of teaching and learning is an efficient way to accomplish multiple tasks. For faculty at certain teaching institutions, where support and rewards for disciplinary research may be rare, the scholarship of teaching and learning provides a different kind of research opportunity

and helps faculty satisfy their natural curiosity about the outcomes of their own instruction. Faculty members are scholars, and the scholarship of teaching and learning is a form of inquiry relevant to the classroom. Faculty also appreciate the opportunity to be involved in cutting-edge teaching initiatives. The current belief system about pedagogy favors the teacher–student relationship as a vehicle for learning (Tiberius, 2002), and the scholarship of teaching and learning fosters that approach.

In spite of the appeal of this scholarship for faculty, the eight chapters in this section describe challenges in maintaining a sense of faculty ownership of this scholarship's infrastructure. By connecting projects with other campus infrastructure and programs, such as teaching–learning centers, the sense of faculty ownership can diminish. All faculty development infrastructures, including those for the scholarship of teaching and learning, work best when they are created and owned by faculty (Cook & Sorcinelli, 2002; Eble & McKeachie, 1985; Sorcinelli, 2002). No lasting changes, including improvements in teaching, occur on a campus without faculty buy-in.

Faculty ownership of infrastructure is important in part because of the relationship between the scholarship of teaching and learning and the campus reward system. The chapters from Elon University, the University of Wyoming, and Youngstown State University all mention the importance of acknowledging excellent scholarship in teaching and learning through the reward system so that faculty who spend time doing research on student learning will get credit in their promotion and tenure reviews. Without faculty advocacy and buy-in for such changes in the reward system, that credit may be hard to achieve.

Faculty ownership
of infrastructure is
important because of
the relationship between
the scholarship of
teaching and learning
and the campus
reward system.

Another important reason for fostering faculty ownership of infrastructure is to counter the resentment of the scholarship of teaching and learning that sometimes comes from colleagues. The chapter from Youngstown State University describes resistance from faculty who prefer to allocate recognition and reassigned time to those who do traditional, discipline-based research. These faculty see the scholarship of teaching and learning as a threat to the type of research they value. That chapter also notes the disappointment shared by leaders of the movement to support the scholarship of teaching and learning when few faculty applied for reassigned time to undertake this scholarship — even though the leadership fought to have the reassigned time included in union contract provisions.

An approach to securing a sense of faculty ownership of infrastructure is to have faculty advisory boards as a key part of the infrastructure. Boards can choose participants in the scholarship of teaching and learning, allocate funds, and oversee programs, as is the case with

most of the institutions featured here. In order to ensure both faculty involvement and collaboration among units, Smith explains that Texas Tech University uses overlapping membership to coordinate the Teaching Academy with the Teaching, Learning, and Technology Center — with Academy faculty serving on Center advisory boards and with the Center director serving in an *ex officio* capacity on the Teaching Academy Executive Council. As at Texas Tech, most teaching–learning center directors are current or former faculty members, chosen for their roles because they are respected teachers and scholars (Sorcinelli, 2002). Their faculty status also assists in the process of ensuring faculty ownership of center initiatives.

The University of Georgia provides an instructive case study regarding the potentially competing imperatives of maintaining faculty ownership of infrastructure while also maintaining resources and recognition from the administration. Georgia Teaching Academy members value their freestanding Academy, which is not on the organizational chart and is not beholden to or dependent upon the university administration. Broder and Kalivoda explain that because the Academy does not receive funds from the university budget, it has the advantage of being able to engage the university community in discussion of sensitive issues related to teaching and learning without administrative oversight, and then advise the administration on policy questions.

Georgia's teaching–learning center, the Office of Instructional Support and Development, does the programming and support for instruction, including initiatives in the scholarship of teaching and learning. It also maintains the Academy website, while the Institute for Higher Education provides meeting space and secretarial support for the Academy. In exchange, the Academy offers cosponsorship and planning support for programs. The disadvantage of this arrangement, of course, is that the Academy faces uncertainty regarding future operational support and, whenever a new administration arrives, there is less assurance that its campus recognition will continue. As a result, members of the Academy have come to believe that more collaboration with the Office of Instructional Support and Development would be desirable, probably in the form of a formal advisory relationship between the two entities. Thus, Georgia appears to be moving gradually toward an arrangement between the Academy and the teaching–learning center that will be similar to the one at Texas Tech.

The Georgia case assumes a clear distinction between faculty and administrators, but that clarity is hard to achieve. Many faculty who value good teaching and are responsible university citizens find themselves assuming administrative positions over time. At both Georgia and Texas Tech, it is a founding member of the Teaching Academy who directs the teaching–learning center. Furthermore, at Georgia, even though the Teaching Academy is independent from the administration, some of the Academy members, including the two chapter authors, have administrative titles. They explain that Academy members with administrative titles participate in the Academy as faculty, not as administrators. Thus, the definition of "faculty" is not always obvious.

A national infrastructure serves to promote and sustain initiatives on campuses.

Maintaining the Scholarship of Teaching and Learning as a Campus Priority

New ideas come and go in higher education just as they do in business and other sectors of the work force. It always seems more attractive for an institution to support an exciting new program (exciting because it is new) than to sustain an existing one, no matter how successful. Furthermore, with many other campus priorities besides the improvement of student learning, there are never enough funds to go around.

The Youngstown State chapter offers a cautionary tale for the future of the scholarship of teaching and learning. Linkon and Russo describe their initiative as fragile and in need of constant effort to maintain its momentum. According to these authors, the Youngstown State administration initially supported initiatives in the scholarship of teaching and learning but then concluded that P–16 partnerships would be more likely to garner external publicity and funding than would these initiatives. The result was a reduction of funding for the scholarship of teaching and learning over time. Youngstown State University appears to be reducing its commitment to the scholarship of teaching and learning, at least in part.

This introduction began by noting that AAHE and the Carnegie Foundation have created a national infrastructure that serves to promote and sustain initiatives in the scholarship of teaching and learning on campuses. Without the continuing attention and sponsorship of AAHE and Carnegie, this scholarship might well lose its visibility and current priority status elsewhere, as at Youngstown State. Those institutions most likely to maintain a priority status for this scholarship are the ones that have developed a strong infrastructure to support it. Though the campus infrastructures for this work differ from one institution to the next, the models in this section provide higher education leaders with wise advice for creating and sustaining an infrastructure.

AAHE and the Carnegie Foundation deserve much credit for their leadership of the national movement in the scholarship of teaching and learning. As Ciccone notes with regard to the University of Wisconsin, the scholarship of teaching and learning used to be a "'boutique operation,' that is, a place where only a few 'shop.'" That is no longer the case. On each of the eight campuses in this section, there are large numbers of shoppers, just as there are on other campuses across the nation, and students' educational experiences are better as a result.

References

Chism, N. V. N. (1998). The role of educational developers in institutional change: From the basement office to the front office. *To Improve the Academy,* 17, 141-153.

Cook, C. E. (2002). Faculty development (instructional development). In J. Forest & K. Kinser (Eds.), *Higher education in the United States: An encyclopedia* (pp. 211-214). Santa Barbara, CA: ABC-CLIO.

Cook, C. E., & Sorcinelli, M. D. (2002, June). The value of a teaching center. Retrieved July 30, 2003, from http://www.podnetwork.org/development/value.htm.

Eble, K., & McKeachie, W. J. (1985). *Improving undergraduate education through faculty development.* San Francisco: Jossey-Bass.

Eckel, P. D. (2002). Institutional transformation and change: Insights for faculty developers. *To Improve the Academy,* 20, 3-19.

Eckel, P. D., Hill, B., Green, M., & Mallon, W. (1999). *On change–reports from the road: Insights on institutional change.* Washington, DC: American Council on Education.

Gaff, J. G., & Simpson, R. D. (1994). Faculty development in the United States. *Innovative Higher Education,* 18(3), 167-175.

Lindblom, C. E. (1959). The science of muddling through. *Public Administration Review,* 19, 79-88.

Sewell, W. H., Jr. (1992). A theory of structure: Duality, agency, and transformation. *American Journal of Sociology,* 98(1), 1-29.

Sorcinelli, M. D. (2002). Ten principles of good practice in creating and sustaining teaching and learning centers. In K. H. Gillespie (Ed.), *A guide to faculty development* (pp. 9-23). Bolton, MA: Anker Publishing.

Tiberius, R. G. (2002). A brief history of educational development: Implications for teachers and developers. *To Improve the Academy,* 20, 20-37.

Wright, D. (2000). Faculty development centers in research universities: A study of resources and programs. *To Improve the Academy,* 18, 291-301.

Contact:

Constance E. Cook
Director, Center for Research on
Learning and Teaching
University of Michigan
cecook@umich.edu

Mutual Benefits, Continuing Challenges

Jane Nelson and Audrey Kleinsasser
University of Wyoming

Since its inception in 1991, the University of Wyoming Ellbogen Center for Teaching and Learning has played a significant role in curricular and instructional innovation and dissemination. Its director and staff are funded by and report directly to the vice president for academic affairs, and they are advised by a broad-based council of faculty and staff. The Center has been a key player in several initiatives, including a summer teaching colloquium and a certificate program for graduate students, an orientation for new faculty, and many faculty development programs. Through a variety of competitive incentive grants programs managed by the Center, faculty have applied for and received nearly one million dollars since 1991 to work on a wide range of projects. The Center maintains media and instructional computing laboratories that are increasingly important to the University's efforts to embed thoughtfully planned instructional technology into teaching. It also maintains the University's writing center, which supports faculty development as well as student writing. The Center's organizational structure enables it to help move academic planning into realization and to assist central administrators in envisioning different course structures and new pedagogies.

The Center is now in what might be called its second generation, with its second director. It is also in its fourth year of the inVISIBLEcollege, a significant component of the scholarship of teaching and learning at the University of Wyoming. The idea of an invisible college is neither new nor original. The term was used to describe the group of scholars who later became the British Royal Society, founded in 1660. The group, members of no known formal college, met to exchange research and ideas. In 1972, Diane Crane wrote *Invisible Colleges,* which explores the way social structures (such as departments, course delivery practices, or the preparation of future faculty) influence the development of ideas. According to Crane, participation in an organization like an invisible college bolsters morale, inspires a sense of purpose, provides criticism, maintains solidarity, and focuses interest on particular issues. Perhaps most important, members of an invisible college see themselves as part of a complex network, not members of a special interest group invested solely in the goals of an academic department.

The Center's goal for inVISIBLEcollege is to create and maintain a high profile, inquiry-oriented faculty development program to foster the renewal of teaching and learning at department, program, and college levels. In each of three academic years since 2000, a new cohort of inVISIBLEcollege members has met regularly, read a common set of books and articles, and implemented inquiry projects about specific aspects of teaching and learning. Readings in each cohort have included Ernest Boyer's *Scholarship Reconsidered: Priorities of the Professoriate (1990);* Glassik, Huber, and Maeroff's *Scholarship Assessed: Evaluation of the Professoriate (1997);* and *Opening Lines: Approaches to the Scholarship of Teaching and Learning (2000),* edited by Pat Hutchings. The members of the first cohort of inVISIBLEcollege developed a working definition of the scholarship of teaching specific to the University of Wyoming: "Scholarship implies peer critique, reflection, and dissemination. The scholarship of teaching enhances student learning through ongoing systematic inquiry." Through the life of this project, we have begun to recognize that one of the essential features of scholarship is "going public."

By embedding inVISIBLEcollege within its established structure, the Center has been able to augment benefits to the scholars in the program. The scholars have access to the time, talent, and services of the five Center staff members and their offices, including significant technological and methodological support for the inquiry projects. Several scholars have received substantial additional resources for expanded inquiry projects through the Center's competitive grants program. For many of its other programs, the Center regularly brings in nationally known scholars on a variety of teaching issues and often creates small-group opportunities for the inVISIBLEcollege participants to meet with these scholars. The participants also benefit from the Center's support of and participation in such national initiatives as the Carnegie

Scholars Program, the AAHE Campus Program, and the AAHE Summer Academy.

For inVISIBLEcollege scholars, perhaps the greatest benefit of being embedded in Center programming has been the increased opportunity for going public with their inquiry projects. Through the course of an academic year, the Center sponsors an average of three events per week that range from one-hour brown bags and two-hour workshops to multi-day colloquia and workshops. As a consequence of the variety and frequency of this programming, the inVISIBLEcollege participants are invited to present their project findings to an array of campus audiences in formal and informal settings. They are also invited to present the results of follow-up projects over the course of several years. An established teaching and learning center helps faculty to sustain their scholarship through several years so that it can gain in depth and meaning.

The Center realized early in the inVISIBLEcollege initiative that the scholarship of teaching and learning yields considerable benefits for students as well as faculty. Many of the competitive grants that the Center now awards include scholarship, and they have led to improvement in pedagogy and increased learning for students. For example, students in nursing and pharmacy now learn standardized patient protocols by participating in role-play clinical scenarios that are videotaped for formative assessment purposes. In another project, a law professor interviewed alumni who are now practicing attorneys to discover how the law school prepared them for writing in the workplace. Based on the professor's work, the law school has identified writing as a top priority in its next round of curriculum revision. Because of successful projects like these, the Center created a university-level project entitled

Warming Up the Chill: Teaching Against the Structures. Funded by a combination of four internal and external grants totaling about $15,000, this project has culminated in a published book, the production of a CD-ROM, and the development of a website featuring the teaching of six University of Wyoming faculty.

Success does not come without challenges, of course. As a result of the improved organizational abilities that accompany the successful sponsorship of multiple projects, central administration has turned to the Center to sponsor and organize numerous teaching-related initiatives that do not have scholarship at their core. Recognizing the importance of participating in these campus projects, the Center sometimes finds ways to incorporate scholarship and to champion philosophical and methodological integrity in the development of these programs.

The greatest challenge for the Center remains the issue of incentives. We acknowledge that the scholarship of teaching and learning is not going to reform the culture of an entire campus. At the University of Wyoming, change seems most effective first at the department level and then at the college level. As a result of local and national engagement in the scholarship of teaching and learning, the nursing and accounting departments at the University of Wyoming have been able to alter their faculty reward systems for tenure and promotion to include this kind of scholarship. The College of Agriculture is beginning to sponsor some multidisciplinary discussion of issues related to the reward system. As these gains become more substantial and include broad changes in the reward system, faculty members will have more and more incentive to participate in Center-sponsored inquiry projects that produce the scholarship of teaching and learning.

References

Boyer, E. L. (1990). *Scholarship reconsidered: Priorities of the professoriate.* Jossey-Bass: San Francisco.

Crane, D. (1972). *Invisible colleges: Diffusion of knowledge in scientific communities.* Chicago: The University of Chicago Press.

Glassick, C. E., Huber, M. T., & Maeroff, G. I. (1997). *Scholarship assessed: Evaluation of the professoriate.* San Francisco: Jossey-Bass.

Hutchings, P. (Ed.). (2000). *Opening lines: Approaches to the scholarship of teaching and learning.* Menlo Park, CA: The Carnegie Foundation for the Advancement of Teaching.

Contacts and URL

Jane Nelson
Director, Writing Center
University of Wyoming
jnelson@uwyo.edu

Audrey Kleinsasser
Director, Ellbogen Center for Teaching and
    Learning
University of Wyoming
dakota@uwyo.edu

For information about the Ellbogen Center for Teaching and Learning, see
http://www.uwyo.edu/ctl

University of Wyoming
Laramie, WY
Doctoral/Research Extensive
http://www.uwyo.edu/

Launching a Center for Learning, Teaching, Communication, and Research

Libby Falk Jones
Berea College

In August 2002, Berea College's Center for Learning, Teaching, Communication, and Research opened in the campus's newly renovated central academic building. The Center's mission is to enhance student learning through services to students, faculty, and staff in all combinations. Five years in the planning, the Center incorporates and extends the work of Berea's Center for Effective Communication (1988-2002). Services provided by the Center include support for:

◆ *learning* (students, faculty, staff): assistance in enhancing written and oral communication, reasoning and problem-solving, studying and test-taking, time management, and research project design/execution;

◆ *teaching* (faculty, labor supervisors, teaching associates, tutors): assistance in teaching approaches, assessment strategies, and instructional technology use for classroom teaching, mentoring, conferencing, and work supervision; and

◆ *professional development* (faculty, staff, student leaders/teaching associates/tutors): assistance in developing leadership, valuing diversities, researching learning and teaching, and preparing for professional reviews.

Our journey in developing infrastructure to support informed and investigative teaching and learning, though not yet complete, has yielded insights we hope might help other institutions. Following are seven such insights.

Develop a Vision Appropriate to Your Institution, its History, and Mission

The Center's mission to serve faculty, students, and staff as they foster student learning makes both theoretical and practical sense. Research on learning suggests the value of holistic approaches: students learn both in and out of the classroom, particularly at a small college. Likewise, teachers — faculty, staff work supervisors, undergraduate peer tutors, and teaching associates — learn when they experience student learning through tutoring, advising, reading the research literature, and conducting research on student learning.

Berea's Center builds on the successful experience of the Center for Effective Communication. The latter provided 14 years of support for campus learning in written and oral communication by various campus constituencies. Other successful campus models on which it builds include a strong program in instructional technology use, several faculty development programs and reading groups that unite faculty and staff, and an active undergraduate research and creative projects program.

Engage All Constituents in Voicing Needs and Planning for the Center

Our Center is the product of recommendations by two different faculty task forces. The first, five years ago, reviewed current programs and recommended extending these into a teaching–learning center. The second, three years ago, built on that recommendation by proposing the new structure. In addition to researching and visiting other institutions' centers, both groups sought extensive input from Berea students, faculty, and staff through written questionnaires and dialogue within classes and departments. While support, including financial support, from upper-level administration (president, provost, deans) has been crucial, even more important has been the student and faculty ownership of the work of learning.

As a Change Strategy, Think Evolution, not Revolution

On a small college campus, everyone wears many hats. Though most delight in the variety of opportunities to fulfill our callings as educators, our heads (and hearts) get weary! Revolution in the form of new programs may be seen less as an opportunity and more as a demand on an already over-taxed system. Evolution, on the other hand, means the gradual development of what's already there. In conception, planning, and practice, our Center has stressed continuity rather than change, emphasizing its role in coordinating existing

services and gradually extending them. Implementation of the full complement of services will be staged over three to five years.

Make Effective Use of Existing Infrastructure

The College's Professional Growth Committee, an elected faculty committee with divisional representation, led implementation efforts for the new Center. In addition to helping to plan the Center's new space in one of our campus's central academic buildings, the committee entered the national dialogue on teaching and learning, sending representatives to the CASTL colloquia and to the Rollins College Conference on Small College Faculty Development. Working with the Center's Director, the committee planned an inaugural event for the Center's first year of operation: a one-day regional conference on the scholarship of teaching and learning.

Another important connection is with the General Studies program. A site for ongoing faculty and student development, our interdisciplinary General Education Program offers a four-year curriculum in which all faculty are expected to teach. The center's faculty associates worked closely with the associate dean of the faculty to plan programs and build resources supporting faculty's ability to teach written and oral communication, critical

> As a change strategy,
> think evolution,
> not revolution.

thinking, and quantitative reasoning, as well as course-specific texts. In the future, the Center plans to connect more closely to the evolving infrastructure of department chairs, currently being built by the dean of the faculty.

Coordinate With, Rather than Compete With, Other Campus Programs

Another example of the evolutionary approach to change involves the Center's staffing. To provide our range of services, Center staff need expertise on pedagogical issues, learning styles, written and oral communication techniques, assessment approaches, disciplinary teaching techniques, instructional technology, and research literature and best practices in learning, teaching, communication, and research. Designating new positions to provide this expertise demands sizable institutional resources, which are difficult to come by, especially in today's economy. In the zero–sum equation of the small college budget, too, winning such resources may provoke resentment from existing programs and undermine a new Center's ability to reach a broad audience. Rather than ask for new, full-time staff positions to supplement the Center's expertise, we have created faculty associate positions and supported them with course release time or stipends. Our Center has benefited from the wisdom, resources, and coordination these individuals bring to our ongoing conversation on learning.

Engage in the Regional and National Dialogue on Learning and Teaching

A center should seek opportunities for faculty and students to share their work with larger audiences, such as the CASTL program. Other options include facilitating regional networking through conferences and email lists, developing book and article discussion groups, sponsoring conference travel, and creating opportunities for attendees to share insights.

Be Patient and Stay Flexible; Celebrate Achievements

Lasting change doesn't happen overnight. Our new Center faces continuing challenges, in the areas of services (providing more direct help for individual faculty, developing more services geared to staff); presentation (providing a clear and compelling message about the comprehensive services the Center offers); leadership (establishing ongoing institutional support for faculty associates as well as clarifying the roles of associates, administrators, and the Professional Growth Committee in overseeing and enacting the Center's work); and resource management (organizing print resources and building a searchable website to make them fully accessible).

It is important to balance the awareness of continuing needs with a celebration of achievements. Stopping by our Center on a May afternoon as we end our first year, visitors find a center of activity and reflection. In our reception area, a student consultant reviews materials for the next year's peer tutor preparation workshop, while a student researcher enters article titles on active learning into a searchable database. On the walls are posters from Communication Across the College (a faculty–staff development program) cohorts and a chart detailing the College's workplace expectations for faculty and staff. Bookshelves hold notebooks with resources for critical thinking, diversity, and writing in the disciplines. In our small meeting room a student consultant coaches a psychology student preparing a PowerPoint research presentation, while in our conference room, a half dozen faculty reflect on the term's teaching surprises. In the kitchen, the coffee perks; outside our doors, a garden beckons. Thanks to the efforts of many, our space and work have become rich educational enterprises.

Contact and URLs

Libby Falk Jones
Director, Center for Learning, Teaching,
  Communication, and Research
Berea College
libby_jones@berea.edu

For information on the Center for Learning, Teaching, Communication, and Research, see http://www.berea.edu/cltcr

For information about Communication Across the College, see http://www.berea.edu/cac

Berea College
Berea, KY
Baccalaureate-Liberal Arts
http://www.berea.edu/

Keeping Falcons as Falcons: Creating a Self-Perpetuating Program

John G. Sullivan, Deborah Thurlow Long, and Rosemary Haskell
Elon University

A story from the Sufi wise-fool, Nasruddin:
Nasruddin had never seen a falcon. One day, a falcon alighted on his windowsill and, strange to say, Nasruddin captured the bird. "My, my," he said, "You are a peculiar pigeon! I'll help you." So he trimmed the falcon's beak and talons, clipped the falcon's feathers, and added a bit of paint. "Now," he proudly proclaimed. "You are a proper pigeon."

Our question is this: How do you take a powerful idea such as the scholarship of teaching and learning and institutionalize it in a way that does not turn a falcon into a pigeon? At Elon University, our falcon arrived in spring 1999, when we launched a three-year initiative in the scholarship of teaching and learning that supported four projects a year, each under the direction of a faculty–student team of researchers. Each project was funded at $6,000 per year — a total of $72,000. The projects were generally successful — teachers and students collaborated on research, design, implementation, and reporting.

As the initial scheme drew to a close, we were charged with institutionalizing the program and its leadership. The honeymoon was over. Competing campus initiatives had emerged. In the words of the song, "How do we keep the music going, how do we make it last?" More importantly, how do we keep falcons as falcons?

Institutionalizing a Program: Project Interweave

The committee charged with oversight of the Carnegie work on the scholarship of teaching and learning at Elon is an appointed group of faculty from different disciplines, referred to as the Elon Carnegie Committee. The Committee has the responsibility of propagating the scholarship of teaching and learning, a function not easily fulfilled by the traditional research and development model we had inadvertently been following. Project Interweave is our attempt to institutionalize the scholarship of teaching and learning at Elon and to address some of the problems encountered in the three-year initiative. Our desire is to "interweave" the scholarship of teaching and learning into the Elon campus culture both across time — from faculty–student team to faculty–student team, and across space — from department to department across campus. The following proposal was accepted by senior administrators:

1. The faculty–student teams would be appointed as Elon Scholars-in-Residence in the scholarship of teaching and learning.
2. Teams would be appointed to two-year residencies.
3. Teams would be staggered in such a way that, in any given year, there would be an experienced faculty–student team and an apprentice faculty–student team, with the experienced team mentoring the apprentice team.
4. The apprentice team would become the experienced team in the second year of the two-year residency, coaching the next team.
5. Teams would typically include at least two faculty members and two or more student associates.
6. Teams would be funded at $5,000 per year, $10,000 for the two-year residency.

In fall 2002, a faculty–student team working on ways to better prepare education majors to teach adolescents was selected from those that had participated in the initial three-year scholarship of teaching and learning project. This interdisciplinary team, comprised of faculty from English, mathematics, physics, and sociology along with two students from education, was appointed for one year to a serve as the first experienced team. An apprentice team was selected to enjoy the full two-year experience during the 2002-2004 academic years. Faculty–student teams were given the following duties:

First Year

◆ Direct a new Carnegie project in order to maintain Elon's momentum in the scholarship of teaching and learning.
◆ Deepen Elon's commitment to partnerships in teaching and learning and in the study thereof.

◆ Work in collaboration with the experienced team, becoming advocates for the scholarship of teaching and learning on and off campus.
◆ Submit results of project for publication or presentation.

Second Year

◆ Become knowledgeable in current research on the scholarship of teaching and learning and share this knowledge with faculty and the new apprentice team.
◆ Continue sharing their scholarship and promoting Elon's faculty–student collaborative approach.
◆ Maintain Elon's national visibility through efforts such as conference presentations, website connections, and networking.
◆ Maintain a close connection with the development of the proposed Elon Center for Creative Teaching and Learning.
◆ Serve on the Elon Carnegie Committee.
◆ Help prepare themselves or others for scholarly opportunities in teaching and learning.

Institutionalizing Campus Leadership

The Carnegie Committee has continued "interweaving" by adding Project Interweave scholars each year and instituting a three-year leadership commitment for the Carnegie Committee chair. The future chair begins as assisting co-chair, moves to chair, and continues as primary co-chair in the third year. The Committee is charged with several tasks:

◆ Overseeing Project Interweave (setting up a mechanism to facilitate proposal submission and overseeing expenditures of funds in collaboration with the Provost's office).
◆ Maintaining contact with national AAHE and Carnegie work in the scholarship of teaching and learning.

- Providing opportunities for Elon faculty and students to present their scholarship nationally.
- Assessing the effectiveness and replicability of Elon projects.
- Ensuring that the Elon Carnegie website is maintained and contributing regularly to the national AAHE WebCenter.

The Way Forward

We are now at a critical point in the evolution of the scholarship of teaching and learning on our campus. In the midst of considerable institutional change and growth, and in the context of competing projects, how can we maintain the enthusiasm and commitment that characterized our initial efforts? How can we keep falcons as falcons? Our continuing work focuses on celebration and communication; time and money; promotion, tenure, and hiring; and national conversations.

Celebration and Communication
Elon University has experienced a pattern of rapid growth over the last decade, with one third of our teaching faculty on staff for less than five years. Thus, communicating to faculty about the exciting nature of the scholarship of teaching and learning is a continuing task. Celebrating Project Interweave is essential to keeping this work visible and vital.

Time and Money
To raise innovation to the level of scholarship, learning must be assessed and results shared with the larger academic community. This process is enormously time consuming and further complicated by the fact that such projects frequently involve several faculty members — often interdisciplinary teams — and students. To do this work, faculty and students

> Continuing work focuses on celebration and communication; time and money; promotion, tenure, and hiring; and national conversations.

need summer stipends, course release and reallocation, and other resources.

Promotion, Tenure and Hiring
Given the time commitment involved, faculty must be convinced that involvement in the scholarship of teaching and learning is worthwhile. A consistent message of support must come from all levels of administration. This support must include official recognition of this scholarship when promotion and tenure decisions are made. Hiring practices should also reflect a commitment to this work, since one of the most difficult tasks we face in this "post-honeymoon" phase is passing on the culture of the scholarship of teaching and learning to new members of the community. Finally, when new faculty arrive, there must be a system in place for initiating them into this work.

National Conversations
Connections with national work in the scholarship of teaching and learning must be maintained. Participation in conferences, workshops, and summer academies provides important networking opportunities that revitalize our work. This is in part why we included the need to stay current in the best practices regarding the scholarship of teaching and

learning in the second year of Project Interweave. We also seek national recognition for Elon University's commitment to this work.

The Challenge of Keeping Falcons as Falcons

We began with the Nasruddin story. At the heart of institutionalizing anything significant and exciting is the key issue of keeping falcons as falcons. If the scholarship of teaching and learning continues to excite passion, then it will not lose its distinctiveness as it becomes institutionalized. We hope that Project Interweave will sustain and nourish this scholarship at Elon during the next few years, but keeping falcons as falcons requires community support and encouragement. This is why we need one another. We welcome ongoing dialogue and support from our colleagues at the national level. Together, we may encourage falcons to fly.

Contacts and URL

Deborah Thurlow Long
Associate Professor of Education
Elon University
dlong@elon.edu

John G. Sullivan
Professor of Philosophy and
  Distinguished University Professor
Elon University
sullivan@elon.edu

Rosemary Haskell
Professor of English
Elon University
haskell@elon.edu

For information about the Carnegie Initiative at Elon University, see
http://www.elon.edu/carnegie

Elon University
Elon, NC
Master's I
http://www.elon.edu/

A Freestanding Teaching Academy

Josef M. Broder and Patricia L. Kalivoda
University of Georgia

In March 1999, Lee Shulman, president of The Carnegie Foundation for the Advancement of Teaching, visited the University of Georgia campus and encouraged our faculty to establish a teaching academy. Thirteen faculty were invited to discuss the foundations of the University of Georgia Teaching Academy. They became charter members of the Academy in October 1999, when they agreed to accept responsibility for the organization. Essentially, these faculty created a freestanding, faculty-organized, and faculty-driven Teaching Academy. This chapter highlights the University of Georgia's experience at creating its Teaching Academy: its history, infrastructure, accomplishments, impact on the university community, and implications for other institutions.

The charter members first considered adopting teaching academy structures from other institutions but felt that the academy concept should not be just an end product but a process of shared ownership and development. They sought to create a structure unique to the University of Georgia and one that would build upon the many good works in teaching and faculty development that had been taking place on campus for two decades. In many ways, the campus infra- structure for establishing a teaching academy was ideal.

Membership to the Academy is by invitation from the members of the Academy. New members are selected from faculty at the University of Georgia who have demonstrated, over a period of not less than five years, a significant commitment to the teaching–learning enterprise. Faculty groups who are routinely nominated for membership include Senior Teaching Fellows and recipients of the University's top teaching awards. Membership in the Academy is permanent. The Academy currently has 143 members from across all academic disciplines and faculty appointments. While some members of the Academy have or may assume administrative appointments after joining the Academy, they participate in the Academy as faculty members and not as administrators.

Campus Infrastructure

As a freestanding entity, the University of Georgia Teaching Academy is not a formal part of the University's administrative structure or faculty governance. As such, the Academy does not receive public funds and does not have official standing in faculty governance. To date, the

Academy has been funded by private grants to the University Foundation, including a $6,000 start-up grant from the President's Venture Fund. The Academy also works closely with University administration and teaching support units, including the Office of Instructional Support and Development, the Institute of Higher Education, and the Office of the Vice President for Instruction.

The decision to create a freestanding academy was shaped largely from campus infrastructure that had been developed over the previous two decades. Catalysts that fostered the creation of the Teaching Academy included: the creation of an office of instructional support and development, enhanced campus-wide teaching awards, the AAHE Peer Review Project, and the CASTL Campus Program. These events and activities were milestones in the University's efforts to promote and recognize teaching and learning as scholarly activities. The result was the nurturing of a growing community of teaching scholars across campus that would later provide the motivation and energy for establishing the Teaching Academy.

Accomplishments

As a freestanding organization, the Teaching Academy developed its own mission and agenda. The Academy's primary objective has been to create a continuous forum for promoting and celebrating excellence in teaching and learning that transcends university administrators, faculty governance, and periodic external reviews. The Academy has sought recognition by faculty and administration as the premiere faculty-organized and faculty-driven organization for teaching and learning. To accomplish this, the Academy has provided campus-wide leadership in three areas. First, the Academy

has promoted the scholarship of teaching and learning and teaching and learning as scholarship, the latter being essential to establishing and achieving broad-based support for the Academy at a Doctoral Extensive institution. Academy members have been active in the Campus Program and in other AAHE initiatives.

Second, the Academy has positioned itself to provide expertise and advice to the university administration on matters related to teaching and learning. With its members consisting of the University's most outstanding, recognized and dedicated teachers, the Academy is in a unique position to provide input on instructional issues and activities. The Academy has contributed input and resources to a number of areas, including:

- support for a proposal to transform a campus-wide teaching award into a professorship;

- criticism of a proposal to establish a separate nontenure track for teaching faculty, which Academy members successfully encouraged the administration not to adopt;

- planning and coordination of the University's annual faculty symposium;

- leadership for the Faculty Survey of Student Engagement;

- mentoring for the Freshman College and Honors Mentor Program;

- input on establishing freshman learning communities;

- input on the University's Outstanding Advisor Award program;

- input on hiring university-level administrators with academic appointments; and

- leadership in developing an Emeriti Scholars Program.

On sensitive issues, the Academy has assumed a role similar to that of the League of Women Voters. Rather than advocate solutions to sensitive issues, the Academy has opted to create forums for deliberations that will better inform university-level administrators.

Third, the Academy has sought to engage its members and the larger university community on issues related to teaching and learning. For faculty engagement to be effective and sustained, there must be opportunities for frequent interaction. To promote interaction among its members, the Academy has sponsored or co-sponsored major teaching forums each semester. These forums feature prominent speakers and include meal functions, small group sessions, a major lecture, panel discussions, and receptions. Preference is given to nationally recognized speakers who are known for their contributions to teaching and learning.

Impact on the University Community

The Teaching Academy has provided a continuous and broad-based faculty forum to promote teaching and learning as scholarly activities. The Academy has served as a sounding board for the administration on teaching and learning issues. While a formal assessment of the Academy's impact has not been completed, external groups have recognized its potential. In 2001, the Academy received one of three commendations awarded to the University from the Southern Association of Colleges and Schools in its Accreditation Reaffirmation report.

To date, the Academy's activities have focused primarily on faculty issues and less on student learning issues. Recently, however, the Academy assumed a more active role in student learning by coordinating the University's Faculty Survey of Student Engagement. As a follow-up to this survey, the Academy will sponsor a forum on student engagement and learning.

Implications for Other Institutions

The formation of teaching academies on university campuses is influenced by institutional differences. For this reason, the University of Georgia's experience with creating a freestanding academy is different from that of other institutions. Anecdotal evidence suggests two contrasting models for creating teaching academies. Institutions can establish and fund an office of instructional support that facilitates the creation of a freestanding teaching academy, or institutions can establish and fund a teaching academy as an academic support unit. The former tends to be organized and driven by faculty while the latter is administratively driven. Academies that operate as teaching support units have more secure funding arrangements but may lack faculty support and participation. They may also lack a measure of independence that allows them to engage the larger university community on sensitive matters related to teaching and learning. Freestanding academies are more independent and have greater involvement of faculty but face uncertainties in funding and operational support. The success of freestanding academies may ultimately depend upon their ability to engage the larger university community and to secure funding.

While the University of Georgia's Teaching Academy is a relatively young organization, its formation has taught us some valuable lessons. First, we learned that a freestanding teaching academy needs a core group of dedicated and energetic faculty to monitor and sustain the momentum of the organization. This core group continuously and tirelessly seeks opportunities for the Academy to engage the larger university community. The academy's membership guidelines should aim to recruit new members to this core group of faculty on a continuous basis. Next, the academy needs holistic and multidimensional recognition by the central administration and the active support of its members. The academy must be proactive in its programs to educate and inform university faculty and administrators. Finally, the academy should choose its programs wisely and minimize controversial activities that may alienate faculty, administrators, or students.

Acknowledgements

The authors would like to thank fellow charter members of the University of Georgia Teaching Academy for their valuable contributions to its formation: Robert Anderson, Jeanne Barsanti, Ron Carlson, Joe Crim, Sylvia Hutchinson, Bill Jackson, Jeremy Kilpatrick, Pat Bell-Scott, Peter Shedd, Fred Stephenson, and Susette Talarico.

Contacts and URLs

Josef Broder
Assistant Dean for Academic Affairs,
   Professor of Agricultural and Applied
   Economics
University of Georgia
jbroder@uga.edu

Patricia Kalivoda
Associate Vice President for Public Service
   and Outreach, Adjunct Faculty Member in
   the Institute of Higher Education
University of Georgia
tlk@uga.edu

For more information on the Teaching Academy's mission, charter, membership, and other activities, see http://teachingacademy.uga.edu/

For an in-depth discussion of the catalysts for development of the Academy, see http://teachingacademy.uga.edu/ documents/unicoi_broder.html

For a summary of the teaching forums and speakers, see http:// teachingacademy.uga.edu/events.htm#past

**University of Georgia
Athens, GA
Doctoral/Research Extensive
http://www.uga.edu/**

The Maricopa Institute For Learning

Maria Harper-Marinick
Maricopa Community Colleges

The Maricopa Institute for Learning (MIL) supports fellowships for Maricopa Community Colleges' residential faculty who are interested in contributing to the scholarship of teaching and learning. The program is administered by the Maricopa Center for Learning and Instruction, a comprehensive faculty development and support center for faculty and administrators of the 10 Maricopa colleges. These fellowships support faculty members with time and resources to conduct applied research in their classrooms and engage in scholarly reflection and dialogue about effective teaching and learning practices. Established in 1998, the Fellowship Program is modeled after the Carnegie Scholars Program that is part of the Carnegie Academy for the Scholarship of Teaching and Learning.

The Model

The MIL Fellowship provided me with a wonderful opportunity to become once again a learner, specifically to focus my learning on the topic of student learning in the discipline of chemistry. The fellowship granted me time to read deeply about current theories of learning and then to reflect on how these theories could be put into practice in the classroom with my students.

(Rosemary Leary, 1999 MIL Fellow, Chemistry, Estrella Mountain Community College).

The primary purpose of the Institute is to create a community of scholars that will engage in classroom-based inquiry, reflective practice, and conversations about the scholarship of teaching and learning. This program addresses the Maricopa vision of a learning organization dedicated to providing "effective, innovative, student-centered, flexible, and lifelong educational opportunities." Six Fellows are selected each academic year, representing a variety of disciplines and colleges within the Maricopa system. The Institute provides a structure for the interdisciplinary team of faculty to examine significant issues in their teaching fields and contribute to the scholarship of teaching and learning. This is accomplished through a variety of experiences and opportunities:

◆ The Institute oversees learning projects that focus on teaching for understanding and investigate how and under what conditions student learning can be fostered, can be tested with students, can be documented and made public, have implications beyond an individual classroom, and are relevant to and extend the scholarship of teaching and learning in an academic discipline.

◆ The Institute offers internal seminars during which fellows refine projects, examine a variety of teaching and learning innovations, and engage in a discourse community.

◆ The Institute hosts external seminars during which fellows attend and participate in national meetings and conferences about teaching and learning.

◆ Finally, the Institute provides resources, including six load hours of release time per semester for fellows, travel funds, a stipend to purchase books and materials in support of their projects, a collection of materials related to teaching and learning research and practice housed in the Center, and access to the Maricopa Learning eXchange, a warehouse of learning ideas and materials.

Factors Making the Institute Successful

Seven principal factors contribute to the success of the Maricopa Institute for Learning. Fellows and participants have identified these seven as important to their work with the Institute.

Reflective Practice

Being part of MIL has been the difference between being reflective about teaching and learning only occasionally and often haphazardly and being reflective consistently and with purpose (Mark Burtch, 2003 MIL Fellow, Mathematics, Scottsdale Community College).

Excellence in teaching has always been a part of Maricopa's mission and one of its core values. The Institute has brought a structure and an environment for faculty to engage in a more systematic analysis of their teaching practices through classroom-based inquiry and reflection. This analysis results in enhanced understanding of effective teaching practices and the factors that contribute to deeper student learning.

Building Community

The experience of the participants in the MIL cadre results in networks of support, dialogue, and innovation, so that the district as a whole has a fertile community of scholars who are willing to try new ideas and bring leading edge practices to our colleges (Martha Bergin, Faculty Developer, Communication, GateWay Community College).

One of the goals of the Institute is to create and nurture a community of scholars. Fellows learn and explore together and grow comfortable sharing their work, successes, and failures. During the pilot year, fellows were asked to participate in a summer retreat and two seminars and to engage in dialogue via a private Web board on the MIL website. Because fellows did not use the Web board as frequently as we had hoped, we learned that if fellows were to establish a connection with each other, they had to come together to work and socialize. As one of the fellows wrote on the program evaluation, "If time is not spent together, then a team can't emerge." Fellows are now asked to participate in monthly meetings, two-day eminars, and summer retreats:

◆ During monthly meetings, the group meets for two to three hours at a location of its choice. In the first half of the meeting, fellows update the group about their projects, especially methodology and implementation issues. Then the group discusses readings on teaching and learning, scholarship, or assessment of student learning. Each month, a different fellow selects the readings and facilitates dialogue about them.

◆ Two-day seminars in both fall and spring have formats similar to the monthly meetings, but these longer seminars allow for richer dialogue and more in-depth discussions. The fellows discuss their projects and the literature, plan conference presentations, and offer formative assessment of the program.

◆ Summer retreats occur after the academic year, and participating faculty are paid a stipend. The goals are to conclude the current projects and help the fellows go public with their work, to acquaint the incoming and outgoing groups, to help the incoming group refine their projects and understand the program's expectations, and to converse about the scholarship of teaching and learning.

Release Time

The most significant part of this experience has been the availability of time. At a community college, the first goal is teaching; time is not often available for reflection on teaching and learning (Maria Chavira, 2000 MIL Fellow, Psychology, Mesa Community College).

The teaching load for faculty at the Maricopa Community Colleges — five courses plus committee responsibilities — leaves little time for research and reflection. Fellows are therefore released from 40 percent of their regular load and asked not to commit to additional activities that would place them on overload. The cost for releasing faculty for six load hours every semester is shared by the fellow's college and the Institute.

Merit-Based Nomination and Selection Process

I was appreciative of the blind selection process. It is an objective and fair process. Since proposals are evaluated on the merit of the ideas and the potential contribution to both the discipline and the scholarship of teaching and learning, it reduces political biases (Ly Tran-Nguyen, 2003 MIL Fellow, Psychology, Mesa Community College).

Candidates are nominated by college presidents, deans, and faculty developers. By selecting their candidates, the colleges publicly acknowledge and commit to the support of those faculty who are innovative and are dedicated to the improvement of teaching and learning. Proposals are reviewed by a committee of 10 to 12 faculty, including former fellows, who represent a variety of disciplines and colleges in our system. Evaluators do not know the identity of applicants or their colleges. Faculty who nominate candidates or help them develop proposals are excluded from the pool of readers.

Faculty Voices

Faculty were part of the team that conceived and implemented the initial model. The leadership was taken by the ACE Learning Team, an intercollegiate Maricopa group sponsored by the American Council on Education. The faculty team was supported by the vice chancellor for academic affairs, the director of the Maricopa Center for Learning and Instruction, an instructional designer, and faculty developers. Pat Hutchings, vice president of The Carnegie Foundation for the Advancement of Teaching, participated in the initial discussions and shared ideas and resources that served as the basis for the development of the Maricopa model. One faculty advocate noted:

> Faculty brought to the table an understanding of the realities and responsibilities of faculty members at Maricopa, the importance of an appropriate support and reward system in terms of release time, the need for clarity in communicating both expectations and responsibilities, and the need for supporting the dignity and professionalism of both faculty and their colleges.

Faculty input has also been essential to the program's evolution and success. Former fellows

> The most significant part of this experience has been the availability of time.

and other faculty known for their creativity and scholarly approach to teaching serve as proposal evaluators. Current fellows participate in the annual comprehensive program assessment.

Administrative Support

The Institute was established as one of the programs within the Center for Learning and Instruction and is managed by the Center's director. It is not supported by grant money. This structure provides a sense of permanence and continuity and demonstrates institutional commitment to faculty professional development. As Anna Solley, vice chancellor for academic affairs, noted:

> At the Maricopa Community Colleges, we take great pride in hiring and supporting quality and diverse faculty. Great teaching is our hallmark and our faculty are respected for their expertise locally, statewide, and internationally. Engaging them in discussions about the scholarship of teaching and learning is one of our priorities and is coordinated by the Maricopa Center for Learning and Instruction, a one-stop resource center for faculty development.

Continuous Evaluation

From its inception, the Institute's elements have been evaluated for their effectiveness in a variety of ways. At end-of-year retreats, for example, both outgoing and incoming fellows are asked to complete written surveys, anonymously, to assess what worked best about the retreat and what needed to be improved. In addition, the incoming fellows plan the next retreat based on their experience and the data collected from the surveys. Outgoing fellows also complete an open-ended questionnaire regarding all components of the program, including clarity of purpose; amount and quality of administrative support; effectiveness of meetings, seminars, and conferences; and usefulness of resources. During the monthly meetings, fellows address issues related to the projects, administrative support, or evolution of the community of scholars. Fellows' feedback serves as the basis for changes made to the model and the infrastructure that supports it.

What Comes Next?

Our priorities now are to connect work in the scholarship of teaching and learning to other initiatives, support the continuing work of former Institute fellows, and involve more faculty in reflective practice and dialogue about teaching for deeper and long-lasting learning. To address these priorities, we have taken several steps:

◆ One of our most respected faculty members is serving as a faculty-in-residence at the Center for Learning and Instruction for a year to explore new initiatives.

◆ A group of current and former fellows has begun to conceptualize "MIL2," which will support Institute participants who want to further their work and make it public. MIL2 will also develop local avenues to engage other faculty in the scholarship of teaching and learning. Our vision is to develop cross-discipline and cross-college faculty learning communities.

◆ Fellows host faculty forums, teaching circles, and dialogue days at their colleges.

◆ We are compiling entries for a publication on the scholarship of teaching and learning at Maricopa, to be distributed to all faculty and to be posted on the MIL website.

Our primary goal has been to establish and nurture a community of scholars who engage in classroom-based research and build community by sharing ideas in reflective discussion circles. Since 1999, 28 faculty have participated in the Institute. Many have published their work and presented at national and international conferences, but most importantly, the Fellows say that this experience has changed the way they approach teaching and learning. As Diane Clark, 2003 MIL Fellow in English from Chandler-Gilbert Community College, noted, "MIL creates an exciting, dynamic environment that fuels our love of teaching and encourages us, as professionals, to continually examine our classroom practices in the search for ways to enhance our students' success. For a teacher, there is no greater gift." We are proud of the Maricopa Institute for Learning Fellows program and would be glad to share additional information.

Contact and URLs

Maria Harper-Marinick
Director, Maricopa Center for Learning and Instruction
Maricopa Community Colleges
maria.harper@domail.maricopa.edu

For more information on the Maricopa Institute for Learning, see
http://www.mcli.dist.maricopa.edu/mil/

For access to the Maricopa Learning exchange (MLX), see
http://www.mcli.dist.maricopa.edu/mlx

To view the selection and evaluation criteria for Institute applicants, see http://www.mcli.dist.maricopa.edu/mil/application.html

Maricopa Community Colleges
Tempe, AZ
Associate's degrees offered at colleges in the Maricopa Community College District
http://www.maricopa.edu/

Building an Infrastructure To Support Instruction

Rosslyn Smith
Texas Tech University

Texas Tech University has established two entities dedicated to supporting instruction, the Teaching, Learning, and Technology Center and the Teaching Academy.

The milestones for the development of the Center and the Academy include the administrative decisions to establish the entities, in 1995 and 1997, respectively; the development in 1998 of the distinctive mission and goals for the Teaching Academy, which serve to differentiate its purpose from that of the Center; the decision in 1999-2000 that the Center would provide staff support and operational funding for the Teaching Academy; and the completion in 1999-2000 of a permanent home for the Teaching, Learning, and Technology Center.

Teaching, Learning, and Technology Center

The Teaching, Learning, and Technology Center provides instructional development opportunities and supports faculty and other instructional staff in the development and application of appropriate technology to teaching. Centrally located in the main library building, the Center serves all colleges and academic areas. Its director is also a vice provost who reports to the provost.

The Center offers a range of programs and services, including confidential teaching consultations, teaching workshops and roundtables, technology short courses, program and course assessment instruction and consulting, customized technology classes, and the Teaching Effectiveness And Career enHancement (TEACH) program for doctoral students going into academic careers. The Center also sponsors a Faculty Fellow and a competitive grants program for faculty of approximately $50,000 annually.

Teaching Academy

Established in 1997, the Teaching Academy seeks to demonstrate, support, promote, and recognize teaching excellence at Texas Tech University. This university-wide organization is composed of faculty who are committed to the improvement of teaching and learning. Membership is selective, with a faculty screening committee considering a candidate's letters of recommendation and paying particular attention to evidence of sustained teaching excellence. Membership in the Academy may

> The initial challenge was to establish unique identities, missions, and goals for the Center and for the Teaching Academy.

not exceed 20 percent of the teaching faculty, and attrition only occurs when faculty retire or leave the university for other employment. Only current Academy members may nominate new members.

Since the Teaching Academy is more of an honorary than an administrative unit, it has no reporting line or independent budget. Most of its funds are provided by the Teaching, Learning, and Technology Center. The Teaching Academy is highly valued by the university administration. As provost William Marcy notes on the Teaching Academy website, "The Teaching Academy is the strongest evidence of Texas Tech's commitment to a quality learning environment....We really cannot overstate the value of teaching excellence and the recognition of those that achieve it."

The Teaching Academy members organize an annual conference and a series of informal discussions about topics related to the scholarship of teaching and learning, and they coordinate the University's participation in several external teaching conferences. The Teaching Academy also sponsors the annual $25,000 Departmental Excellence in Teaching Award,

and the Academy's Executive Council serves as the selection body for the Chancellor's Distinguished Teaching Award.

Why it works

Perhaps the best explanation of why it works for the university to have both a teaching and learning center and a teaching academy is that the Center and the Teaching Academy complement one another. Their coordination is reflected in the fact that the Teaching Academy and the Center often co-sponsor programming, and Teaching Academy members frequently serve on Center's advisory committees and present at Center programs, where they model exemplary practice.

Challenges

The major initial challenge was to establish unique identities, missions, and goals for the Center and for the Teaching Academy. The Center was established prior to the Teaching Academy and therefore had a defined mission at the time the Academy was established. The director of the Center, also a member of the Teaching Academy, served on the first Teaching Academy Executive Council. The council drafted the mission and goal statements for the Teaching Academy, and they subsequently voted to make the director of the Center an ex-officio member of the council, an arrangement that encourages close cooperation and articulation of responsibilities and programs.

The Teaching Academy's operations and programs are largely dependent on the Center's budget, which allows the institution to leverage its existing staff and financial resources in the face of budget constraints. Had we foreseen the extent to which the Teaching Academy and the Center would collaborate, we might also have planned for dedicated space for a Teaching Academy office within the Center and requested supplemental funding for Teaching Academy functions and support.

Impact

The collaboration between the Center and the Teaching Academy has had a tangible impact on the institution and on individual faculty and students:

- ◆ Supported by the Center, Teaching Academy members, students, and other faculty have attended conferences such as the Wakonse South Teaching Conference and the AAHE Summer Academy. Attendance at these conferences has contributed to the development and implementation of curricular models related to the improvement of introductory chemistry and business math courses and the development of a cross-disciplinary service-learning project, to name just a few examples.

- ◆ The Teaching Academy and the Center have collaborated on teaching conferences, which focused on the scholarship of teaching and learning and featured nationally known speakers.

- ◆ Members of the Teaching Academy led an institutional self-study on the evaluation of teaching effectiveness, a project funded by the Kellogg Foundation that was also part of the University's participation in the CASTL Campus Program.

- ◆ Texas Tech has been selected as an AAHE/Carnegie Cluster Leader; our cluster topic is Scholarly Inquiry about Active Pedagogies. A former chair of the Teaching Academy Executive Council serves as the coordinator of this cluster, and the Center provides the clerical and operational support for the work of the cluster.

These events have shaped the growth of the Teaching, Learning, and Technology Center and the Teaching Academy and have contributed to the collaborative relationship between the two entities.

Future Directions

Given their success thus far, the Teaching, Learning, and Technology Center and the Teaching Academy will continue to make the teaching mission of the University visible to the public, a vital function in this era of budget constraints and accountability. By doing so, they will continue to play an important role in the recruitment of both faculty and students and the enhancement of the quality of student learning at Texas Tech University.

Acknowledgements

I wish to express my thanks and acknowledge the valuable input from the current, future and past chairs of the Executive Council of the Teaching Academy, Marjean Purinton, Timothy Floyd, Debra Laverie, Daisy Floyd, and James Brink, as well as the associate and assistant directors of the Teaching, Learning, and Technology Center, Edward Anderson and Katherine Stalcup.

Contacts and URLs

Timothy Floyd
(for inquiries about the Teaching Academy)
Chair, Teaching Council, 2003-2004
Texas Tech University
timothy.floyd@ttu.edu

Rosslyn Smith
(for inquiries about the Teaching, Learning,
   and Technology Center)
Vice Provost/Director; Chair, Executive
   Council, 1998-1999
Texas Tech University
rosslyn.smith@ttu.edu

For more information on the Teaching
Academy and the Center, see
http://www.academy.ttu.edu/ and
http://www.tltc.ttu.edu, respectively.

Texas Tech University
Lubbock, TX
Doctoral/Research Extensive
http://www.ttu.edu/

Furthering the Scholarship of Teaching and Learning The Wisconsin Way

Anthony Ciccone

University of Wisconsin-Milwaukee

"Advancing the practice of teaching through scholarly inquiry into student learning"

(UW System/UW-Milwaukee Leadership Site mission statement)

In June 2003, the joint UW System/UW-Milwaukee Scholarship of Teaching and Learning initiative, begun at UW-Milwaukee in 1999, reached an important milestone. In a climate of severe budget cuts, the UW System Board of Regents took time to engage in a 90-minute discussion of the scholarship of teaching and learning. The regents examined a case study presented by Pat Hutchings, vice president of The Carnegie Foundation for the Advancement of Teaching; willingly participated in a "think-pair-share" activity; asked thoughtful questions about teaching and learning; and, most importantly, asked how they could further the scholarship of teaching and learning leadership site initiative in Wisconsin. How were we able to get to this point? How did we build the infrastructure that has positioned us to make significant progress in supporting the scholarship of teaching and learning across the UW System?

Building infrastructure for the scholarship of teaching and learning in Wisconsin became the mission of two faculty development offices, the UW-Milwaukee Center for Instructional and Professional Development and the UW System's Office of Professional and Instructional Development. The first lesson learned about building infrastructure for this work lies herein: the scholarship of teaching and learning works in Wisconsin because it is tied to traditionally successful faculty development offices that have this scholarly perspective on teaching and learning in their philosophy and programs. Both the Center for Instructional and Professional Development and the Office of Professional and Instructional Development operate in that "free space" between faculty and administration, charged with finding a *lingua franca* that explains the needs and desires of one group to the other. The language of the scholarship of teaching and learning, as imprecise as it still is, expresses the deep concern faculty have for student learning and their effectiveness in facilitating it, and the sincere interest campus and System administrators have in increasing student success in measurable ways.

The UW-Milwaukee faculty consider the scholarship of teaching and learning to be a major professional development initiative and define it as understanding, explaining, and valuing teaching and attention to student learning as scholarly, intellectual work. By emphasizing this work's scholarly aspects, the campus definition allows us to create credible models within the research institution context. The UW-Milwaukee Center's Scholars Program, now in its fourth year, redirects existing faculty development funding to five faculty per year who model systematic inquiry projects. The Scholars serve as a "think tank" for campus and system-wide initiatives in the scholarship of teaching and learning. The results of their work can be found in their presentations at conferences and workshops as well as in Center publications.

As an integral part of the UW System Administration, the Office of Professional and Instructional Development depends for its success on the ability to construct an agenda that advances System, campus, and individual faculty priorities. Created in the late 1970s as a visible sign of the collaboration the newly created UW system was to foster, the Office has always believed that individual professional growth can inform institutional change. Building infrastructure for the scholarship of teaching and learning thus meant bringing national models (e.g., the Carnegie Scholars) to the attention of UW faculty and campuses through its own conferences and the financial support it provided for local programs. It also meant refocusing its principal programs for individuals, the Wisconsin Teaching Fellows and Teaching Scholars Programs, around work in the scholarship of teaching and learning.

The Center for Instructional and Professional Development and the Office of Professional and Instructional Development have a long history of collaboration. Indeed, the Center

had been created in 1981 under an Office grant program that funded the development of campus teaching improvement centers. After learning about the nature of scholarly work in teaching and learning through AAHE and CASTL programs, leaders in these offices recognized its value as an organizing principle for faculty development. A "Going Public" grant from AAHE in 2000 helped the Center design creative ways to use the work of UW-Milwaukee Center Scholars to advance discussions of this scholarship on other campuses and to help the System campuses build on each other's strengths.

In July 2002, a joint Office/Center Steering Committee defined the purposes and outlined the structure of a system-wide Leadership Site on the scholarship of teaching and learning, to be housed at UW-Milwaukee. The committee, which was composed of Center Scholars, Wisconsin Teaching Scholars, and administrators, used AAHE support to attend the 2002 Summer Academy and plan for the year ahead. Once official support was received from both the UW System and UW-Milwaukee administrations, three areas of infrastructure were addressed simultaneously: continued development of the "flagship" program in the scholarship of teaching and learning at UW-Milwaukee; restructuring of the Office of Professional and Instructional Development to make connections with campuses through this scholarship more visible and effective; and establishment of the actual leadership site.

The continued development of infrastructure at UW-Milwaukee required solidifying campus sources of funding, finding ways to increase participation, creating opportunities for committed teaching and learning scholars to continue useful work, and creating connections to existing campus priorities. UW-Milwaukee provost and UW System professional development allocations were redirected to the Center for expanded programming in the scholarship of teaching and learning. The result has been continued support for Center scholars, who now direct new initiatives in this scholarship, and Center leadership of committees on assessment and student success.

Restructuring the Office of Professional and Instructional Development to make connections with campuses through this work more visible and effective required redefining grant programs, creating a more direct link with campus programs, and establishing ways for campuses to benefit from and contribute to the work of others. The Office's Executive Committee and the UW System approved $17,000 in grants to each system unit to create, or further, campus-based work in the scholarship of teaching and learning. They encouraged campuses to create teams for this work that included former Teaching Scholars and Fellows. Finally, the Office provided a substantial part of the resources needed to create the leadership site at UW-Milwaukee.

The leadership site includes a coordinator, staff support, an Executive Committee, and an Advisory Council. The council, composed of representatives from every campus-based project in the scholarship of teaching and learning, is the conduit for crucial communication between individual campuses and the leadership site as well as among campuses. The first year's modest budget will also provide funding for a train-the-trainers program and ultimately a "Scholarship of Teaching and Learning 101" project that will guide the work of individual faculty in systematic inquiry.

The scholarship of teaching and learning perspective, which has challenged us to redefine the value of teaching improvement in terms of its effects on student learning, is gradually becoming the *lingua franca* of professional development in Wisconsin. It is no longer just a "boutique" operation, that is, a place where only a few "shop." Every system unit has an ongoing program in the scholarship of teaching and learning, funded by the Office of Professional and Instructional Development and local offices. In 2003-2004, more than 1,000 faculty and teaching staff will participate in some type of program related to this scholarship, and many will design and implement scholarly projects on first-year experience programs, service-learning, or interdisciplinary courses, for example. Individual projects will help us understand, among other topics, how students revise their writing, how they understand the value of participation in discussion, and how they learn through online discussions. Finally, the leadership site will help us understand how work in the scholarship of teaching and learning can be done effectively across a large state system.

The work has not been without its challenges. Campuses vary in mission and culture, and administrators must support faculty initiative without co-opting it. The goal of creating a leadership site in Wisconsin, however, helped the Office of Professional and Instructional Development and the Center for Instructional and Professional Development crystallize a new understanding of their work — advancing the practice of teaching through scholarly inquiry into student learning. The initiative has succeeded to this point because it has built on campus and system strengths, redirected existing funding sources, created and employed human and intellectual capital, and connected this work to existing or newly formed initiatives on campuses. The scholarship of teaching and learning perspective works in a multi-campus system because it provides us with better ways to understand the relationship between teaching and student learning on one hand, and between teaching and the process of scholarly inquiry on the other. With its focus on student learning, the scholarship of teaching and learning may finally help us connect faculty, instructional, and organizational development.

Contacts and URLs

Anthony Ciccone
Director of the Center for Instructional and
  Professional Development
University of Wisconsin-Milwaukee
ciccone@uwm.edu

Renee Meyers
Department of Communication, Coordinator
  of Leadership Site
University of Wisconsin-Milwaukee
meyers@uwm.edu

Jude Rathburn
Department of Business, Coordinator of
  UW-Milwaukee's Student-Faculty
  Partnerships grant
University of Wisconsin-Milwaukee
jude@uwm.edu

Connie Schroeder
Associate Director of the Center for
  Instructional and Professional
  Development
University of Wisconsin-Milwaukee
connies@uwm.edu

For more information about the Center for Instructional and Professional Development, see www.uwm.edu/dept/CIPD

University of Wisconsin-Milwaukee
Milwaukee, WI
Doctoral/Research Extensive
http://www.uwm.edu/

Organizing and Bargaining for Scholarship of Teaching and Learning

Sherry Linkon and John Russo
Youngstown State University

In a 2000 address to the American Association of State Colleges and Universities, Lee Shulman, president of The Carnegie Foundation for the Advancement of Teaching, used Youngstown State University as an example of a campus that was actively developing scholarship of teaching and learning projects. Youngstown State University had begun to organize programs related to this scholarship in 1999. By fall 2002, the University had created a new center for teaching and learning. Youngstown State had also approved specific contract language in its union agreement providing reassigned time for the scholarship of teaching and learning and clarifying its use in faculty promotion. But the development of this work has proved fragile in the midst of reductions in state funding, contested visions, episodic administrative support, and outright resistance from "traditional" scholars. This leaves the future of this scholarship at Youngstown State uncertain.

Youngstown joined the Carnegie Academy for Scholarship of Teaching and Learning in 1998, when the program first started. By the end of the 2000-2001 academic year, the University had two Carnegie Scholars, and it had hosted a one-day conference where several scholars met with faculty members, sponsored a year-long seminar for faculty who wanted to explore methods in this scholarship, developed a series of informal "teaching lunches," and drafted an initial proposal to establish a center for teaching and learning. Those efforts created a core group that approached Youngstown's new president with a proposal to create the Center for the Advancement of Teaching And Learning at Youngstown State. The new president had been unaware of the activities in the scholarship of teaching and learning on campus until he heard Shulman's speech, but he quickly recognized that this work could bring recognition to the university and increase opportunities for outside funding. In summer 2001, the administration agreed to establish the new center and to fund a full-time director position. A planning committee was created with two representatives from each of the six undergraduate colleges at the university and from the administration.

Even as the committee began its work, however, tensions appeared between conflicting visions for the Center. Several administrators believed that the Center should be tied to partnerships with P-12 schools because more outside funding was available for projects including P-12 educators. For some committee members, any reference to P-12 partnerships raised questions about the whole enterprise, while others who worked closely with P-12 projects believed that such partnerships could strengthen the Center. Similarly, some committee members questioned the centrality and usefulness of the scholarship of teaching and learning, while others who were already active in this scholarship believed that it should be the guiding principle in the Center's work. A compromise was reached, built around the image of three interlocking circles representing related but largely separate activities: faculty development, the scholarship of teaching and learning, and classroom research on the P-12 level.

In an effort to accommodate the multiple interests of committee members and administrators, the planning committee drafted a job description for the director position that attempted to incorporate all three areas, as well as the administration's interest in generating outside funding and recognition. Some committee members hoped to shape the position toward greater emphasis on faculty development and the scholarship of teaching and learning through their choice of a director, though ultimately the broad job description may have perpetuated the administration's vision of the Center as geared to P-16 partnerships and fundraising. At the same time, committee members and administration leaders wrestled over whether to hire a director as a faculty member or as a professional staff person, reflecting continued uncertainty about the center's purpose.

These tensions made clear the importance of university-wide outreach to faculty, focused on determining their interests and enlisting their support for the Center. The committee consulted with faculty through department meetings and a series of needs assessment surveys. The committee asked faculty what they wanted

from a center for teaching and learning, identified faculty needs, and explored faculty concerns. The committee then developed a list of priorities, including support for assessing student learning, teaching with technology, grant development, mentoring, and understanding and applying the scholarship of teaching and learning on campus. Work with P-12 teachers emerged as a low priority for faculty.

By June 2002, the committee had hired a director for the Center and submitted proposals summarizing the faculty data to both the administration and the faculty union. The committee also requested an appropriate physical space and a substantial operating budget. The Center received the budget but no space. As of spring 2003, the Center still did not have a home at Youngstown State. Given significant state funding cuts, the Center lost funding for its administrative assistant position as well as a significant portion of its operating budget.

Faculty and university administrators had different priorities for the Center, which created some initial obstacles for the new director. When he arrived on campus, the provost asked him to work on several activities related to P-16 partnerships and institutional assessment. Confusion also arose about whether the provost or the planning committee was responsible for directing the Center's development and providing direct guidance. Several conversations and memos between all of those involved generated clearer priorities, including greater emphasis on providing resources and opportunities to faculty.

The Center's Planning Committee offered a proposal to the negotiating team for a new faculty contract in spring 2002. This proposal emphasized the need for two things — time and rewards. The scholarship of teaching and learning was added to the contract's list of activities that could be considered in promotion and tenure decisions. The committee also suggested that the new contract include reassigned time for faculty who wanted to pursue projects related to this scholarship, distance learning, or faculty development. Eventually, the Center's proposal was included, and Article 24.4 (Professional Development and Scholarship of Teaching and Learning) of the faculty contract, which had previously supported "institutional research" and generic "faculty development," was revised to provide reassigned time for "professional development related to teaching, and scholarship of teaching and learning, and initial distance learning projects." The new language offered reassigned time on a competitive basis for faculty engaged in the scholarship of teaching and learning, and although the contract already guaranteed significant reassigned time for discipline-based research, some faculty saw the new language as taking support away from traditional research.

By early 2003, union leadership had changed, and the new group was even more resistant to the idea of providing reassigned time for the scholarship of teaching and learning. Resistance grew when the call for applications for reassigned time drew few proposals, especially in the College of Arts and Sciences, the largest college on campus. By late spring, the negotiating team — without notifying faculty or the Center's Advisory Board — added traditional research to the list of activities that could be supported in Article 24.4. This could undermine access to reassigned time for those who wish to pursue the scholarship of teaching and learning in the future.

Today, the news from Youngstown State is mixed. In spring 2003, the Center sponsored a series of workshops, guest speakers, and infor-

> A secure future for the Center will most likely depend on results, including faculty participation in teaching and learning activities.

mal conversations. Sixteen faculty members representing five of the six colleges applied for the first Scholarship of Teaching and Learning Summer Institute. The institute will help faculty develop proposals for reassigned time under Article 24.4 as well as grants and presentations. The Center is also planning a faculty learning community centered on the scholarship of teaching and learning.

Frustration still exists among some who played key roles in developing the Center. The committee's expectations may have been too high, and the process may have moved too quickly. Faculty members' requests for more time to work on teaching did not ultimately translate into applications for reassigned time, and the gains made in the union contract were less significant than the committee had hoped. Administrators' assurances that the Center would be a high priority for support proved to be empty. The Center's budget for staff and operations was cut by almost two-thirds less than one year after the center officially opened, and the Center still has not been assigned a space other than a faculty office for the director. Meanwhile, administrators have created a new position focused on grant development for P-16 partnerships. The Center and its director's position survived the latest budget cuts, but a secure future for the Center will most likely depend on results, including faculty participation in teaching and learning activities.

Perhaps these frustrations should have been expected. While some of the Center's core group continues to organize and encourage colleagues to participate, many have grown weary and shifted to other, related organizing projects, such as the Visible Knowledge Project. The central lesson of Youngstown State's experience is that successful projects require ongoing organizational efforts to gain support from both faculty and administrators. Yet in the face of lukewarm support from both the administration and colleagues, it is uncertain whether campus leaders can sustain that level of commitment.

Contacts and URLs

Sherry Linkon
Coordinator of American Studies
Youngstown State University
sllinkon@ysu.edu

John B. Russo
Center for Working-Class Studies, Labor
   Studies Program, College of Business
   Administration
Youngstown State University
jrusso@cc.ysu.edu

For more information on the Center for the Advancement of Teaching And Learning at Youngstown State (CATALYST), see http://www.ysu.edu/catalyst/

For more information about the Visible Knowledge project, see http://crossroads.georgetown.edu/vkp/

Youngstown State University
Youngstown, OH
Master's I
http://www.ysu.edu/

INTRODUCTION TO SECTION TWO
Collaborating for Change

Devorah Lieberman
Wagner College

Scholars in higher education seeking ways to introduce sustainable change into campus cultures claim that collaboration is a common ingredient necessary to adequately embed and sustain campus-wide change (Eckel, Green, Hill, & Mallon, 1999; Eckel, Green, & Hill 2001a, 2001b; Trowler, Saunders, & Knight, 2003). This literature often assumes that how and when collaboration occurs is consistent across institutions. Institutional change through collaboration, however, may emerge from different circumstances and may be sustained by different support systems. This section addresses how individuals and units in seven institutions collaborated to foster and further the scholarship of teaching and learning. The authors examine institution-specific approaches to collaboration as well as the relationship between collaboration and sustainability.

The seven institutions in this section have actively participated in the CASTL program and have advanced the scholarship of teaching and learning on their campuses through collaborative practice. Each institution represents a variety of demographics, including institutional size, geographic location, mission, and source of funding. Six institutions

are colleges and universities: Buffalo State College, The Citadel, Middlesex Community College, University of Montana Missoula, Rider University, and University of Maryland College Park. The seventh is the WebCenter, a virtual organization coordinated by AAHE, which furthers collaborations across and among all institutions participating in the Campus Program.

Common questions posed to each of the seven institutions provided a framework for their written case studies. Key persons at each institution responded to the following questions:

◆ How has collaboration served (or not served) to further scholarship of teaching and learning on your campus?

◆ What are specific examples of collaboration that occurred on your campus in relation to the scholarship of teaching and learning?

◆ What have been the key elements of these collaborations?

◆ What are lessons learned about collaboration that your campus could share with others?

Emergent Themes

Based on qualitative analysis, eight themes emerged across the institutions' case studies. Though the emergent themes often cut across all chapters in this book, an element of each focuses on collaboration within the process. Collaboration, for the purposes of this project and analysis of the case study data, refers to the interactions between and among individuals within the campus community whose efforts and activities were intended to deepen, broaden, and sustain the scholarship of teaching and learning.

The eight themes are: held open campus discussions; involved deans, provost, and president; involved students; communicated results through specific example and evidence of success; involved teaching and learning centers; related funding and support; included diversity of participants; and impacted promotion and tenure.

Held open campus discussions - *A forum for campuswide discussion about the scholarship of teaching and learning was provided, either in a one-time session or as a year-long series.*

Five campuses that began their work in the late 1990s address the importance of beginning discussions and collaborations around the scholarship of teaching and learning in ways that are open and accessible to all on campus. Open campus discussions create a nonthreatening and inclusive environment. On many campuses, the entire campus community was invited to participate in these beginning discussions and ongoing collaborations.

Involved deans, provost, and president – *Upper-level administrators assumed leading facilitative roles, provided funding, or did not derail faculty doing the scholarship of teaching and learning.*

Five campuses cited the importance of collaborating with the provost, president, and deans throughout the process of introducing and embedding the scholarship of teaching and learning on campus. When actively involved in this introductory process, upper-level administrators were more likely to make scholarship of teaching and learning activities part of their units' agendas.

Involved students - *Some campuses intentionally included students as collaborators, either as participants in discussions or as co-researchers.*

Collaborations were evident both in data collection, such as faculty working together on a project and faculty involving students in research, and in dissemination, such as co-authored publications and units jointly presenting on campus and at national conferences.

Communicated results through specific examples and evidence of success - *All campuses reported discipline-specific or interdisciplinary collaborations that resulted in greater understanding across the campus, published outcomes, or changes in teaching and learning practices within the campus.*

Though campuses documented their success and communicated their results in different ways, most strategies related to oral and written dissemination on campus, national presentations, and publications. The criteria for disseminating their results were the same criteria used for all forms of scholarship: peer review and contributions to a body of literature.

Involved teaching and learning centers - *Institutions identified critical roles of Teaching and Learning Centers in leading campus collaborations or serving as one of the collaborating offices.*

Four institutions addressed the importance of collaborating with campus-based Teaching and Learning Centers. In these examples, Teaching and Learning Centers took the lead in furthering campus-wide collaborations around the scholarship of teaching and learning.

Related funding and support - *Campuses cited the importance of financial support to add legitimacy to individual activities or larger collaborations. Funding and support were critical for sustainability.*

Campuses invested funds in the scholarship of teaching and learning initiatives in different ways. Critical funds enabled faculty to pursue these activities as individuals or units, brought national speakers to lead sessions and workshops on campus, or provided support for faculty and students to attend or present at national conferences on the scholarship of teaching and learning. Every campus that provided financial support for scholarship of teaching and learning collaborations and activities reported that these funds added legitimacy and prestige to the scholarly work.

Included diversity of participants - *Campuses citing the importance of interest from a wide range of participants highlighted the faculty senate as a source of legitimacy.*

Collaborating with participants in different roles was important in introducing and institutionalizing the scholarship of teaching and learning. The collaborations involved existing constituencies, such as pivotal upper-level administrators, faculty senates, academic planning councils, and departmental units. Other institutions created opportunities for diverse faculty to form their own learning communities. For example, University of Montana Missoula included multiple departments in its AAHE Summer Academy team, The Citadel created an interdisciplinary academy, and Middlesex Community College formed an interdisciplinary faculty group. The AAHE WebCenter intentionally created space for these campus-based communities to interact.

Impacted promotion and tenure - *Campuses that included scholarship of teaching and learning as legitimate scholarship for promotion and tenure were more likely to have long-term, campus-wide change.*

For most campuses, recognition through the promotion and tenure process was crucial. Those campuses that had successfully integrated scholarship of teaching and learning into their promotion and tenure guidelines commented on the critical nature of collaborating with appropriate groups throughout this process. For example, Buffalo State College worked with its college senate, academic council, and CASTL advisory committee.

Future Challenges

All the institutions addressed challenges of collaboration facing them in the future. Four central challenges include the place of this scholarship vis-à-vis other forms of scholarship, the promotion and tenure system, second-generation collaborators, and funding.

Supporting scholarship of teaching and learning in the dominant context of traditional research.

In general, campuses identified a continuing need to explain to campus constituencies that the scholarship of teaching and learning is not a required form of scholarship and that it does not replace traditional scholarship. Rather, it is an option available to faculty that has the same rigorous criteria used for doing and evaluating traditional scholarship. This issue must be addressed and re-addressed.

Embedding scholarship of teaching and learning into the promotion and tenure system.

Several case studies also addressed the importance of campus-wide acceptance of scholarship of teaching and learning by embedding it into their promotion and tenure guidelines. They articulated the need for intentional and thoughtful collaborations in order to achieve the outcomes.

Providing ongoing funding.

Facing reduced budgets, institutions may regard the scholarship of teaching and learning as less important than discipline-based research and regard it as a candidate for cuts. Campus case studies uniformly addressed the need for continued funding for individual faculty and for collaborative groups focused on the scholarship of teaching and learning. Because areas of scholarship that receive campus-based funding are perceived as the most worthy, faculty pursue the scholarship that is supported by the administration. The Citadel respondents echoed the funding need when they noted that their Carnegie group working on the scholarship of teaching and learning had grown yearly since 1998, but that without continuing financial support, a campus cultural shift toward acceptance of the scholarship of teaching and learning is very difficult.

Developing a second generation.

Campuses raised issues of the next generation of scholarship of teaching and learning collaborations. Several campuses commented on the need for more intentional and thoughtful collaborations as campuses transition from early adopters to campus-wide adoption. Collaboration is critical if campuses are to avoid clashes between early and mainstream adopters. Middlesex Community College noted that as they ended the third year of their efforts the challenge was finding within their campus group roles for charter members who had completed projects.

Lessons learned

The following actions were recommended by chapter authors most frequently as important ways to initiate and sustain campus-wide collaborations. Each lesson learned was threaded throughout the emergent themes:

◆ Help partners feel a return on the investment of time, funds, or energy.

◆ Create a safe setting that supports inquiry and peer review.

◆ Engage enthusiastic participants without overwhelming the few skeptics.

◆ Bring national leaders in this scholarship to campus to meet with collaborating campus constituencies.

◆ Include students in the collaborative process.

◆ Collaborate top-down, bottom-up, and horizontally.

◆ Include on collaborative teams faculty members and students from diverse disciplines.

◆ Educate the campus community continually about the elements of this scholarship and the criteria to evaluate it.

◆ Involve the upper-level administration, faculty leaders, and promotion and tenure committees, especially at doctoral/research intensive institutions.

◆ Align the scholarship of teaching and learning with the institutional mission.

◆ Encourage the scholarship of teaching and learning through thoughtful, collaborative, and intentional introduction and embedding.

◆ Use online technologies to provide crucial support for groups seeking to collaborate and promote campus-wide scholarly work.

References

Eckel, P., Green, M., Hill, B., & Mallon, W. (1999). *On change III: Taking charge of change: A primer for colleges and universities.* Washington, DC: American Council on Education.

Eckel, P., Green, M., & Hill B. (2001a). *On change IV: What governing boards need to know and do about institutional change.* Washington, DC: American Council on Education.

Eckel, P., Green, M., & Hill, B. (2001b). *On change V: Riding the wave of change: Insights for transforming institutions.* Washington, DC: American Council on Education.

Trowler, P., Saunders, M., & Knight, P. (2003). *Change thinking, change practices: A guide for heads of departments, programme leaders and other change agents in higher education.* York, England: Learning and Teaching Support Network.

Intentional and thoughtful collaborations provide transition from early adopters to campus-wide adoption.

Appendix A. Campus-Specific Emergent Themes and Challenges about Collaboration

Emergent themes across chapters	Univ. of Montana Missoula	University of Maryland College Park	Buffalo State College	The Citadel	Middlesex Community College	Rider University	AAHE WebCenter
Held open campus discussions	1999.	1999; brought in national speaker to lead discussion.	1998; published campus document on the definition of "peer review."		1998; worked toward defining this for the campus.		Assisted campuses to serve as resources for each other.
Involved deans, provost, and president	"Vertical" credibility; fruitful discussions.		Office of Academic Affairs and the Advisory Committee involved.	Upper administration recognized the scholarship of teaching and learning.	Provost assisted in developing the themes.	Provost deeply involved.	Senior administrators on campuses approved of participation.
Involved students	"Horizontal" credibility.			Students benefit from improved teaching.			
Communicated results through specific examples and evidence of success	Redesigned courses integral; some programs revised.	Campus joined AAHE Campus Cluster; specific departments embraced scholarship of teaching and learning: Physics Education Resource Group, Behavioral and Social Sciences Teaching Fellows.	"Going Public" colloquium established; introduced at new faculty orientation; creativity week established; supported publications within the scholarship of teaching and learning; campus publication devoted to this scholarship; appointed a Reflective Practice Fellow, a Collaborative Teaching Fellow, and an Applied Learning Fellow.	CASTLE started an annual regional conference; CASTLE has ongoing workshops; five departments studied student procrastination and the relationship to performance on quizzes.	Annual campus publication: *Explorations from a Community of Practice*.	Writing Across the Curriculum-found higher grades correlated with greater participation among students.	Posted the "successes" from each campus in order to make public; online journals emerged, e.g., George Mason University, Indiana State University, Metropolitan State University, Portland State University, Georgetown, Knowledge Media Lab.
Involved teaching and learning centers	Center for Teaching Excellence.	Center for Teaching Excellence supports scholarship of teaching and learning; Lilly Program & Center sponsor a Fellowship Program.		CASTLE formed by using centralized/ pooled resources.		BRIDGE-SELECT-Science Center for Innovative Instruction.	
Related funding & support		Scholarship of teaching and learning funding source.	Course release for Campus Coordinator of scholarship of teaching and learning; five to six scholarship of teaching and learning Fellowships annually.	Funding for speakers, workshops, projects; funding for release time to undertake future planning.	Course release.	Provost committed funds to further scholarship of teaching and learning; support travel to national BRIDGE; committed 1.8 million to SELECT.	

Appendix A. *Continued*

Emergent themes across chapters	Univ. of Montana Missoula	University of Maryland College Park	Buffalo State College	The Citadel	Middlesex Community College	Rider University	AAHE WebCenter
Included diversity of participants (e.g., faculty senate and other forms of faculty leadership)	Summer Academy team comprised diverse departments; senate approved scholarship of teaching and learning.	Three campus Carnegie Scholars led continued discussion and communicated results.	Pivotal administrators and faculty leader involved.	CASTLE (Citadel Academy for Scholarship of Teaching and Learning and Evaluation) invited many partners (e.g., Departments of Biology and Education).	The movement here started with a Pew National Fellow and a Carnegie Scholar.	CASTL Fellow-Interdisciplinary collaborations.	The institutional leadership adopted "proto" public space; The AAHE WebCenter facilitated interactions.
Impacted promotion and tenure			Began to review and assess faculty scholarship for scholarship of teaching and learning; revised some of the promotion and tenure criteria.				
Identified future challenges — Sustaining this in the campus culture	Focus on "traditional research."	Continues to have a focus on "traditional research."		Underlying feeling that scholarship of teaching and learning may not be valued; continues to be a cross-disciplinary research challenge.	The culture of peer review is not as well established here as at research institutions.		
Embedding scholarship of teaching and leraning into the promotion and tenure system	Ongoing issues.			The administration must continue to support scholarship of teaching and learning in promotion and tenure.		Ongoing challenge.	
Transitioning to second-generation collaborations	Ongoing challenge.		Ongoing challenge.				
Providing ongoing funding	Ongoing challenge.	Ongoing challenge.	Ongoing challenge.	Ongoing challenge.	Ongoing challenge.		

Contact

Devorah Lieberman
Provost and Vice President for
Academic Affairs
Wagner College
dlieberm@wagner.edu

Unlocking the Potential of Collaborations

Cheryl Albers
Buffalo State College

Buffalo State College has learned many lessons during five years of work expanding a campus culture that supports the scholarship of teaching and learning. Several highly effective collaborations are directly related to our achievements in developing infrastructures that promote this scholarship. Two principles guided this collaborative work: valuing diversity and maximizing returns. It would be nice to claim that we began our work agreeing on these ideals. The reality is that we learned their importance as they surfaced in the process of institutional change.

Two extraordinary collaborative endeavors, policy reform and a fellowship program, have resulted in systemic change at Buffalo State College. First, our success in developing official policy guidelines for reviewing and assessing faculty scholarship hinged on coming to agreement on the nature and role of the scholarship of teaching and learning. Building this consensus required attending to the diversity of interpretation of this scholarship evident throughout the campus and accepting differing levels of interest and investment among groups and individuals. Second, our fellowship program institutionalized support for this scholarship at a time of shrinking budgets. Accommodating difficult financial circumstances taught us the necessity for maximizing returns on invest-

ments of time, energy, and money. The fellowships provided both financial returns for individual scholarship and systematic investigations of topics that strengthened the overall academic milieu of the college. Further returns resulted as the fellows provided faculty development for colleagues based on the results of their scholarship.

The Context

Buffalo State College joined the Campus Program in 1998. An advisory committee of representatives from a wide cross section of the campus led the first year's activities. In spring 2001, central administrators provided a course release for a Campus Programs coordinator. The collaboration of the coordinator, an advisory committee, and the Office of Academic Affairs created a powerful force for planning and fostering a campus context supportive of the scholarship of teaching and learning.

This expanded collaboration focused on creating awareness and understanding of this scholarship throughout the campus community. A wide variety of activities was undertaken, including a campus publication promoting the work of faculty and staff involved in this scholarship, a half-day faculty development seminar led by a consultant on the purposes and benefits of this scholarship, and lunch-time workshops where faculty and staff designed classroom-based investigations. As 2001 came to a close, the advisory committee and the coordinator reflected on refocusing efforts. While attempts to create awareness and understanding were favorably received by a cross-section of the campus community, many people remained either unaware or unconvinced of the value of the scholarship of teaching and learning. In addition, individuals were justifiably concerned about the lack of policies and funds to place this scholarship on par with more traditional forms of scholarship.

This assessment of our progress led to a three-pronged effort to achieve systemic change. First, we needed to continue efforts to reach faculty and staff who were unaware or unconvinced of the credibility of the scholarship of teaching and learning. Second, we wanted to revise the guidelines for promotion and tenure review to provide parity among all forms of scholarship. Third, we needed to establish a vehicle for visible, ongoing administrative support for this scholarship in the Office of Academic Affairs.

Policy Development: A Lesson in Valuing Diversity

Buffalo State's first issue, policy revision, was accomplished through a collaboration among the significant campus structures for faculty governance (the college senate), academic planning (the academic council), and support for the scholarship of teaching and learning (CASTL Campus Programs Advisory Committee). The document that emerged from debate and negotiations among various components of the college community stressed:

- the credibility of multiple forms of scholarship;

- the identification of characteristics that unite and characteristics that distinguish various forms of scholarship;

- acknowledgement that not all faculty will undertake this form of scholarship;

- the premise that the criteria for assessing scholarship are more important than its classification; and

- preservation of departmental rights to determine acceptable products of and criteria for assessing the quality and significance of scholarship.

Lessons Learned about Establishing Collaborations to Create Policy to Support the Scholarship of Teaching and Learning

Revising our promotion and tenure policy to provide parity among various forms of scholarship brought into play the diversity in understanding of and interest in the scholarship of teaching and learning. Successful collaboration required an awareness of and willingness to work with differences among individuals, departments, and governing structures. Our experience resulted in the following observations.

Early administrative/faculty collaboration is pivotal to the success of policy revision. Changes that are viewed as the initiative of any one campus constituent run the risk of being resented or stonewalled by other constituencies.

Open discussion of difference regarding the meaning and role of the scholarship of teaching and learning results in greater satisfaction with the final policy. For example, the definition of peer review was the focus of considerable debate at Buffalo State College.

Encouraging such discussions during policy development results in a clearer interpretation during policy implementation.

Policy change does not create an automatic buy-in throughout the campus. An element of the campus will remain unaware of the opportunity to participate in the policy development stage, or will be aware but choose not to participate in the process. In addition, the negotiation of the final product often results in a minority opinion that remains even after the policy is approved.

Uniformity is an unrealistic goal. There are disciplinary differences in the manifestation of scholarship. Successful policies need to set mutually agreed upon standards that apply across disciplines while preserving departmental prerogative to determine the quality and significance of scholarship.

Fellowships:
A Lesson in Maximizing Returns

The second issue we faced involved finding a way to institutionalize ongoing support for the scholarship of teaching and learning. In times of economic turmoil, the institution needs to have strong justification for the expenditure of resources to create new infrastructures. In 2001, the program coordinator presented the provost with an idea to accomplish this goal. The proposal was for fellowships to be awarded to faculty each year in recognition of their strengths in a particular area of teaching and learning. During the year, fellows were to work on specific scholarly projects in their area of expertise that addressed specific campus needs. Institutional needs emerged in a number of ways. During a strategic planning process, faculty and staff identified an institutional

> Early administrative/
> faculty collaboration is
> pivotal to the success of
> policy revision.

strength in applied learning programs, such as internships, service-learning, and student teaching. A suggestion to adopt a requirement that all students be involved in applied learning led to a need to assess the content of existing programs and consider models to maximize learning in applied settings. The need to coordinate and support first-year programs was an outcome of a Middle States accreditation review and the growth of a recently launched Learning Communities program. Other needs, such as working with departments to create a climate to foster the scholarship of teaching and learning, developing avenues for faculty and staff to go public with the results of their scholarship, and developing links between the program for undergraduate research and these initiatives, were related to wider institutional goals to facilitate new forms of scholarship. The lack of an institutional structure to support teaching restricted the availability of a faculty development program designed to strengthen pedagogical skills. To address this need, fellows designed and conducted faculty development activities based on their scholarship and expertise.

Administrators and the advisory committee considered institutional needs and identified four areas of expertise—collaborative teaching, applied learning, assessment, and reflective practice—that would be most effective in developing scholarly projects to address these issues. A format was created for nominations and criteria for selection were determined. Submissions were solicited through e-mail, newsletters, flyers, department chairs, and deans. In spring 2002 the review committee determined that proposals in three of the four areas were suitable for funding..

In their final form, the fellowships in the scholarship of teaching and learning involved:

◆ the provision of visible rewards and recognition for this scholarship;

◆ promotion of projects and activities that directly advanced the mission of the institution;

◆ a vehicle for significant professional development of fellows;

◆ motivation and support for the fellows' individual scholarship through monthly meetings with the CASTL advisory committee;

◆ college-wide faculty development activities planned and conducted by fellows with the support of the associate vice president for undergraduate studies; and

◆ opportunities for the fellows to "go public" with their work throughout the year, including new faculty orientation, the Faculty and Staff Scholarship and Creativity Week, the second edition of the Buffalo State College publication on the scholarship of teaching and learning, and the national AAHE/CASTL colloquium.

In the 2002-2003 fellowship program cycle, during which each fellow was awarded $5,000, Reflective Practice Fellow Susan Birden, assistant professor in educational foundations, assembled cases of best practice, making public the work of teachers who successfully address issues of diversity in the classroom. She reviewed course syllabi from a range of depart-

ments to identify innovative approaches to addressing academic diversity across disciplines. She also conducted reflective interviews with teachers of these courses. These data will inform the work of the Buffalo State Equity and Diversity Council as they promote faculty development based on strategies that have been successful in our campus context.

An orientation workshop for faculty teaching in Learning Communities is an outcome of work of the Collaborative Teaching Fellow, Scott Johnson, associate professor in criminal justice. The workshop synthesizes the extensive body of knowledge on student development and learning theories and presents new data identifying key factors that support and hinder teaching in first-year programs at Buffalo State. This workshop is based on the analysis of the fellow's interviews with faculty involved in academic programs such as learning communities, first-year seminars, and peer mentored classes. This study provided student affairs, academic affairs, and the Center for Interdisciplinary Studies with vital information for improving the success of first-year initiatives on campus.

A multidisciplinary, applied learning student guidebook, *Inquiry and Scholarship of Internships,* was written by Applied Learning Fellow, Lori Till, assistant professor of hospitality administration. The guidebook enables faculty to maximize student learning in applied settings. The project gathered data on the course objectives, pedagogical content, instructional methodology, and assessment techniques used in applied learning classes throughout campus, information useful to the Faculty Advisory Board for Internships. The results of this study will serve as an important baseline for assessing the impact of a recently awarded national grant to strengthen service learning.

Lessons Learned on the Collaborative Establishment of Fellowships to Support the Scholarship of Teaching and Learning

The institutionalization of support for the scholarship of teaching and learning requires individuals and groups to dedicate resources, including time, energy, and money, to planning and operating a vehicle for support. *Collaborators need to be convinced that valuable returns will result from their contribution.* Returns might include progress toward the institutional mission, professional growth, enhanced professional standing, or progress toward promotion. Sometimes we needed to pay more attention to the returns to individuals and groups, but at other times the returns were so obvious that the demands on fellows became overwhelming. Lessons include the following:

Most department members perceive a fellow's contribution to the institution as a credit to the department. However, resentment can surface if the fellowship is viewed as a distraction from the "real work" of the department. It is important to advise fellowship applicants to discuss their proposal with departmental chairs, colleagues, and members of the personnel committee. *A clear understanding of the potential impact of scholarly projects for improving teaching and learning throughout the campus can result in viewing a fellow's work as complementary to, rather than competing with, departmental demands.*

Fellows are selected for their expertise in a specified area of teaching and learning. However, their projects often necessitate developing new skills or learning new research methods. For example, one of our first scholars had never used qualitative methods for gather-

> Two principles guided this collaborative work: valuing diversity and maximizing returns.

ing data. Her training and experience in philosophical and historical research techniques left her unsure of how to conduct, record, and analyze interviews. *Under these circumstances fellows need mentors and collaborators to maximize returns.* Studying and applying new research techniques resulted in significant professional growth for this particular faculty member.

All members of the campus community need to be aware of the benefit to the institution of the fellow's scholarship. Without this, members of the campus community may get suspicious of how the data gathered from individuals and departments will be used. Two of our first fellowship studies began by reviewing syllabi for classes focused on diversity or applied learning. In spite of the fact that these documents are in the public domain, some faculty expressed concern over the close examination of their syllabi. Explaining the relationship of the study to the overall college mission helps convinced skeptics of the benefits of these contributions to institutional research.

Caution needs to be used to prevent the fellowships projects from morphing into an unmanageable size. When various members of the institution are convinced of the potential value of fellows' work, many demands can be made on their expertise. As news of our fellows and their projects spread, additional institutional needs related to their areas of expertise emerged. All of the fellows experienced difficulties setting boundaries that allowed them sufficient time and energy to devote to their original project.

Concluding Notes

Sound planning entails learning from experience as well as considering the future. Reflecting on past experience has convinced us of the importance of valuing diversity and maximizing returns in furthering collaborative efforts that would extend a campus culture supporting the scholarship of teaching and learning. Looking forward, we anticipate some new and some ongoing challenges.

First, continued efforts will be required to convince some members of the campus community that the scholarship of teaching and learning is valid scholarship. Both applied research and the scholarship of teaching and learning are still misunderstood and devalued by some individuals. Valuing diversity in interpretations of this scholarship does not extend to those who discount its legitimacy.

Second, the success of our collaborative efforts was made possible by supportive administrators. The departure and arrival of new administrators provides a potential threat to maintaining this vital component.

Third, we face the challenge of sustaining momentum on existing projects, while beginning new ones. Encouraging new initiatives must not detract from attending to ongoing work.

Finally, current and future collaborations are ultimately dependent on funding. Funding for the scholarship of teaching and learning can be tied to a center or program that is part of the campus infrastructure, such as a center for teaching effectiveness, an interdisciplinary unit, or an office of academic affairs. However, in difficult budget situations, funding for any initiative is increasingly dependant on its contribution to achieving the institutional mission. Buffalo State's strategic and continuous promotion of the potential of the scholarship of teaching and learning to address the mission of the college will be necessary to convince funding sources of its value.

Contact and URLs

Cheryl Albers
Associate Professor of Sociology and
    Coordinator for CASTL Campus Program
Buffalo State College
albersCM@BuffaloState.edu

Visit the Buffalo State College SOTL website at http://www.buffalostate/orgs/castl/

The full document regarding policies about the scholarship of teaching and learning is available at http://www. buffalo.edu/orgs/senate/dops-final.htm

**Buffalo State College
    (SUNY at Buffalo)
Buffalo, NY
Master's I
http://www.buffalostate.edu/**

The Citadel Academy for the Scholarship of Teaching, Learning, and Evaluation: An Interdisciplinary and Collaborative Approach

Suzanne T. Mabrouk, Virginia M. DeRoma, Kenneth P. Brannan, Terry M. Mays, Harry D. Davakos, Michael Barrett, Alix G. Darden, and L. Christine Fudge
The Citadel

In Spring 2000, Citadel faculty interested in the scholarship of teaching and learning formed a campus-wide group, now known as The Citadel Academy for the Scholarship of Teaching, Learning, and Evaluation. Twenty-five percent of the entire faculty are actively involved in The Citadel Academy. Twelve percent of the entire faculty are engaged in research on teaching and learning. The Citadel Academy consists of faculty previously involved in individual or departmental scholarship of teaching and learning work and other interested faculty. Thirteen of the fifteen academic departments are represented.

Essential Elements for Collaboration

The Citadel Academy's mission is two-fold: to inform the entire faculty about the scholarship of teaching and learning and its benefits in the classroom and to sustain the efforts of those actively involved in this scholarly work. To accomplish these goals, meetings at the beginning of the academic year and workshops throughout the year are advertised to the entire faculty. Newcomers are subsequently encouraged to join The Citadel Academy so that they will receive regular email advertisements about bimonthly meetings.

To encourage the scholarship of teaching and learning on a college campus, the following elements are needed: institutional support, enthusiastic leadership, and regularly scheduled programs and activities.

Institutional Support

The two most important factors for a successful collaboration are the financial support and philosophical support of the institution. Funding enables workshops with outside speakers and attendance at conferences. In publicly recognizing the scholarship of teaching and learning, the administration must identify it as valuable in tenure and promotion decisions. Administrative recognition can provide the necessary respect for faculty activities, such as the awarding of internal funding and promotion and tenure. At The Citadel, administrators have demonstrated their public support through attendance at workshops and bimonthly meetings; promotion of The Citadel Academy events at general faculty meetings; and, as of fall 2003, the award of one course load reduction per semester for a facilitator of The Citadel Academy who prepares materials for The Citadel Academy's semimonthly meetings.

Enthusiastic Leadership

The Citadel Academy leaders should be interested faculty or staff members. Leaders need to provide effective organization and guidance of collaborative activities as well as actively recruit additional collaborators from different disciplines. Experience indicates that passive leaders can discourage participation and slow the development of new research projects. Therefore, leaders should be self-starters.

Regularly Scheduled Programs and Activities

The Citadel Academy's goal is to promote research about teaching and learning and to offer programs that enable and sustain the work. Therefore, The Citadel Academy holds bimonthly meetings for its members and at least one workshop per year for any interested campus faculty member. The regular meetings have moved from discussions of literature about the scholarship of teaching and learning

to faculty presentations of ongoing classroom research to discussions of a cross-disciplinary research project and presentations of effective classroom techniques. In 2001, The Citadel Academy started an annual conference for the region where presentations have addressed qualitative assessment methods, assessment of critical thinking, the relationship between student motivation and performance, and the relationship between teaching style and student performance. Due to these regular events, The Citadel Academy members feel encouraged to initiate and continue work on the scholarship of teaching and learning.

Centrality of Collaboration

Centralization of efforts has enabled integrated perspectives, pooled resources, enhanced visibility, and a campus support group.

Integrated Perspectives

Cross-disciplinary collaborations facilitate the exchange and use of models from diverse disciplines. Such collaborations also encourage faculty to focus more on teaching methods and less on the specifics of the discipline. For example, in fall 2002, faculty and graduate students from five disciplines—biology, chemistry, civil and environmental engineering, physics, and psychology—conducted a research project on student procrastination and its correlation with performance on immediate and delayed quizzes. The project enabled the faculty to generalize their findings to multiple disciplines and learn more about the intrinsic motivation of current students.

> The two most important factors for a successful collaboration are financial support and philosophical support by the institution.

Pooled Resources

Through the establishment of a sanctioned campus group, The Citadel Academy members have access to related books, an extensive web site on group activities and scholarly materials, internal and external speakers, bimonthly meetings, a meeting room, and a graduate assistant. These resources have become a focal point to draw collaborators together.

Enhanced Visibility

Centralization has enhanced the visibility of collaborations and offered authentication of the scholarship of teaching and learning. Through the establishment and subsequent visibility of The Citadel Academy, both the Faculty Tenure and Promotion Committee and the Research Committee have begun to recognize scholarship of teaching and learning in disciplines in which traditional research has been more normative. For example, half of the research conducted by two recently tenured professors was in the area of teaching and learning. The Research Committee recently funded two research projects in teaching and learning. These outcomes should encourage faculty to further pursue this kind of work.

Support Group

A central organization provides a support group to faculty who are new to the scholarship of teaching and learning. At the bimonthly academy meetings, faculty can share problems as well as accomplishments in a collegial and accepting atmosphere. Members feel acknowledged and supported and some members not previously involved in this research have initiated projects.

Successful Collaborative Practices

Based on our experience, two collaborative practices portend well for the scholarship of teaching and learning: dual focus of research and education and identification of collaborative research with wide appeal.

Dual Face of Research and Education

A successful program format used for several years alternates presentations of effective classroom techniques and research methods with bimonthly research meetings. To facilitate the current research, one type of meeting focuses on a related classroom technique or research method (e.g., statistics, abstract thinking skills, and the grading and design of "thought papers"). During the research meetings, faculty members develop expertise in designing and conducting human subject research.

Collaborative Research with Wide Appeal

For fall and spring programs, The Citadel Academy members select a specific research project that appeals to the majority. Identifying a project coordinator; employing graduate assistants; keeping the project open to interested participants, regardless of previous skills; and establishing reliable communication procedures have ensured project success. For example, faculty are currently developing a project to assess the critical thinking skills of their students. Faculty are consulting the literature for established testing methods and presenting their findings at the regular meetings. Interested faculty will develop a tool to assess the critical thinking skills of their students. Participation in the regular meetings has led to cross-disciplinary collaborations on other projects as well, as seen with faculty from biology and education.

Current Challenges

Establishing an effective collaboration among participants and administrators marks the beginning of a successful program in the scholarship of teaching and learning. Three challenges await any new group launching a program on a college campus: membership, leadership, and advocates.

Membership

Attracting a large core of committed faculty from across the entire campus has been surprisingly challenging. Although meetings early in the year attract many participants, attendance rarely exceeds 10 percent of the entire faculty per meeting. As the school year wanes, so does attendance. Misconceptions about the scholarship of teaching and learning and its value, time constraints, and a lack of interest in either The Citadel Academy or the larger work may explain attendance problems. To increase participation, core members have met with all new faculty members during orientation sessions and addressed colleagues during departmental meetings. Meetings at the beginning of the year and workshops continue to be advertised to the entire faculty.

Cross-disciplinary collaborations facilitate the exchange and use of models from diverse disciplines.

Leadership

The Citadel Academy has found that attracting and sustaining leadership is also challenging. Lack of time and other demands discourage some potential leaders. The leadership has been coming from a small percent of the faculty who have already been actively involved in this work. To decrease the commitment, leadership is being decentralized so that individuals oversee discreet functions. Each person manages one of the following tasks: scheduling facilitators or speakers, coordinating a research project, or working with other area schools to plan a conference.

Advocates

So far, few core members participate in regional or national conferences related to the scholarship of teaching and learning due to a lack of time or interest. Because participation in these conferences can rejuvenate members and provide fresh ideas to stimulate the entire group, The Citadel Academy started an annual conference in 2001. This event has gathered not only Citadel faculty but also faculty throughout the region. Continuing to encourage faculty to participate in other scholarship of teaching and learning conferences, The Citadel Academy fully funds some members to attend the annual Colloquium on Scholarship of Teaching and Learning prior to the national AAHE meeting each spring.

Funding Issues

Since The Citadel Academy's inception, The Citadel has not only promoted the scholarship of teaching and learning, but also supported the work financially. Yearly funds of approximately $25,000 have provided for on-campus workshops, faculty participation at national and regional meetings, a graduate assistant to handle daily operations, and reference materials. Support for individual faculty research projects (maximum award per person: $3,000), presentation of research (maximum award per person: $2,500), and faculty development (maximum award per person: $2,000) is available through campus grants; and those not funded in that way can be directed to the Provost's Academic Impact Fund.

Administrators continue to be committed to elevating the importance and the on-campus visibility of faculty members' scholarly projects on teaching and learning. The institutional involvement is vital because, as a teaching institution, The Citadel needs to respect the scholarship of teaching and learning in tenure and promotion actions and in decisions related to resource allocation. To this end, the administration will continue to financially support The Citadel Academy's operations.

Challenges for the Future

Now that The Citadel Academy is focusing on cross-disciplinary research in teaching and learning, leadership will continue to be a challenge. Leaders must be willing to devote time and energy to coordinating and leading a study with the initiation (literature review, research design, and data collection), completion (statistical analysis), and publication of a study accomplished in a short time frame. The coordinator should also skillfully involve co-investigators in all aspects of the project. To continue The Citadel Academy's mission, facilitators will provide guidance while new leadership emerges.

Contacts and URLs

Suzanne T. Mabrouk
Associate Professor of Chemistry
The Citadel
mabrouks@citadel.edu

Virginia M. DeRoma
Assistant Professor of Psychology
The Citadel
virginia.deroma@citadel.edu

Kenneth P. Brannan
Professor and Department Head of Civil and
    Environmental Engineering
The Citadel
ken.brannan@citadel.edu

Terry M. Mays
Assistant Professor of Political Science
The Citadel
terry.mays@citadel.edu

Harry D. Davakos
Associate Professor of Health, Exercise,
    and Sport Science
The Citadel
harry.davakos@citadel.edu

Michael B. Barrett
Associate Professor of History
The Citadel
michael.barrett@citadel.edu

Alix G. Darden
Associate Professor of Biology
The Citadel
alix.darden@citadel.edu

L. Christine Fudge
Director of the Writing and Learning Center
The Citadel
fudgel@citadel.edu

Minutes from all past meetings are available on the The Citadel Academy for the Scholarship of Teaching, Learning, and Evaluation (CASTLE) website at http://www.citadel.edu/carnegie/

The Citadel
Charleston, SC
Master's I
http://www.citadel.edu/

Sustaining a Community of Practice at Middlesex Community College

Phyllis S. Gleason and Jessie W. Klein
Middlesex Community College

Seated around a table in a quiet room, 10 faculty members talk about teaching and learning, how the two converge, and how they collectively and individually have pursued the scholarship of teaching as members of the Carnegie Group at Middlesex Community College.

The sense of collegiality is palpable; the conversation is animated, thoughtful, as they discuss a session two of the group are to present at the upcoming national American Association for Higher Education conference. The session title, "Collaborative Scholarship," reflects the spirit and the substance of the Middlesex group (Kolbe, 2001).

The Beginning of Our Collaboration

Since fall 1998, faculty members at Middlesex Community College have sustained an effective, evolving, cross-disciplinary community of practice in which participants have shared teaching and learning experiences in the context of relevant teaching and learning literature. A Carnegie Scholar, Donna Killian Duffy, professor of psychology, and Joan Kleinman, professor of computer science, created a Carnegie group as a new kind of professional

development opportunity for Middlesex faculty. According to Kolbe (2001), the group "developed into an interdisciplinary community of practice, providing a forum for critical reflection and collaboration with colleagues, fostering the evolution and deepening of ideas about their teaching"(4).

All academic divisions at Middlesex— Humanities, Social Science, Health, Technology, Math and Science, and Business—are represented in the Carnegie Group. When asked about the initial draw and sustained commitment given the considerable time and energy participants must devote, founding members cited many aspects of the experience.

"I've spent 20 years trying to find a group to talk about teaching with, and the group provides the time and the purpose for colleagues to get together."

"For a faculty member in the health field, it's a break from the isolation we sometimes feel. The collegiality of a group from a variety of disciplines is very supportive."

"Our Carnegie Group works because it is not only a place to discuss the scholarship of teaching and learning, but also a place to take care

of our souls. We have bimonthly meetings that open with time spent on sharing our frustrations and successes in the classroom."

"*It is an antidote to the isolation of our profession and the lack of time for pedagogical discussions within our departments and divisions.*"

"*The culture that the group has developed encourages continued attendance because of its camaraderie and cohesiveness.*"

"*The sharing nature of the group is nourishing; it reinforces the teaching experience in a less formal setting. It offers a unique opportunity to discuss issues of teaching and learning both in great depth and over time. Even though there is diversity of opinions, all ideas are heard and responded to.*" (Kolbe, 2002, 45)

Common Definitions and Ground Rules

The Middlesex Carnegie Group began by developing its own definition of the scholarship of teaching and learning and searching for a theme that would interest all its participants. Using the metaphor of a trip, we realized through our discussions that we had different learning styles and thought processes, so some of us needed a road map while others were more interested in hitting the road and seeing where the trip would take us. Because we recognized each person's unique perspective, our meetings created a safe environment for exchanging ideas. After many conversations and discussions about our classrooms, we realized that many of our past efforts had been met with frustration despite our willingness to explore new teaching and learning paradigms.

As we read and discussed scholarly articles, we grappled with the disconnect between theory

> The group is an antidote to the isolation of our professions and the lack of time for pedagogical discussions within our departments and divisions.

and practice. As anecdotal evidence amassed, we came to realize that "student motivation" is a critical factor thwarting learning. This revelation focused our thoughts and efforts, and we agreed that motivation should serve as the unifying theme for our projects.

After more research, the charter members of the group narrowed its theme to intrinsic motivation, the desirable form of motivation in students. The book *Why We Do What We Do,* by Edward Deci (1995), was distributed to the group for summer reading. The motivation theme was embraced by the provost and the Academic Council, who also chose to read Deci's book. In its second and third years, the group researched the types of environments that foster intrinsic motivation in students. Our research and discussions on motivation led to a two-part seminar for Middlesex faculty, staff, and administration. In this seminar that investigated links between research and theory on motivation and teaching practices, the 35 participants described their techniques for cultivating intrinsic motivation, and each member received a compilation of these ideas. The Carnegie Group participants have reflected on the strength of the group and its most successful practices. Collaborating on workshops and presentations was one kind of success. For example, members presented a workshop on the CASTL Campus Program and the concept of the scholarship of teaching at the statewide Massachusetts Teaching and Learning Conference for Community Colleges in April 1999.

A second source of success is that the collaborative nature of the Carnegie Group has changed campus culture. Evidence of our success includes the steady growth in membership since 1998 with 17 current active members, including five of the original eight. Further evidence of the sustainability of this project includes the increasing diversity of disciplines and backgrounds of participants, the focus on a single goal within the scholarship of teaching and learning, and the adoption of the group's goal into the individual practices of the members.

Our president and vice presidents are aware of the benefits that the Carnegie Group brings to the faculty. Their support of the initiative is evinced in the award of a course release during the first year to allow for the necessary time commitment.

The administration expects each member to ultimately complete a project. With that under-

standing, each Carnegie member conducts research to better understand student learning in his or her classroom. Although charter members initially read and discussed general articles on motivation, subsequent research topics became more focused. They included an investigation of the value of using media to enhance students' intrinsic motivation and the value of using case studies, problem-based learning, distance learning, and a motivation-based curriculum to enhance student engagement. These projects were compiled into a 2001 monograph entitled *Explorations from a Community of Practice.* More recent Carnegie Group members are in various stages of their investigations with probable completion and publication in 2004. While researching our projects and preparing them for publication, we have embarked on a new collaborative adventure: peer review. The activity emerged as members of the groups learned to give and receive constructive comments.

Growing Pains

Like any other maturing group, the Carnegie Group has experienced some growing pains. The charter members spent the first year reading many articles on the scholarship of teaching and learning and deciding without any previous models how the group should proceed. Subsequent groups have spent less time reading and discovering the tenets and applications of this scholarly work, focusing instead on preparation for their projects and college-wide presentations.

Although we thoroughly enjoyed collaborating on presentations, the group grappled for a period with the opposing tension of giving back to the Middlesex community while completing our own projects. In some ways, we still

---

Our community of practice creates a safe setting that supports inquiry and peer review.

---

struggle to find that balance. For instance, because the second group was not as well versed in the basics of the scholarship of teaching and learning as the first group, the entire group had to rethink priorities. In order to overcome the discrepancies in the full group's knowledge, we arranged end-of-the-semester retreats to focus on "back to basics." At the retreats, we spent time discussing some seminal articles, reviewing our personal goals for membership, and making plans for the future direction of the group. These extended sessions have become bonding experiences that strengthen our collegiality.

As we ended our third year with the publication of the *Explorations from a Community of Practice,* we struggled to find a role for the five charter members who had completed their projects. The charter members now act as mentors to the newer members, helping them with projects and giving moral support as they struggle with the frustrations of balancing teaching loads with research. The charter members also had a seminal role in Middlesex's selection a cluster leader in the AAHE/Carnegie Campus Program.

Recent research by Wenger, McDermott, and Snyder (2002) suggests that communities of practice move through five stages of development: potential, coalescing, maturing, stewardship, and transformation. Having gone through the first two stages at the end of our fourth year as a community of practice, we are somewhere between the maturing and stewardship stages. We are ready to move our work to a more public, national position by becoming a cluster leader. The charter members of our community of practice will lead the development of a Summer Institute for the Scholarship of Teaching and Learning, which will set the stage for collaborations across different colleges and for enabling other faculty to gain an understanding of the basics of this scholarship.

We will also formalize a peer review process for supporting the work of faculty. In its publication *Greater Expectations: A New Vision for Learning as a Nation Goes to College,* the Association of American Colleges and Universities suggests that higher education should "help college students become intentional learners who can adapt to new environments, integrate knowledge from different sources, and continue learning throughout their lives" (2002, p. xi). The report suggests that higher education institutions model this intentionality for their students. Faculty members who focus on the scholarship of teaching and learning become more intentional in their view of student learning; and through reviewing each other's projects, they can then integrate different sources of knowledge. Faculty groups collaborating across institutions can become a powerful source for lifelong learning.

The collaborative nature of the Carnegie Group has changed campus culture.

Collaborating into the Future

As a cluster leader, Middlesex faces two main challenges. First, we need to move from only a "Middlesex" perspective to a more national perspective. We must sustain our local community as we branch out to a larger, nationwide group in our role as cluster leader. To do this, we must maintain a balance between performing public activities and supporting our local community needs for mentoring, peer review, and exchange of ideas. A second, greater challenge in the future may be funding. We are hopeful about funding, however, because since its inception in 1998, our Carnegie Group has grown every year, and despite the current statewide budget crisis, our administration continues to be committed to the continuation of the group.

Although colleges typically have faculty development programs to help professors learn new approaches and stay current, there are few settings where faculty members can, over time, join in a community to collaboratively study their craft. In our community of practice, we have designed strategies that create a safe setting that supports inquiry and peer review. Through our role as a cluster leader in the Campus Program, we hope to share our strategies with the wider education community and to collaborate with our core members in developing even more strategies to benefit students' educational experiences.

References

Association of American Colleges and Universities. (2002). *Greater expectations: A new vision for learning as a nation goes to college.* Retrieved May 5, 2003, from http://www.greaterexpectations.org

Deci, E. (1995) *Why we do what we do.* New York: Penguin Books.

Kolbe, C. (2001). *Carnegie scholarship of teaching project has national and local presence. The Learning Community.* Bedford, MA: Middlesex Community College, 4-5.

Wenger, E., McDermott, R., & Snyder, W. M. (2002). *Cultivating communities of practice.* Boston: Harvard Business School Press.

Contacts and URLs

Phyllis S. Gleason
Professor of English
Middlesex Community College
gleasonp@middlesex.mass.edu

Jessie W. Klein
Professor of Science
Middlesex Community College
kleinj@middlesex.mass.edu

Middlesex Community College
Bedford, MA
Associate's
http://www.middlesex.cc.ma.us/

Developing Collaborative Practices at Rider University

Phyllis M. Frakt, Don Ambrose, Jean Kutcher, and Arlene Wilner
Rider University

Rider University encourages collaborative practices to support the scholarship of teaching and learning through a growing number of programs. This chapter highlights examples from three recent additions to faculty development programming: Rider BRIDGE, Rider SELECT, and the Center for Innovative Instruction. These programs support collaboration among Rider faculty across disciplines and between faculty and instructional technology specialists. Collaboration also occurs more broadly, linking Rider faculty to faculty at other institutions and professionals in related fields, especially K-12 teachers.

The overall success of these programs is demonstrated by growing participation and longstanding interest in them, classroom innovation and improvements in student learning, and emerging recognition and scholarship. But discussions and collaborations across traditional boundaries generate other welcome benefits, such as observation of parallels and analogies among disciplines and creation of "comfort zones" outside established departmental cultures. Important bulwarks to sustain success appear to be expert faculty leadership, budgetary support and incentives, and diversity of programming.

Successful Collaborative Practices

Rider faculty can select among several new and longstanding projects that encourage the scholarship of teaching and learning. Three new programs broaden opportunities to bring innovations to our classrooms and promote collaborations.

Rider BRIDGE

Rider BRIDGE (Bridging Research, Instruction, and Discipline-Grounded Epistemologies) targets assignment design to improve student learning across the disciplines. Facilitators promote a collegial and structured setting for small groups of faculty to discuss the assumptions of their varied disciplines, course goals reflecting these assumptions, and instructional strategies to meet established goals. Faculty participants then experiment with instructional changes to produce evidence of deeper student understanding. Given the disciplinary range of faculty participants and the diversity of their student audiences, instructional changes vary widely. One faculty participant revised writing assignments to encourage novice students to adopt disciplinary practices in responding to painting. Another participant provided seniors in a capstone accounting course with opportunities to interview practitioners about applications of textbook topics. Evidence of effects on student learning has come from quantitative measures (such as higher scores on freshman biology exams) and qualitative measures (such as increased class participation in a communications class). Unanticipated results occasionally provide opportunities for rethinking conventional practices. In one such instance, a professor decided to cover fewer topics more thoroughly through geological case studies. A less easily definable indication of success is the increased confidence and optimism reported by many participants, supporting Lee Shulman's claims about the value of making teaching community property.

Rider SELECT

The Rider Science Education and Literacy Center (Rider SELECT) encourages collaboration among education and science faculty members to improve K-12 science and math education. A group of education and science faculty meets regularly to learn about the inquiry approach and to mentor one another as they integrate it into courses. In this collaboration, education faculty mentor scientists and mathematicians in implementing inquiry instruction, while scientists and mathematicians serve as content experts to education faculty. In further collaborations, Rider faculty enhance the content knowledge of K-12 teachers, while K-12 teachers model inquiry teaching in their classrooms. SELECT has begun assessing changes in education students' attitudes toward science and their use of inquiry methods in student teaching. Assessment tools include Science Course Attitude Inventory, Horizon Teacher Survey (modified by ETS), and instruments from the Expert Science

Teaching Educational Model (ESTEEM). So far, the Science Course Attitude Inventory has revealed some statistically positive changes in students' attitudes, for example, that logical thinking can be applied in science as well as in other fields, that science is a complex subject that they have the ability to learn, and that good writing is important in science. The Horizon Teacher Survey has shown that teacher preparation students feel prepared to use the inquiry method to teach science. Using ESTEEM model instruments, SELECT expects to assess changes in field study students, student teachers, novice teachers, and their mentors.

Center for Innovative Instruction

The Center for Innovative Instruction promotes experimentation with pedagogical strategies and instructional technology. Led by an instructional methodologist and an instructional technologist, Center initiatives blend teaching strategies and models with technology applications. These initiatives include department workshops, consultation with individual instructors and faculty inter-

---

Important bulwarks to sustain success appear to be expert faculty leadership, budgetary support and incentives, and diversity of programming.

---

est groups, extensive course revision, and Web-based instructional improvement resources. Faculty participation is growing, largely through the identification of "resident experts" who present instructional innovations at faculty workshops and through an electronic instructional improvement catalog. Participants have made significant revisions to courses and teaching methods, as described in year-end reports. For example, instructors in the Marketing and English Departments have experimented with cooperative learning, concept attainment, and creative visual metaphors. The Center for Innovative Instruction provides access to these reports and other instructional improvement resources on a CD version of the catalog and on its website.

Ingredients of Successful Collaborations

Several ingredients contribute to the success of these programs. Starting with Writing Across the Curriculum in the 1980s, programs have depended on dedicated and prepared faculty leadership to ensure quality and credibility. Current program leadership includes a CASTL Fellow, a faculty member with expertise in curriculum and instructional improvement, and staff dedicated to instructional technology.

Program leaders cite the importance of administrative support, particularly to provide incentives for faculty participation. BRIDGE offers stipends for faculty participants, workload release for the director, and operating funds for supplies and refreshments. SELECT provides stipends to redesign and pilot new inquiry-based courses, physical space for inquiry teaching and learning, instructional technology support, and faculty development opportunities.

Center for Innovative Instruction course revision teams are eligible for course releases.

In addition to immediate incentives for participation in campus programs, several forms of longer-term incentives sustain progress. Faculty engaging in the scholarship of teaching and learning are eligible for funding for travel to professional meetings, summer research, and leaves. A BRIDGE participant, for example, was awarded a summer fellowship to refine her study of the effects of student debates on critical thinking in an introductory history course. Research leaves can be structured to include teaching if that teaching is part of a research agenda. Moreover, most academic departments include scholarship of teaching and learning as an option for promotion and tenure considerations.

An array of external grants and recognition provides funding, publicity, and external connections. BRIDGE received a $5,000 Going Public grant from the American Association for Higher Education. A BRIDGE participant was selected to present her project to revise a business policy course at the 2003 Charles M. Hewitt Master Teacher Competition. SELECT was launched with a $350,000 Congressional appropriation through the Fund for the Improvement of Post-Secondary Education. To establish a virtual learning community, SELECT also received a three-year, $1.8 million High Tech Work Force Excellence Grant from the New Jersey Commission on Higher Education. Bristol-Myers Squibb contributed $750,000 for the Bristol-Myers Squibb Center for Science Teaching and Learning, the facility that houses SELECT and other faculty development programming, and for professional development for K-12 science and math teachers. Johnson & Johnson awarded a $10,000 grant to support a summer research team of a

K-12 teacher, an education student, and a faculty member. The Martinson Family Foundation donated $21,500 for planning a Mathematics Teaching Institute.

Diversity of participants and activities also contributes to success. It is not our institutional philosophy for everyone to be involved in the same approach. A healthy range of activities provides multiple opportunities for different kinds of collaboration. Through a multi-disciplinary team structure, BRIDGE both uncovers unforeseen parallels between disciplines and confirms discipline-specific insights. A business law professor, seeking to deepen students' understanding of disciplinary conflicts, adopted a history professor's design for structured student debates about primary sources. A chemistry professor, on the other hand, recognized that persuasive student lab reports differ from accepted rhetorical and evidentiary principles in literary interpretation or historical analysis. Through collaboration with faculty and staff experts, faculty in the Center revise courses to incorporate technology or to clarify learning goals. Through science and education collaborations, SELECT brings faculty together to adopt the inquiry model to improve K-12 math and science education. Beyond these prominent interdisciplinary programs, however, the university recognizes that some faculty will remain interested in traditional collaborations within their home disciplines.

Changing the Campus Culture

Some faculty are relieved to discover that the university officially supports the scholarship of teaching and learning as well as more established forms of research. Some faculty eagerly join interdisciplinary discussions to revitalize approaches to their classrooms. Later, they dis-

cover that collegial discussion and classroom innovation can lead them to a form of scholarship that was absent from their graduate training or previously unrecognized in their home departments. Like other institutions that place an emphasis on teaching, Rider welcomes this form of cultural change, recognizing that change is a relative term and requires ongoing nourishment.

Some faculty are led to collaborative activities by classroom frustrations that inevitably befall even the most dedicated teachers. Interactions with like-minded and sympathetic colleagues across disciplinary boundaries can provide distance from sometimes constraining departmental cultures. Hypothetically, these frustrations might degenerate into unproductive exercises in blame, with likely targets as ill-prepared students, questionable high school curricula, or market-driven admissions. Vigilant and focused program leadership and rigorous program design have minimized the blame game, another welcome cultural change.

Remaining Challenges

To encourage the scholarship of teaching and learning to move on to the community stage and beyond, the Provost's Office is planning to spotlight projects through a luncheon series. Each program also plans current operations and future expansion on campus and beyond. SELECT, which already supports collaboration between Rider faculty and K-12 educators, envisions a regional network of partners from school districts, other higher education institutions, and industry to design and deliver inquiry- and standards-based teacher preparation and professional development. Although BRIDGE professors have already presented assignment design projects at campus forums and via Web postings, they are encouraged to present at scholarly conferences and to publish in print journals. Providing periodic seminars and frequent electronic dissemination of ideas and practices on campus, The Center for Innovative Instruction is currently revising ways to prioritize, structure, and promote its services.

A final and unexpected challenge is to determine the limits of programming. Ongoing program development creates precedents for institutional attention and budgetary support, comparisons for parity, and potential competition. Beyond inevitable budgetary constraints, the Provost's Office must encourage careful overall planning to avoid overwhelming our faculty audience, discouraging other welcome contributions to scholarly life, or diluting support for existing programs. At some point we may face a surprising question: in order to provide a well-balanced array of programs to support faculty interests, how much programming in support of the scholarship of teaching and learning is actually enough?

Endnote

The Science Course Attitude Inventory is from the University of Oregon's NSF-funded Workshop Biology Program (http://yucca.uoregon.edu/wb/). The original Horizon Teacher Survey can be found at www.horizon-research.com. (The original survey was modified by ETS for purposes of this study.) Original ESTEEM instruments are described in J. Burry-Stock (1995) Expert Science Teaching Educational Model (ESTEEM) Instrument Manual, Center for Education, Western Michigan University, Kalamazoo, MI.

Contacts and URLs

Phyllis M. Frakt
Vice President for Academic Affairs and
    Provost
Rider University
frakt@rider.edu

Don Ambrose
Professor of Graduate Education
Rider University
ambrose@rider.edu

Jean Kutcher
Administrative Director of the Teaching
    and Learning Center
Rider University
jkutcher@rider.edu

Arlene Wilner
Professor of English
Rider University
wilner@rider.edu

Websites for more information about Rider
programs:

Rider BRIDGE –
http://www.rider.edu/~bridge

Rider SELECT –
http://tlc.rider.edu/select/index.htm

The Center for Innovative Instruction –
http://ghost.rider.edu/cii

Instructional technology –
http://ghost.rider.edu/innovate

Other faculty development programs –
http://tlc.rider.edu, click on Programs

**Rider University
Lawrenceville, NJ
Master's I
http://www.rider.edu/**

Lessons Learned at The University of Montana-Missoula

Betsy W. Bach, William T. Borrie, Mark S. Cracolice, and
Steven E. Gaskill
The University of Montana-Missoula

The scholarship of teaching and learning was first introduced at the University of Montana-Missoula in spring 1999, when we began Campus Conversations to conceptualize and define this term for our campus. Our initial stocktaking effort, coordinated by individuals in the Provost's Office and the Institutional Research Office, included eight two-hour sessions where 5 to 15 participants at a time responded to discussion questions using Group Systems software, an online Delphi technique where participants submit comments and read and respond to comments made by others. Transcripts of the eight sessions were reviewed, and comments from each session were clustered into a number of themes that were inductively derived. Widespread participation included faculty members, academic staff, academic deans, and executive officers.

Faculty members raised several issues and concerns pertinent to the scholarship of teaching and learning during our stocktaking. Issues related to faculty roles, rewards, and recognition for engaging in this scholarship; use of effective teaching strategies and assessment of student learning; the need for training and development for improving and assessing effective classroom teaching; and the desire to recruit and enroll quality students. Despite repeated attempts to bring faculty together in a retreat to discuss and elaborate upon these points, our efforts began to lose steam and limped along in spring 2000.

Luckily, our efforts were resuscitated with the hiring of a new provost and chief academic officer in fall 2000. Aspects of the scholarship of teaching and learning were reflected in the Academic Trajectories, which were developed through active solicitation of ideas and feedback from all campus constituents. Faculty concerns raised during our initial Campus Conversations were newly reflected in three different areas of academic planning: learning opportunities that support the individual styles and life circumstances of students; engagement with the community and society evidenced throughout teaching, research, and service activities; and a dynamic, intellectual environment that fosters creativity, innovation, and humanity.

To promote engagement, a team consisting of four faculty members, one student, and one administrator participated in the 2002 AAHE Summer Academy to develop a plan to broaden campus conversation about student learning and its relationship to faculty roles and rewards. Since returning to campus, that team, including the authors of this chapter, has collaborated with faculty from the Center for Teaching Excellence and the First-Year Experience Task Force and with others to discuss and implement the scholarship of teaching and learning.

The Importance of Vertical and Horizontal Collaboration

Although the thought of one more committee meeting may be less than motivating to many faculty members, administrators, and students, collaboration is essential in moving forward the scholarship of teaching and learning and related efforts. In our case, collaboration has involved a series of face-to-face meetings. Our collaborative efforts have been vertical and horizontal to ensure that input is broad-based. Vertical collaboration, an important part of our discussions about this scholarship, played an important role in developing our current plan. The composition of the AAHE Summer Academy team, which included faculty members, a student, and an administrator, enabled us to discuss campus culture from multiple perspectives and levels of insight. It also provided us with a base from which to solicit additional support from the constituencies we represent. For example, during the academic year, faculty from our team met with both the provost and the Executive Committee of the Faculty Senate to discuss this scholarship, while our student member campaigned for the topic among teaching assistants and student leadership, and our administrator highlighted team efforts with the academic deans.

Horizontal collaboration is essential for engaging in participative decision-making. We learned that the seeds of change must be planted and discussed with our respective faculty/administrative/student groups. As any change is cause for uncertainty and confusion, allowing others to discuss campus culture with those of similar status allowed for more open and less politicized communication. Perhaps the most rewarding conversations have come in separate discussions held in the Faculty Senate and with the academic deans, where teaching and scholarship have been discussed with great enthusiasm.

Members of the Summer Academy team have been active on campus, working within departments and across disciplines in developing a broad dialogue. In many cases, the results of these interactions are achieving concrete results. For example, the Department of Health and Human Performance has revised several lab classes, from multiple demonstration labs to individual, term-long research and service projects involving students in design, data collection, analysis, and presentation. The projects have been collaborative between classes and across campus. In 2002, 16 undergraduate students were selected via a peer review process to present their projects at regional and national meetings, such as the Northwest American

> The encouragement and enthusiasm of students are reinforcing and proof-positive of the importance of the scholarship of teaching and learning.

College of Sports Medicine and the National American College of Sports Medicine meetings. Faculty and guest speakers have discussed the concepts of the scholarship of teaching and learning. The result has been an ongoing commitment by faculty to first engage in the principles of scholarly teaching and then to begin evaluating their teaching methods for effectiveness. The immediate results have been much greater student involvement in meaningful projects, an increase in community engagement, more class discussion and integrative work, and an overall feeling of community.

The encouragement and enthusiasm of students are reinforcing and proof-positive of the importance of such initiatives in the scholarship of teaching and learning. Not only was this scholarship perceived to be customer responsive to the needs of undergraduate students, but graduate students also recognized the role of the scholarship in raising the profile of excellence in college teaching, a major motivation for their pursuit of an academic career. The scholarship of teaching and learning communicated the centrality and seriousness with which faculty members pursue this part of their duties, and seems consistent with a "research culture." The essential role of students in good scholarly work on teaching and learning aligned with campus encouragement of undergraduate research and provided an accessible and understandable context in which to introduce the purpose and methods of research. In our experience, collaboration is essential for laying the groundwork for culture change. It must be vertical, both top-down and bottom-up, as well as horizontal. Collaboration undergirds any effort to change culture. Although collaboration can be frustrating, and subsequent change may be slow, collaboration is essential for communicating expectations and desired outcomes.

Helpful Collaborative Practices

Three specific strategies allowed us to work collaboratively to promote our campus conversation: vertical collaboration with our provost; horizontal collaboration between deans and the Faculty Senate; and use of specific examples to anticipate and mitigate skepticism. Without a doubt, support from our provost has done the most for our ability to vertically collaborate. She provided the funds for the team to attend the AAHE Summer Academy, and she has encouraged the team as we act upon the goals we set during the academy. Her support has also been public, which has helped facilitate discussions with faculty and other campus groups. Because her public support has demonstrated a commitment to and interest in promoting the scholarship of teaching and learning, administrators and faculty members have taken notice.

Congruent with her academic plan to promote engagement, the provost is fostering a campus atmosphere where open discussion about teaching and learning is strongly encouraged. Engagement Awards, established in 2001, encourage faculty to increase student engagement through the use of scholarly teaching. Other projects to promote engagement are under development, one of which requires each academic unit to establish a plan for engagement with first-year students.

While the endorsement and financial support of our provost acted as an important catalyst and foundation for scholarship of teaching and learning activities, it was not without its own caution. Regardless of institution, change introduced from the top is often viewed with suspicion; undertaking a change such as this one could be perceived as buying in to a provost's plans, skeptically viewed as a political action, or seen as an insincere interest in the improvement of teaching practices. However, the initiation and conduct of the scholarship of teaching and learning extends beyond the presence of a particular provost. Actively introducing this scholarship to the institution's academic officers such as deans and senior academic administrators is an important counter to this perception, given their history and support from within the faculties. This also serves as horizontal collaboration. On our campus, endorsement from the Faculty Senate helped counter a perception that the scholarship of teaching and learning was soft research and a resort of last option for research activity.

Admittedly, faculty on the team had some initial skepticism about the scholarship of teaching and learning as a useful and necessary component of good higher education teaching. Having faculty from diverse departments on the Summer Academy team helped allay fears that this scholarly work was primarily the domain of the arts and humanities. This strategy was deliberate and employed to mitigate initial skepticism from faculty members. Furthermore, the AAHE and Carnegie's provision of discipline-specific examples of successful scholarship from biological, geo-chemical, and business programs helped faculty relate to the strengths and weaknesses of their own classroom practices. The identification and collection of campus examples of the scholarship of teaching and learning was also a priority. In particular, documentation of these scholarly activities in promotion and tenure materials was sought from several faculty members to serve as models.

Challenges

The context for valuing the scholarship of teaching and learning offers many challenges, especially in developing criteria for promotion and tenure and in hiring practice.

The University of Montana-Missoula is in the midst of a significant cultural shift to a stronger emphasis on graduate education and external funding. For example, from the 1995–1996 to the 2002-2003 academic year, the university more than doubled its grant funding from 24 million to 60 million dollars. As state financial support dwindles, faculty members are feeling pressured to bring in funding from outside sources. A primary challenge, therefore, is to encourage faculty to devote time to the scholarship of teaching and learning in the face of a shifting rewards system increasingly focused on success in obtaining external funding, unless, of course, the external funding were for the scholarship of teaching and learning.

Another challenge is redefining assessment of teaching so that faculty who engage in scholarly activities can be recognized and rewarded for their efforts. Departments vary greatly in how the teaching component of their faculty's workload is assessed. Some departments look only at summary statistics on student evaluation forms; others have more extensive evaluation systems in place. Yet, very few, if any, departments have a definition of scholarly teaching written into their promotion and advancement standards. The evaluation of quality scholarly teaching also remains problematic on a broader scale. Given the trend for simply counting publications in a traditional research evaluation, qualitative criteria to evaluate teaching effectiveness are often wanting, making evaluation difficult.

Changing the campus culture requires that new faculty members with balanced interests in both the scholarship of teaching and discovery be hired. Certainly one of the most important decisions made in any organization comes when new employees are chosen. If the organization decides to make a commitment to a change in culture, the hiring process needs to reflect that change. Steps are being taken in the Provost's Office to ensure that faculty members are hired with expertise in both teaching and research. Candidates for tenure-track positions are informed about the importance of teaching and are encouraged to use the Center for Teaching Excellence upon their arrival on campus. However, faculty hiring decisions at UM-Missoula are still primarily a departmental decision, with only some input from those recognized on campus as leaders in the scholarly teaching community. If scholarship is truly to be reassessed, we must rise to the challenge of overcoming the "more of the same" mentality in hiring new faculty, where committees composed of faculty with traditional ideas of scholarship set the future of the university.

The current administration understands that implementing change requires leadership from the top but also groundwork at the student and faculty levels. The leadership has provided support for scholarly activities and improved teaching with student and community engagement. The groundwork is ongoing. Departmental discussions and extended vertical campus conversations continue to promote the scholarship of teaching and learning and its positive effect on both student and faculty learning.

Contacts and URLs

Betsy W. Bach
Interim Dean
Davidson Honors College, University of
    Montana - Missoula
betsy.bach@umontana.edu

William T. Borrie
Associate Professor, College of Forestry &
    Conservation
University of Montana - Missoula
bill.borrie@umontana.edu

Mark S. Cracolice
Department of Chemistry and Director,
    Center for Teaching Excellence
University of Montana - Missoula
mark.cracolice@umontana.edu

Steven E. Gaskill
Associate Professor, Department of Health
    and Human Performance
University of Montana - Missoula
steven.gaskill@umontana.edu

For more information on the University of Montana - Missoula's Center for Teaching Excellence, see www.umt.edu/cte/history.

For information on the Provost's Academic Plan, visit http://www.umt.edu/provost/pdf/AcademicPlanFall2003.pdf

The University of Montana-Missoula
Missoula, MT
Doctoral/Research Intensive
http://www.umt.edu/

Technology as Collaborative Practice: Protopublicity, Multivocality, and Knowledge Brokering

Darren Cambridge
American Association for Higher Education

Technology has played a central role in the collaborative practice of Campus Program participants and staff since the program's beginning. Technology provides a key means by which campus participants make their practice more public and more global, moving from working in local communities of practice focused on the scholarship of teaching and learning of individuals to the establishment of more broadly based and further-reaching groups to promote change (Cambridge, 2003). As "academic publics," participants in the campus projects influence institutional and disciplinary structure and culture, and as constellations of communities of practice they cultivate ideas across organizational and disciplinary boundaries. Mediating these activities, technology enables collaboration in three main ways: providing spaces through which to manage the transition from private to public; integrating multiple media for multivocal representation of practice; and offering tools for brokering knowledge.

Managing "Publicness"

Going public is a central activity in the scholarship of teaching and learning. Being "made public" is one of the three distinguishing characteristics of scholarship in Lee Shulman's definition: Scholarship is "public, susceptible to critical review and evaluation, and accessible for exchange and reuse by other members of one's scholarly community" (Shulman, 1998, p. 5). Going public is also a key stage in the collaborative work of transforming institutions to better support the scholarship of teaching and learning. Campus groups need to become academic publics, making campus and discipline-based scholarship visible to key decision makers and arguing for changes in policy that further support that work. Group members also

> Building communities of practice based on common identity at the local level is essential to cultivating the scholarship of teaching and learning.

need protopublic spaces in which to hatch and mature ideas, strategies, and representations in dialogue with like-minded others before moving into more fully public venues to address audiences who may be unfamiliar or resistant (Eberly, 2000).

The AAHE Campus Program WebCenter serves as a protopublic space in which Campus Program participants share and develop work in progress. In the WebCenter, participants upload and download documents, participate in threaded discussions, refer each other to sources that have influenced their practice of the scholarship of teaching and learning, receive personalized recommendations based on their use of the system, and learn about the activities and interests of other campus groups and individual participants. Although the system is open to individuals who are not formally members of Campus Program groups, there is a necessary process to accessing the WebCenter. Users must complete a fairly extensive profile detailing their work on the scholarship of teaching and learning and how they would like to collaborate with other users. While all contributions to and interactions within the system are visible to other registered users and clearly attributed to the author, they are not accessible to the general public. The registration process ensures that all those

interacting within the WebCenter's spaces have asserted their identity as scholars of teaching and learning. The WebCenter serves as an incubator, where Campus Program participants can develop representations of their work in relative safety. When the work is mature and ready to be used to persuade external audiences, it can be made public in other forums.

The most recent version of the WebCenter provides several levels of protopublicity. Participants choose whether to share resources and discussions with only members of their campus group, with the members of their cluster of campus groups focusing on a common interest area, with a set of individuals they define, or with all registered users. Participants may make their work increasingly public as it becomes increasingly mature.

Technology can provide a venue through which mature work can be made fully public on the Web. Several Campus Program groups have launched peer-reviewed online journals that focus on the scholarship and teaching and learning. George Mason University publishes *inventio*, Indiana University South Bend issues the *Journal of Scholarship of Teaching*, and San Jose State offers *TeaL: A Journal of Scholarship on Teaching and Learning*. The Knowledge Media Lab of The Carnegie Foundation for the Advancement of Teaching has focused on defining new genres for the representation of the scholarship of teaching and learning, such as electronic portfolios. The Knowledge Media Lab online gallery exhibits various kinds of electronic portfolios, created by Carnegie Scholars in conjunction with the Media Lab staff, that model how faculty can select and organize materials, including digital video, to illustrate key issues around their teaching, reflections, and inquiries. The Media Lab's Snapshot tool provides a browser-based, easy-

---

Electronic portfolios illustrate how the scholarship of teaching and learning online can be highly collaborative.

---

to-use interface for constructing simple electronic portfolios. The Lab has incorporated the formats of some of the model portfolios displayed in the gallery into its Snapshot tool as templates, making "going public" in this emergent genre more accessible. For example, Barbara Mae Gayle, a member of the cluster focusing on supporting scholarly work at learning-centered universities, composed and published in a matter of days a portfolio tracking her students' development as public speakers. Gayle's portfolio uses the course anatomy format, developed by earlier Carnegie Scholar Bill Cerbin and built into the Snapshot tool, which interweaves videos capturing her students' performance over time with her own reflections on the course.

Representing Multivocality

Electronic portfolios illustrate how the practice of the scholarship of teaching and learning online can be highly collaborative. They weave together the work of multiple authors. Portfolios produced with the Snapshot tool are truly collaborative texts, the product not only of the teacher-scholar whose work is represented, and of her students, whose work may be examined and excerpted, but also the technology developers who built the tool that made that representation possible and the scholars whose models informed the templates.

As made clear from the accounts in other chapters, producing institutional change to support the scholarship of teaching and learning requires cooperation of many agents coordinating diverse needs and perspectives. When multiple media are combined within online texts, the multivocality of this work can be powerfully captured, as illustrated by the Scholarship of Teaching and Learning Tutorial

(http://webcenter.aahe.org/sotl_tutorial/home. html). The Indiana University Bloomington group received a Campus Program Going Public grant to develop a multimedia introduction to the scholarship of teaching and learning. Written by two faculty members and an administrator working with a Web designer, the tutorial provides an effective introduction to the theory and practice of the scholarship of teaching and learning and offers the Indiana group's process as a model for other campuses. Through steaming audio and video recordings, the voices and images of many change agents at Indiana are shared with the reader.

The developers of the tutorial also included forms through which readers could share their own ideas and experiences with others, interactively participating in the evolution of the text. Texts on the Web can also become multivocal by enabling readers to become co-authors, responding to and expanding texts. In the resources section of the WebCenter, participants can annotate resources submitted by their peers, adding their own perspectives, offering feedback on works in progress, and drawing connections to work on their own campuses.

Brokering Knowledge

Building communities of practice based on common identity at the local level is an essential step in cultivating the scholarship of teaching and learning. The challenges campuses face are powerfully addressed when scholars share knowledge and build relationships across traditional academic dividing lines: discipline, institutional type, and organizational role. Technology can play a key role in brokering knowledge between communities of practice (Brown & Duguid, 2001). The Reports and

Recommendations sections of the WebCenter were designed to aid AAHE staff in brokering knowledge between groups and to help individual participants locate others with whom they might have common interests. Campus Program groups posted several rounds of reports on the WebCenter over the course of the program.

AAHE used the supports and barriers described by campuses in their first reports to help point other campuses to critical and similar issues. Also used were the mapping progress reports, filed regularly in the next stage of the program, to identify major areas that campuses needed to attend to in order to support change that fosters the scholarship of teaching and learning. From the patterns in the areas on which campuses chose to focus and the results of their efforts, the domains and leaders of the new Campus Clusters were identified. For example, groups on campuses as diverse as Buffalo State College, Elon University, New Jersey City University, and Western Washington University all highlighted in their mapping progress reports the power of students playing an active role in the scholarship of teaching and learning. Recognizing this emergent theme, Campus Program staff chose it as the focus of a Campus Program cluster led by Western Washington, entitled "Collaborating in the Scholarship of Teaching and Learning: Sustaining the Student Voice."

Technology offers tools for brokering knowledge.

The recommendation system of the WebCenter, although not continued in the current version, was built to use collaborative filtering, a technology which finds patterns in activity by comparing one person's use of the system with that of all the other users (Cambridge, 1999). When a participant asked for recommendations, the system located a group of other users whose patterns were similar and recommended alternative resources, references, and discussions that had been commonly utilized by members of that group. This is the same technology that Amazon.com uses to recommend books. Unlike Amazon, the WebCenter is a protopublic space, so the system could also recommend users within the similar group to the participant, who could then read their profiles and contact them to discover what they have in common and might share. Because the system looked for statistical patterns rather than logical connections, it could help participants discover connections they might not otherwise have thought to explore.

The experience of the Campus Program suggests that online technology supports the work of groups seeking to promote change. It supports the scholarship of teaching and learning by providing protopublic spaces for the incubation of practice, venues for the publication of mature work products, new genres that powerfully represent the diversity and complexity of that work, and tools with which to make connections with others encountering similar challenges. While AAHE was confident that technology would be important to facilitating change when the Campus Program began, these key roles only became clear as the result of the collective ingenuity and reflective practice of Campus Program groups.

References

Brown, J.S., & P. Duguid. (2001). Structure and spontaneity: Knowledge & organization. In *Managing industrial knowledge: Creation, transfer, and utilization* (pp. 44-67). I. Nonaka and D. Teece (Eds.) Thousand Oaks, CA: Sage.

Cambridge, D. (1999). *Supporting the development of a national constellation of communities of practice in the scholarship of teaching and learning through the use of intelligent agents.* Paper presented at the Computer-Supported Collaborative Learning Conference, Stanford University.

———. (2003). *Techne in action online: Rhetoric and the WebCenter.* Unpublished doctoral dissertation, University of Texas, Austin.

Eberly, R. (2000). *Citizen critics.* Urbana, IL: University of Illinois Press.

Shulman, L. S. (1998). Course anatomy: The dissection and analysis of knowledge through teaching. In *The course portfolio: How faculty can examine their teaching to advance practice and improve student learning* (pp. 5-12). P. Hutchings (Ed.) Washington, D.C.: American Association for Higher Education.

Contact and URLs

Darren Cambridge
Director of Web Projects
American Association for Higher Education
darren@darrencambridge.net

To visit the AAHE WebCenter, see
http://webcenter.aahe.org/chef/portal

To read *inventio*, see
http://www.doit.gmu.edu/inventio/

To read *Journal of Scholarship of Teaching,* see http://www.iusb.edu/~josotl/

To read *TeaL: A Journal of Scholarship on Teaching and Learning,* see
http://cfdc.sjsu.edu/itl/journal/

To visit the Knowledge Media Lab, see
www.carnegiefoundation.org/KML/

Interdisciplinary Practices to Enhance the Culture of Teaching and Learning at a Doctoral/ Research Extensive University

Charles E. Sternheim
University of Maryland College Park

If the scholarship of teaching and learning is to flourish at a doctoral/research extensive university, the campus culture for teaching and learning must be increasingly valued across disciplinary and even institutional boundaries so that this scholarship is encouraged and rewarded. Multiple and diverse collaborative efforts are needed to bring about this cultural change. Some initiatives require extensive planning, action by high levels of the administration, or external funding, but other efforts do not. At Maryland, we have tried a number of different approaches ranging from modest programs to more complex initiatives.

Modest Programs That Can Have a Major Impact

Faculty members at the University of Maryland have made unique contributions to the scholarship of teaching and learning. In fall 2001, the entire campus community was invited to a conversation with three resident Carnegie Scholars: Spencer Benson from cell biology and molecular genetics, and Emily Van Zee and Deborah Roberts from curriculum and instruction. All three presented their research. The Center for Teaching Excellence at Maryland wants to encourage further creative and collaborative initiatives, so in spring 2001 a Scholarship of Teaching and Learning Fund of moderate size was established. The Fund provides basic financial and technical support for developing ideas that can serve as pilot studies in teaching and learning or as the basis for grant applications that will help develop these ideas. An Advisory Committee of faculty members from several colleges administers the Fund.

One fund-supported project, Integrating Visual Materials into the Teaching and Learning of History, illustrates the potential effectiveness of institutional units working together to further the scholarship of teaching and learning. The project team from three campus units will design, implement, and assess a pilot collaboration between the College of Arts and Humanities, the Office of Information Technology, and the Department of History that uses the Maryland Interactive System for Image Searching to distribute digital images for use in history courses. Faculty will explore the many possibilities of new and evolving technical solutions. The programming team will respond to needs articulated by faculty in an iterative development process.

The College of Behavioral and Social Sciences Teaching Fellows Program is another example of a project that was created without a major effort on the part of administrators or faculty. This program was developed to invite faculty members in departmental pairs or individually to explore specific teaching issues of concern to the college, to reflect on ways to improve teaching, and to enhance the college culture around teaching. Participants examined issues including models for teaching portfolios, peer review and support models, and student feedback as a way to assess the effectiveness of teaching. This collaborative program required comparatively little effort and money to establish and has paid large dividends. For example, the college's Teaching Course Feedback System was developed by participants in the program, and it continues to be used throughout the college. The system has also been made available online for use by other institutions.

Complex Initiatives

The Academy for Excellence in Teaching and Learning is the outgrowth of a faculty-led initiative to build a community of scholars committed to fostering a culture of excellence in teaching and learning at Maryland. The creation and development of the Academy required the approval and support of high-level administrators. These administrators selected members of the Academy from a group of university educators committed to teaching and learning as a key component of scholarship at Maryland.

The mission of the Academy is to interact with campus and external communities on a broad range of teaching and learning issues and serve as an advisory body to the provost and the campus leadership; to promote and undertake scholarly dialogues, innovative projects, and critical studies that contribute to the improvement of undergraduate and graduate teaching and learning on campus; and to seek opportunities to communicate and collaborate with organizations and institutions that share its commitment to educational excellence and scholarship. An inaugural group of 18 Academy Fellows, selected in the 2002-2003 academic year, chose the theme of shared learning through student-faculty interactions. The goal is to identify innovative practices and models for shared learning experiences that students consider to be especially effective or transformative.

Some initiatives supporting the scholarship of teaching and learning require extensive planning and external funding. A noteworthy example is the Physics Education Research Group. Under the direction of Edward F. Redish, the Research Group is an ongoing, combined effort of the Physics Department and College of Education to study the learning and teaching of physics from elementary school through the university level. The group consists of faculty members, postdoctoral associates and fellows, graduate students, undergraduate students, and administrative staff. At a weekly seminar, speakers from within and outside the University present their research on issues relevant to physics education. Graduate students in the program can earn a Masters in Science Education or a Ph.D/Ed.D. in Science Education.

The Lilly-CTE Fellowship Program is an example of a collaborative program that was founded and developed with funds from an external foundation and for which continued funding is provided by the Center for Teaching Excellence. This program provides the opportunity for 10 faculty members annually to develop specific interests in undergraduate education. Each year, the group has included an interdisciplinary team of faculty that meets throughout the academic year and chooses a few specific projects or topics. For example, the 2002-2003 Lilly-CTE Fellows have gained the provost's support for the creation of a high level University Commission to look closely at the state of teaching on campus. The fellows recommended that the Commission be charged with examining institutional expectations, administrative roles and responsibilities, and engagement of students as stakeholders. One potential goal is to explore innovations in education based upon the scholarship of teaching and learning to help us better meet the needs of an increasingly talented student body that demands a more challenging education.

Future Plans

The University of Maryland participates as core member of two AAHE/Carnegie clusters of institutions for the next three years. Over the past three years Maryland's Campus Program has greatly benefited from working with people beyond our campus on issues related to the scholarship of teaching and learning. One current cluster, led by Western Washington University, focuses on faculty and student collaboration in the scholarship of teaching and learning, with a special focus on sustaining the student voice in a campus-wide learning community. Our campus will focus on undergraduate research and developing a scholarship of teaching and learning unit within the Maryland Center for Undergraduate Research. Partnering with students, we will catalog the different modes of undergraduate research experiences on campus and identify specific

experiential components that impact student learning. We aim to formulate specific research questions to further our understanding of the learning processes embedded in undergraduate research and provide funding to facilitate the exploration of these questions.

We have also become a core member of the cluster led by Indiana University Bloomington, a research university consortium on the advancement of the scholarship of teaching and learning. A major goal of this cluster is to cultivate scholarly productivity that is held to the same standards of rigor, relevance, and review as other kinds of scholarship. This goal will be reached by supporting a rich and varied community of scholars of teaching and learning.

Maryland will continue to educate administrators, faculty members, and students about the scholarship of teaching and learning and the ways it can contribute to campus culture. Faculty from different disciplines need examples of projects that reflect the characteristics of this scholarship to see how these projects may differ according to discipline and research par-

One fund-supported project illustrates the potential effectiveness of institutional units working together to further the scholarship of teaching and learning.

adigms. The Center for Teaching Excellence plans to hold an additional workshop on the scholarship of teaching and learning each semester and provide for individuals who have ideas about research that looks closely at the teaching and learning process. In addition, the Center will advise interested members of the campus community about publishing rigorous scholarship related to these issues and will work more closely with undergraduates in a continuing program on faculty-student collaboration in teaching and learning.

Acknowledgements

The success of our campus program is due, in large part, to the continuous encouragement and support by Robert L. Hampton, formerly Associate Provost for Academic Affairs and Dean for Undergraduate Studies. Arjang A. Assad, Spencer A. Benson, Neil A. Davidson, Susan L. Gdovin, James D. Greenberg, Francine H. Hultgren, Edward F. Redish, Emily H. Van Zee and Richard E. Walker have also contributed in important ways to the development of the scholarship of teaching and learning at the University of Maryland. Arjang A.Assad, James D. Greenberg, Edward F. Reddish, Eden H. Segal, Emily H. Van Zee and Richard E. Walker provided very helpful comments on a draft of the manuscript.

Contacts and URLs

Charles Sternheim
Professor, Acting Senior Associate Dean, College of Behavioral and Social Sciences, and Faculty Associate, Center for Teaching Excellence
University of Maryland College Park
csternheim@psyc.umd.edu

Center for Teaching Excellence
(James Greenberg, Director and Susan Gdovin, Associate Director):
http://www.cte.umd.edu/index.html

The Scholarship of Teaching and Learning Fund: http://www.cte.umd.edu/grants/SOTLawards.html

The Course Feedback Survey: http://www.bsos.umd.edu/eval/CourseEvalLogin.asp

The Academy for Excellence in Teaching and Learning:
http://www. rhsmith.umd.edu/dit/aetl/test/

The Physics Education Research Group:
http://www.physics.umd.edu/perg/

Lilly-CTE Fellowship: http://www.cte.umd.edu/programs/lilly/index2.html

The Maryland Center for Undergraduate Research:
University of Maryland College Park
College Park, MD
Doctoral/Research Extensive
http://www.umd.edu/

INTRODUCTION TO SECTION THREE
Instituting Policies

Duane Roen
Arizona State University

In this section, scholars from a range of universities and colleges describe efforts to change their institutional cultures. Although those changes represent relatively high-level policy shifts, the institutions' efforts are clearly driven by strong commitments to student learning. The institutions in this section have achieved productive synergies with coalitions among leaders who understand that effective teaching is teaching that results in better student learning. Further, these institutions have a critical mass of leaders – faculty, administrators, regents, or elected government officials — who understand the distinction between scholarly teaching and the scholarship of teaching and learning.

The terms *scholarly teaching* and the *scholarship of teaching and learning* represent important concepts. As Lee Shulman (2000) notes, scholarly teaching, which focuses on student learning, is well grounded in the sources and resources appropriate to the field. It reflects a thoughtful selection and integration of ideas and examples, and well-designed strategies of course design, development, transmission, interaction and assessment. Scholarly teaching should also model the methods and values of a field, avoiding dogma and the mystification of evidence, argument, and warrant.

Shulman continues that the scholarship of teaching and learning occurs when "our work as teachers becomes public, peer-reviewed and critiqued, and exchanged with other members of our professional communities so they, in turn, can build on our work. These are the qualities of all scholarship" (p. 49).

Policies Reconsidered

Promotion and Tenure

Many authors in this section address issues related to promotion and tenure because promotion and tenure decisions are among the most important ones that colleges and universities make. On the institution's balance sheet, each positive decision can entail millions of dollars in future salary and support. Perhaps more important, though, is that each tenure decision affects the quality of teaching, research, and service that an institution can offer. Granting tenure makes an investment in a faculty member and predicts that the faculty member will be productive until retirement. The executive vice president and provost of Arizona State University, Milton Glick, sometimes says about faculty productivity that having a colleague quit and leave is a shame, but a bigger shame is having a colleague quit and stay.

These chapter authors offer diverse perspectives on promotion and tenure policies. For instance, in Chapter 5, Cheryl McConnell describes Rockhurst University's careful efforts to broaden the scope of faculty roles and the rewards — especially promotion and tenure — that sustain those roles. Readers who visit the Rockhurst website will find model language for considering the scholarship of teaching and learning in promotion and tenure decisions.

In Chapter 2, Milton Glick describes the convergence of two changes at Arizona State University. In addition to more widespread valuing of teaching and learning in the institution's guidelines for promotion and tenure, Arizona State University has a relatively new president who has highlighted the teaching mission of the university. Although the scale of these changes is smaller than that in Georgia, it is nonetheless multi-campus because Arizona State University comprises four campuses. Furthermore, Arizona State, as well as the other universities in Arizona, enjoys a fruitful collaboration with the Board of Regents in focusing on students' learning.

In Chapter 7, Constance Post analyzes Iowa State University's broadened criteria for reviewing faculty roles and rewards. Even though responses to the revised criteria vary widely, there seems to be consensus that they have encouraged faculty to engage in conversations about teaching and learning and to consider changed policies.

Institutional initiatives result from wide-ranging, prolonged conversations.

Peer Review of Teaching

Because colleges and universities are placing increasing emphasis on teaching and learning, carefully evaluating the work in that arena is important. Although student course evaluations can provide valuable information about the effectiveness of faculty members' teaching, they do not tell the full story. Institutions acknowledging that the story needs more details are embracing additional means for evaluating teaching, including peer review and self-evaluations such as those found in teaching portfolios (Cambridge, 2001; Hutchings, 1998; Seldin, 1997). In Chapter 3, Maxine Atkinson, Alton Banks, Judy C. Peel, and J. Douglas Wellman describe the processes and procedures that North Carolina State University uses in reviewing faculty's important work with students. The future of peer review looks bright at North Carolina State because so many people at so many levels have been involved in the conversations. In Chapter 2, Milton Glick focuses on the addition of peer review to student evaluation of the effectiveness of teaching at Arizona State.

Combinations of Policy Changes

In Chapter 1, Dorothy Zinsmeister describes an effective set of partnerships in the University System of Georgia, which consists of 34 institutions. The Georgia commitment to the scholarship of teaching and learning includes a wide array of stakeholders who value the overall mission of higher education. The University System of Georgia has a long record of innovative leadership, and Zinsmeister has vividly portrayed part of that record. In particular, institutions in the University System of Georgia have revised combinations of policies related to recruitment and hiring, promotion and tenure, tangible forms of rewards and recognition, and opportunities for continuing development.

In Chapter 6, Charlotte Ravaioli and Lansdale Shaffmaster describe substantial changes in hiring, promotion, and tenure at Keystone College. In 1998, when Keystone began offering baccalaureate degrees in addition to the associate degrees that it had offered for years, the institution decided to review faculty roles and the qualifications for fulfilling those roles. The result is a set of policies and procedures that reflect the complex teaching mission of the institution.

In Chapter 4, Jennifer Meta Robinson describes the scholarship of teaching and learning initiative at Indiana University Bloomington — a program honored with the prestigious Hesburgh Award in 2003. The chapter offers details that indicate the institution's leadership in changing policies regarding the scholarship of teaching and learning.

Four Common Practices Leading to Policy Changes

Four common practices emerge in the chapters in this section. First, institutional initiatives have resulted from wide-ranging, prolonged conversations. For instance, the conversations in the 34-campus University System of Georgia involved faculty, staff, deans, senior campus administrators, the governor, the system chancellor, and the board of regents. At the other end of the numerical spectrum are Rockhurst University and Keystone College. Both are small, private institutions; yet, like the Georgia System, they involved a wide range of stakeholders in conversations that led to changes in policies and procedures for promotion and tenure. Somewhere between a 34-campus system and the small, private institutions is Arizona State University. The conversations at Arizona State have involved faculty and admin-

istrators at all levels in the organizational chart. At Indiana University Bloomington, another large institution, prolonged conversations between the administration and the faculty have led to shared authority for policy changes.

Second, committed leaders can make a difference. Across the chapters in this section, leaders play crucial roles in facilitating change. For instance, at Indiana University Moya Andrews, vice chancellor for academic affairs and dean of the faculties, and George Walker, former vice president for research and dean of the university graduate school, worked with colleagues to shift resources to support the scholarship of teaching and learning. Walker is also well known for his leadership role in national conversations about the scholarship of teaching and learning. Another example of the importance of leadership comes from Arizona State University, where changes in promotion and tenure policies resulted from the tireless work of president Michael Crow and of campus leaders, including members of the Task Force on Promotion and Tenure and the Academic Senate.

Third, external support can also make a difference. Intellectual and moral support from external agencies is important. Institutions contemplating change or engaged in change frequently draw on the resources of organizations such as AAHE and Carnegie. These resources include Web and print materials and participation in events such as the AAHE Summer Academy, an important venue for colleges and universities to engage in national conversations about the scholarship of teaching and learning.

Fourth, faculty roles and rewards are inextricably linked. If institutions expect to sustain initiatives, there must be rewards for engaging in those activities. In the institutions represented in this section, policy changes have led to a greater valuing of teaching and learning and of the scholarship of teaching and learning. At Rockhurst University, Keystone College, Iowa State University, North Carolina State University, the University System of Georgia, and Arizona State University the rewards come in the form of promotion and tenure, among the most meaningful forms of reward for faculty.

Building Consortia to Effect Policy Changes

In addition to the efforts of individual institutions or state systems, such as those included in this section, national consortia of institutions are working for more widespread change. For instance, at the 2003 AAHE Summer Academy, as part of the Carnegie Academy for the Scholarship of Teaching and Learning (CASTL) Campus Program, scores of institutions collaborated in 12 well-defined clusters to plan initiatives that build on the kinds of foundations described in this section. The clusters have the potential to build powerful networks of institutions that can encourage and support widespread policy changes.

For example, the cluster of which my campus is a core member is The Research Consortium for the Advancement of the Scholarship of Teaching and Learning. With Indiana University Bloomington as cluster leader, core members included as of summer 2003 Arizona State University, Georgia State University, Iowa State University, Northwestern University, University of British Columbia, University of Illinois Champaign-Urbana, University of Maryland College Park, and University of Nevada Las Vegas. The cluster's mission state-

---

Intellectual and moral support from external agencies is important.

---

ment, composed by the institutional representatives who participated in the 2003 AAHE Summer Academy, indicates a strong commitment to offering models for enhancing research universities' focus on student learning:

> Consistent with the longstanding mission of research universities, the scholarship of teaching and learning offers far-reaching possibilities for integrating discovery, learning, and public engagement. The international AAHE - Carnegie cluster of major research universities and disciplinary societies will further the emerging recognition of the scholarship of teaching and learning as a powerful and integral component of the research university's mission and identity. The scholarship of teaching and learning must be held to the same standards of rigor, relevance, peer review, and dissemination as other forms of disciplinary research and creative activity. It also must bring the same levels of rewards. We intend to make a significant contribution toward the transformation of the academy through the advancement of the scholarship of teaching and learning.

Available on the AAHE WebCenter, the plans for this consortium, as well as those of the other 11 clusters who met in 2003, bode well for the future of the scholarship of teaching and learning. They constitute mechanisms for supporting over 90 institutions seeking to enact policies that will benefit even more institutions over the long term.

Author Note

I thank my colleague Judy Grace for many engaged conversations about this section of the collection. Her insights, as always, were invaluable.

References

Cambridge, B.L., Kahn, S., Tompkins, D. P., & Yancey, K. B. (Eds.) (2001). *Electronic portfolios: Emerging practices in student, faculty, and institutional learning.* Washington, DC: American Association for Higher Education.

Hutchings, P. (Ed.). (1998). *The course portfolio: How faculty can examine their teaching to advance practice and improve student learning.* Washington, DC: American Association for Higher Education.

The Research University Consortium for the Advancement of the Scholarship of Teaching and Learning. (July 2003). Mission statement. Retrieved July 20, 2003 from http://chef.aahe.org/chef/portal

Seldin, P. (1997). *The teaching portfolio: A practical guide to improved performance and promotion/tenure decisions* (2nd ed.). Boston, MA: Anker.

Shulman, L. (2000). From Minsk to Pinsk: Why a scholarship of teaching and learning. *The journal of scholarship of teaching and learning* (JoSoTL), (48-53). Retrieved June 26, 2003, from http://titans.iusb.edu/josotl/VOL_1/NO_1/SHULMAN.PDF

Contact

Duane Roen
Director, Center for Learning and Teaching Excellence and Professor of English
Arizona State University
duane.roen@asu.edu

Not There Yet: Supporting Professional Development, Teaching Excellence, and the Scholarship of Teaching and Learning

Dorothy Zinsmeister
University System of Georgia

The year was 1994. Governor and former history professor Zell Miller and the far-sighted and enlightened Board of Regents of the University System of Georgia, led by chancellor Stephen Portch, were gathered around the table, all with similar interests in mind. The governor wanted to move the university system to a new level of excellence at the same time that the board and chancellor were crafting a new vision for the system that moved academic excellence to the forefront and recognized the need for a world-class faculty to achieve its goals. The governor was soliciting ideas for professional development, and, more importantly, was willing to fund them. Meanwhile, using its new vision document as a blueprint, the system was poised to offer a plan and a budget that included:

written criteria and procedures for promotion and tenure (teaching given priority for instructional faculty), awards to recognize professional excellence (especially in teaching and service to students), provisions for professional travel, developmental reassignments and leaves, training and mentoring programs for teaching assistants, and programs or centers for faculty and staff development programs and centers.

At the April 1996 Board of Regents meeting, a task force of faculty, staff, deans, and senior administrators from a representative group of public institutions in Georgia presented recommendations for faculty/staff development. Referencing specific goals in the system's vision statement and strategic plan, the recommendations were part of a complementary, comprehensive package of policy directions focused on the need to recruit and retain top quality faculty and staff who would provide the best education and services possible to students of the University System of Georgia. More specifically, the recommendations required system institutions to clarify or establish clear institutional policies, criteria, and procedures for recruitment and hiring; evaluation, including annual, pre-tenure, promotion and tenure, and post-tenure reviews of faculty; rewards and recognition of outstanding performance; and opportunities for continuing development. Comprehensive in nature, the recommendations addressed the need for policies that supported and recognized the work of faculty throughout their careers from the time they were hired to the time they retired.

After board members questioned recommendations, debated issues, and cited anecdotes and stories from personal experience, they called for the adoption of the recommendations made by the task force. Board action ultimately resulted in a legislature-funded Professional Development Initiative. At the same time, the legislature approved two additional Special Funding Initiatives. The Connecting Teachers and Technology Initiative related professional development directly to the integration and effective use of technology into instruction, and the Distinguished Professor Initiative provided a campus resource to improve the overall quality of instruction.

Making the Right Investments

To implement the recommendations approved by the board, the System Professional Development Initiative split responsibility and accountability between the institutions and the System Office. With direction and guidelines from the chancellor, institutions focused attention on crafting or refining policies and procedures that clearly delineated processes for recruiting, hiring, evaluating, and supporting faculty through the span of their careers. In one of his boldest moves, the chancellor instructed the presidents to set aside one percent of full-time employee salaries to support faculty and staff professional development programs. Clearly, policy changes at the system level

---

Interdisciplinary contact contributes to common understandings.

---

resulted in policy changes at the institutional level.

While campuses developed policies, the system office focused attention on providing system-wide leadership to support teaching and learning and on demonstrating support for teaching and learning activities on campuses. The system allocated resources to support and to move forward these initiatives in a variety of ways.

Convenings played an important role. The first System Teaching and Learning Conference, hosted in fall 1996, introduced to system institutions prevailing issues in higher education presented by some of the best thinkers and most creative educators in teaching and student learning. Nominated to attend the conference by their vice presidents for academic affairs, institutional teams of faculty leaders returned to their campuses with a well-conceived project that addressed a teaching and learning need of the institution.

Faculty participants at the Teaching and Learning Conferences gave conference planners an important piece of advice: "Our administrators need to hear this, too!" This suggestion prompted the inclusion of issues related to teaching and learning at the annual System Administrators Workshop. Attended primarily by deans and department chairs, the workshop has periodically provided a forum for discussing strategies for initiating, developing, supporting, and sustaining scholarship of teaching and learning activities on campuses.

Awards have played a part in the system strategy. In 1996, the system implemented Regents' Teaching Excellence Awards that recognize both individual faculty and departments for strong commitment to teaching and to service to students. The Regents' Research in Undergraduate Education Awards (now called Regents' Scholarship of Teaching and Learning Awards) followed two years later with criteria that clearly reflect the attributes of the scholarship of teaching and learning. The Regents' Award is the highest honor for faculty at Georgia's public colleges and universities. Recipients are honored by the chancellor and the Board of Regents each year at the May board meeting. Since the inception of the awards, the number and quality of the nomination portfolios submitted by institutions has steadily increased.

Course development support proved important in faculty development. The Connecting Teachers and Technology Initiative serves to increase the number of courses that integrate technology into the instructional process by preparing teachers to use various technologies, to teach via distance learning networks, and to explore the contributions of technology to instruction. To maximize the effective use of available funds, the Professional Development and Connecting Teachers and Technology Initiatives pooled resources and offered professional development grants to support areas of strategic interest to the system. As part of these efforts, $431,000 was awarded in 1998 to faculty at system institutions to support course development technology enhancement projects in four strategic areas: Teacher Preparation, Internationalizing the Curriculum, Information Technology, and Foreign Languages.

Interdisciplinary contact contributes to common understandings. The system provides opportunities for disciplinary committees to meet annually to discuss issues related to the core curriculum and the major. For example, the Academic Committee on Biological Sciences hosts 34 members, one representative from each of the system institutions. Since 1996, the Professional Development Initiative has funded 25 grants to academic committees to promote and enhance faculty development activities that focused on student learning and the scholarship of teaching and learning in the various disciplines.

Lastly, a focus on excellent teachers at each system school rounds out these initiatives. The Distinguished Professor Program Initiative funds one position ($45,000 from special funding with a matching $25,000 in private funding generated by the institution) at each of the University System of Georgia's 30 state universities and two-year colleges. The goals of this initiative are to identify, compliment, reward, and focus public attention on excellence in teaching; to improve the quality of instruction, especially with technology; and to foster faculty development.

Worth the Effort

So what has the University System of Georgia accomplished from 1996-2003 as a result of the strategic implementation of these Initiatives? First, institutions have stronger policies in place that more clearly define performance expectations for faculty during critical times of review — annual, pre-tenure, promotion, tenure, and post-tenure reviews. Second, language that honors and rewards scholarly teaching and the scholarship of teaching and learning has been incorporated into tenure and promotion policies at most institutions. Third, the Regents' Awards for Teaching Excellence and the Scholarship of Teaching and Learning attest to the strong commitment the system has toward impacting student learning and ultimately fostering the academic success of students. Fourth, the number of faculty offering high quality instruction of online courses has increased, as has the number of online courses. The core curriculum is offered online and courses and programs of economic importance to the state are available to students who cannot travel to a campus or who need more flexible class scheduling. Fifth, system-wide Academic Advisory Committees are having conversations about and defining learning outcomes for the courses that are part of the System's common core curriculum. Each academic committee is reviewing those core courses for which it has responsibility, and preparing a set of learning outcomes that are common to all the institutions. For example, biologists at all 34 institutions are working to agree on the intentions of the core biology course(s), that is, what students need to know and be able to do when they complete the course(s). Finally, one significant outcome of the Distinguished Professor Program was the establishment of Centers for Teaching and Learning or other centralized support for faculty at many of the institutions.

Lessons Learned

What advice does the University of Georgia System have to offer from what it has learned?

◆ Think strategically. Tie new initiatives to existing activities; it will strengthen what you are already doing and result in a more comprehensive plan to achieve your goals.

◆ Start small and gradually expand your activities. Although some funding is necessary to support your work, large sums of money are not necessary to get started.

◆ Provide opportunities for faculty to meet across disciplines as well as within disciplinary groups. The conversations will be very

different, but both will inform the participants.

◆ Invite campus leaders to serve on an advisory committee to help plan and implement your professional development initiative.

◆ If you already offer grants to faculty for research projects, reframe the request for proposals to include language that supports teaching and the scholarship of teaching and learning.

◆ Invite several institutional leaders to attend a meeting or conference that considers issues for change in higher education. Their advice and perspectives can inform your work and they can become a voice for change on their campus.

Final Thoughts

In 2001, funding for the Distinguished Professor Program was permanently incorporated into the operating budgets of each of the participating institutions — as were the Connecting Teachers to Technology and Professional Development Initiatives. Did the system design a perfect professional development program? No, of course not. If we could do it again, we would do some things differently. For example, providing adequate time for new initiatives to become self-sustaining as part of the culture of the system institutions would be a high priority. Because institutions need opportunities to develop ownership of new initiatives, they should be challenged to think strategically about sustaining them. Our professional development program could always be better, but we have an excellent track record so far in systemically supporting the scholarship of teaching and learning.

Contact and URLs

Dorothy Zinsmeister
Senior Associate for Academic Affairs
University System of Georgia
dorothy.zinsmeister@usg.edu

For more about the recommendations, see
http://www.usg.edu/admin/regents/minutes/

For information on projects, see
http://www.usg.edu/admin/acadaff/fac_dev/

For more about grants to disciplines, see
http://www.usg.edu/admin/comm/

For more about reward recipients, see
http://www.usg.edu/admin/acadaff/fac_dev/

Award criteria and nomination portfolios of award recipients can be
found at http://www.usg.edu/admin/acadaff/fac_dev/awards.html

For more about online courses, see http://www.usg.edu/facstaff/

For more about learning outcomes, see
http://www.usg.edu/admin/comm/charge03.phtml

For more about selection of core course learning outcomes, see
http://www.usg.edu/admin/comm/acaddocs/charge03.phtml

University System of Georgia
Atlanta, GA
http://www.usg.edu/

Faculty Roles and Rewards in the New American University: Redefining/Refining the Institutional Mission

Milton Glick
Arizona State University

On February 18, 2002, the Academic Senate at Arizona State University voted to approve the recommendations of the institution's Task Force on Promotion and Tenure, which had worked for many months drafting and revising the recommendations with much input from stakeholders. The revised guidelines emphasize excellence in research/creative activity and teaching, encourage attention to the scholarship of teaching and learning, and call for the peer evaluation of teaching to supplement students' course evaluations. The Academic Senate's vote, which came after many months of discussion, constitutes an important endorsement for the work of the Task Force. The discussion and vote also served to increase university-wide attention to teaching and learning.

Soon after Michael Crow became the 16th president of Arizona State University, he offered a vision of the New American University that includes the following features: (1) embracing its cultural, socioeconomic, and physical setting; (2) becoming a force, not just a place; (3) cultivating entrepreneurship; (4) conducting use-inspired research; (5) focusing on the individual student; (6) practicing intellectual fusion or interdisciplinarity; (7) embracing social embeddedness; and (8) developing global engagement (Crow, 2002, pp. 1, 6). In the same document President Crow offered the following principles for the institution:

◆ *Teaching is our prime directive.* We are teachers. I am a teacher; you are teachers; the institution is a teacher. I can't think of anything more important than that. That is the prime directive.

◆ *Scholarship is our pathway to better teaching.* Scholarship, in whatever form each of us takes it, is essential to the quality of our teaching. There's a whole range of things that scholarship means, but all of us must be creatively engaged in pushing back the edges of whatever it is we do if we hope to be great teachers.

◆ *If teaching is our prime directive, creative expression in all forms is our highest goal.* We have a responsibility to be creative.

◆ *We must be an institution built around openness and access to our learning environment for all.* Whatever we're doing, the energy we create, the creativity that we stimulate, the teaching we do, if we sequester it, hold it inside, or wall it off, it's greatly diminished.

These principles underpin promotion and tenure policies that strengthen the connection between teaching and scholarship broadly defined.

New Conversations

Thanks to the insightful and dedicated effort of the Task Force on Promotion and Tenure, the support of the Academic Senate, and the vision of its new president, ASU is now the site of multiple, overlapping conversations on teaching and its rewards. In departments and colleges across Arizona State's four campuses, faculty members, chairs, deans, and central administrators are discussing interrelated questions:

◆ How can all of us at Arizona State collaborate to encourage effective teaching that maximizes learning?

◆ How can we most effectively combine student course evaluations, peer teaching reviews, and other forms of evaluation (e.g., teaching portfolios) to fairly and comprehensively assess teaching and the learning that results from it?

◆ How can we secure Arizona State's future as a New American University?

◆ What support can we provide to enhance faculty success in teaching, research/creative activity, and service so that faculty members have long, productive careers at Arizona State and in their fields?

◆ How can policies help us to achieve a desirable balance among our commitments to teaching, research/creative activity, and service?

◆ How can we most effectively serve our many stakeholders?

Because the conversations addressing these and other questions are lively, engaged, and thoughtful, we are very optimistic about the future of the university.

Walking the Talk

Besides fostering conversations, we are also taking concrete action. During 2002-2003, for instance, departments developed procedures for the peer review of teaching, and some began implementing the procedures. Many examples illustrate these new policies and procedures, but a few are especially useful here. For instance, the College of Liberal Arts and Sciences specifies that probationary reviews during the second and fourth years include not only student evaluations of teaching but also another form of evaluation of teaching, such as peer evaluations or independent reviews of teaching materials. Departments in the College of Education, under the leadership of associate dean Sarah Hudelson, have collaboratively developed detailed peer-review policies and procedures that draw on Boyer's (1990) four categories of scholarship and Glassick, Huber, and Maeroff's (1997) six criteria for assessing scholarship. Another example is the Department of Theatre in the Herberger

---

Conversations and changed practices have led us to clarify procedures for promotion and tenure.

College of Fine Arts, which has designed peer review that, among other things, pays attention to the match between the course learning goals and the class and the place of the class in the learning of the whole semester.

It is interesting to see how this development and implementation have led to further conversations about the value of assessing our crucial work with students. In some departments, such as those in the College of Education, the conversations have expanded to consider the peer review of teaching as a means to encourage ongoing discussions about teaching and learning.

Simultaneously, conversations and changed practices have led us to clarify procedures for promotion and tenure. For instance, we have revised the template for the letter that we send to external reviewers so that they are fully aware of the kinds of details helpful to promotion and tenure committees at Arizona State. We are also developing workshops and Web resources to support faculty applying for tenure and the chairs and deans who help construct the documentation for faculty members' activities in teaching, service, and research/creative activity.

Additionally, the conversations have prompted us to enhance efforts to support faculty so that they are successful at times of tenure and promotion and throughout their careers at our university. We are collecting models of support, such as mentoring programs that already exist at Arizona State and at other universities. Further, we are collecting print and Web resources and developing workshops for senior faculty and administrators at all levels so that they can learn about strategies for providing ongoing support for colleagues. We are also developing networks of support that cross

department and college boundaries so that faculty can enjoy multiple perspectives on how to be maximally successful in the institution. For instance, these networks could make it easier for junior faculty to find others who have specialized skills and knowledge in a certain approaches to teaching or who have an interest in interdisciplinary research projects.

External Support

In January 2002, leaders from AAHE and Carnegie came to Arizona State to facilitate conversations about relationships between faculty roles and rewards and the scholarship of teaching and learning. Although our Academic Senate, our Center for Learning and Teaching Excellence, and our Center for Research on Education in Science, Mathematics, Engineering, and Technology had already led such conversations in recent years, the perspectives of AAHE and Carnegie leaders were quite helpful. Further, in July 2002, we sent a seven-member team from the Main, East, and West campuses to the annual AAHE Summer Academy to explore strategies for implementing the new guidelines for promotion and tenure within the context of the New American University. Those few days of discussion did much to move us forward, and our participation in the CASTL Campus Program for the past few years has helped to further raise our awareness about the role of the scholarship of teaching in research universities and to provide moral support for policy change. Further, our reporting on CASTL activities at our university via the AAHE WebCenter has helped us to assess our progress in engaging in the scholarship of teaching and learning.

External encouragement has helped us sharpen our focus and expand our support. During a

May 2003 visit by Nadya Fouad of the University of Wisconsin-Milwaukee, we discussed with diverse groups of faculty and administrators an even wider range of support for faculty on all of our campuses — support that will more effectively help faculty as they engage in teaching, research/creative activity, and service. Also the Arizona Board of Regents has for the past few years encouraged our attention to faculty roles and rewards in the New American University by emphasizing learner-centered education. The Board has offered $25,000-$100,000 grants for faculty who wish to develop and assess learner-centered approaches.

Building Synergy for Change

If we had known that all the talking and the doing were going to be as invigorating as they have been, we may have begun the process earlier. A confluence of factors has made our recent efforts fruitful, however, and we look forward to what will happen in the future. Among the factors that have led to change, five stand out as important: the Task Force on Promotion and Tenure studied a wide range of models and listened to the voices of a wide range of faculty; the Academic Senate thoroughly discussed the proposed changes recommended by the Task Force; Arizona State's president has provided leadership in emphasizing relationships between teaching/learning and research; the university has drawn on the resources of external organizations that can support discussions of teaching and learning; and the Arizona Board of Regents has provided financial support for learner-centered education. We realize how important it has been for us to bring all of these forces together to build a synergy for change.

References

Ad hoc Committee on Evaluation of Teaching. (2001). *Proposed guidelines for evaluating teaching.* Retrieved June 25, 2003, from http://www.asu.edu/provost/reports/final_tenure_promo.doc

Boyer, E. (1990). *Scholarship reconsidered: Priorities of the professoriate.* Menlo Park, CA: The Carnegie Foundation for the Advancement of Teaching.

Crow, M. (2002, September 13). Four guiding principles drive Crow's vision for ASU. *ASU Insight* (1) 6.

Glassick, C., Huber, M., & Maeroff, G. (1997). *Scholarship assessed: Evaluation of the professoriate.* San Francisco: Jossey-Bass.

Our reporting via the AAHE WebCenter has helped us to assess our progress in engaging in the scholarship of teaching and learning.

Contacts and URLs

Milton Glick
Executive Vice President and Provost
Arizona State University
glick@asu.edu

The recommendations and the Senate's discussion of them are available at: http://www.
asu.edu/provost/reports/final_tenure_promo.doc and
http://www.asu.edu/provost/asenate/minutes/Summ021802.htm

For the New American University vision statement, see
http://www.asu.edu/ia/inauguration/address/c.htm

For peer review of teaching information, see
clasdean.la.asu.edu/faculty/review/chk_prob_fac.doc and
http://theatre.asu.edu/faculty/PeerObservation.doc

For details about the Board of Regents' attention to "Learner-Centered Education in the Arizona University System," see
http://www.abor.asu.edu/4_special_programs/lce/ABORactions
_lce.htm, which offers examples of learner-centered practices
from the three universities in the state.

Arizona State University
Tempe, AZ
Doctoral/Research Extensive
http://www.asu.edu/

Peer Review of Teaching: Developing a Program in a Large, Research-Extensive, Land-Grant Institution

Maxine P. Atkinson, Alton J. Banks, Judy C. Peel, and J. Douglas Wellman
North Carolina State University

This chapter recounts the development of university-wide guidelines for peer review of teaching at North Carolina State University. Following a description of the context in which the guidelines arose, we describe the work of the faculty committee that spearheaded the proposal, the principles for which we advocated, the procedures we recommended, and the early stages of the new system's implementation.

The past decade has seen a wave of initiatives to improve teaching and learning at North Carolina State University, including but not limited to:

◆ First-Year College, created to improve students' transition into college and choice of major, now enrolling one third of the first-year class;

◆ Inquiry-guided Learning, a campus-wide faculty development program funded by the Hewlett Foundation and the University and aimed at changing teaching to improve students' critical thinking and engagement in their studies;

◆ First-year Inquiry, a program of small seminars taught by experienced faculty trained to teach for critical thinking through guided questioning, now reaching approximately one third of first-year students;

◆ Faculty Center for Teaching and Learning, a university faculty development unit created in 1998 in the Office of the Provost;

◆ Learning and Research Center for the Digital Age, situated in the North Carolina State libraries and supporting applications of educational technology;

◆ Distance Education and Learning Technology Applications, part of a new vice provost's office, supporting on- and off-campus teaching with technology;

◆ Honors Program, completely overhauled, with a new director recruited in a national search; and

◆ Service-Learning, situated in the Faculty Center for Teaching and Learning and supporting faculty involvement through extended training coupled with support for student reflection leaders and community liaisons.

All those involved in these reforms, including faculty, administrators, staff, and graduate and undergraduate students, recognize that the key to their success and sustainability is faculty involvement. If faculty members other than early adopters are to make the necessary commitments of time and energy, the reward system for teaching must be supportive. However, at North Carolina State, as at comparable institutions, numerous forces work against a supportive environment for teaching. First and foremost is the dominance of research. Research primacy is driven by an interlocking set of institutional conditions, including declining state funding prompting increasing pressure for funded research; a long-standing drive for AAU status; a commitment to expanding graduate education, in line with the university's role as one of two research-extensive institutions in the 16-campus state university system; and the professional incentives for faculty as members of national and international disciplinary guilds. In addition, North Carolina State's size, with approximately 30,000 students and 1,500 faculty members, and its decentralized campus culture work against efforts to reform the faculty reward system.

A confounding factor unique to North Carolina State is its history of course evaluations. Decades ago, a university-wide evaluation system was exploited to produce a listing of "NC State's One Hundred Worst Professors" published in the Raleigh newspaper. This searing experience led to the abandonment of the centralized system in favor of college and departmental course evaluations and fostered resistance to any centralized faculty evaluation approaches. In part because of this history with course evaluations, when the University of North Carolina System responded to legislative pressure in 1993 and required peer review of teaching, North Carolina State departments established their own approaches. The efficacy of their varied peer review programs was unclear.

Thus, as the waves of teaching reform washed over the campus in the 1990s, the faculty reward system for teaching consisted of widely diverse course evaluation instruments, an unknown array of peer review protocols, the judgments of department heads and voting faculty, and a variety of teaching awards. These means of evaluation were insufficient to support widespread faculty investment in innovative teaching.

Proposal Development

In 1998, following establishment of the Faculty Center for Teaching and Learning, the university standing Teaching Effectiveness and Evaluation Committee was reconstituted into two committees, an advisory committee for the teaching center and the Committee on the Evaluation of Teaching. This decision was based on the argument that formative and summative faculty support, effectiveness, and evaluation should not be conflated and that there was sufficient work to justify a committee focused on each. This decision proved to be critical, and both committees worked effectively to support campus reform efforts in teaching and learning. For its part, the committee developed a new university-wide course evaluation instrument and succeeded in overcoming numerous challenges on the way to achieving campus endorsement. Unfortunately, implementation has been stymied by budget cuts and other problems. The committee also promoted university awareness of the scholarship of teaching and learning. Finally, and the subject of this chapter, the committee advanced the case for university guidelines for the peer review of teaching.

The committee's peer review work was led by a five-member subcommittee, including three faculty members and two ex officio administrators, the vice provost for faculty development, and the director of the Faculty Center for Teaching and Learning. Over a two-year period, the subcommittee consulted the literature such as Chism (1999a, 1999b) and Hutchings (1995), reviewed North Carolina State's official and informal peer review programs, and systematically examined the protocols developed by the 63 NC State academic departments as required by the University of North Carolina System in 1993. In its final report, the subcommittee made the following recommendations:

◆ Departmental policies should recognize both formative and summative evaluations of faculty teaching, and any single review should serve only one of these purposes.

◆ Schedules for peer review of teaching should be differentiated by instructor rank; first-year reviews for tenure-track assistant professors and instructors in their first appointment should be strictly formative in nature.

◆ Departments should provide mentoring for junior faculty.

◆ The university should consider developing an optional cross-disciplinary mentoring program.

◆ Student course evaluations should be considered as necessary but not sufficient for assessing the value of the course material, the pedagogical aspects of teaching, and the overall fit of the material in the main body of the subject.

◆ Departments should have leeway to craft peer review procedures, but all should adhere to the following best practices: openness and transparency; mutually agreed upon and strictly followed procedures; writ-

ten feedback at both formative and summative stages; multiple sources, multiple methods, and multiple times without sole reliance on classroom visits; consideration of teaching materials and teaching philosophy; prompt discussion of both summative and formative reviews; and training for peer reviewers.

◆ Teaching/course portfolios should be an option for faculty to include in their reappointment/promotion/tenure dossiers.

◆ Guidance, including information on a website, should be provided on request for departments developing peer review procedures.

Implementation

On the basis of the literature review, examination of peer programs, and its own deliberations, the subcommittee concluded that certain conditions must be in place for a peer review of teaching to be implemented widely and in a sustainable manner, including administrative buy-in, faculty buy-in, reviewer training, department head training, rewards/recognition for reviewers, modification of faculty activity reports to include service as peer reviewer, and periodic college review of departmental peer review programs.

In June 2001, the subcommittee submitted its report to the full Committee on the Evaluation of Teaching. Following committee approval, the report was submitted to the provost, who undertook a number of actions. The provost developed a Peer Review of Teaching website for guidance to departments. For college deans, he emphasized in the 2001 reappointment/promotion/tenure process memorandum the need for examination of departmental criteria and process documents, the importance of mentoring, and the importance of full participation in departmental consultation. In addition, he requested that each dean describe the approaches to mentoring in each academic department. Finally, he included mentoring and peer review teams as examples of resources in individual faculty members' Plan for Professional Development, part of the reappointment/promotion/tenure documentation.

Due to turnover in the Office of the Provost, changes in the Evaluation of Teaching Committee, and repeated budget cuts, no additional steps have been taken since 2001 to institutionalize peer review of teaching at the university level. Although it is possible that colleges and departments have instituted changes, no systematic effort has been made to monitor such change. As conditions permit, this assessment of progress should be one of our next steps.

In the end, if the reward system for faculty at North Carolina State University has a strong and sustainable peer review of teaching component, it will be the result of faculty initiative supported by administrative moral and financial backing. As such, it will be part of this university's strong and sustained faculty-led effort to raise the stature of teaching and learning at this "people's university."

References

Chism, N. V. N. (1999a, March). Peer review as 'habits of the heart.' *The Teaching Professor, 13*(3), 3.

Chism, N. V. N. (1999b). *Peer review of teaching.* Bolton, MA: Anker.

Hutchings, P. (Ed.). (1995). *Making teaching community property.* Washington, DC: American Association for Higher Education.

Contacts and URL:

Maxine P. Atkinson
Associate Professor and Associate
    Department Head in Sociology and
    Anthropology
North Carolina State University
maxine_atkinson@ncsu.edu

Alton J. Banks
Director, Faculty Center for Teaching and
    Learning
North Carolina State University
alton_banks@ncsu.edu

Judy C. Peel
Associate Vice Provost for Faculty
    Development
North Carolina State University
judy_peel@ncsu.edu

J. Douglas Wellman
Professor and Head, Department of Parks,
    Recreation and Tourism Management
North Carolina State University
doug_wellman@ncsu.edu

For information on the North Carolina State University Peer Review of Teaching, see http://www.ncsu.edu/provost/peer_review/

North Carolina State University
Raleigh, NC
Doctoral/Research Extensive
http://www.ncsu.edu/

Multiple Sites of Authority

Jennifer Meta Robinson
Indiana University Bloomington

What can an anthropologist using the ethnographic method tell us about hands-on learning? What can we learn when a feminist literary critic thinks of his classroom as a text? What new perspective can we gain when a cultural studies instructor examines her classroom as a community? The potential suggested in using such discipline-based "habits of mind" on questions in higher education rests at the center of the scholarship of teaching and learning that is finding purchase at Indiana University Bloomington (Walker, 2003). There, scholarly conversations within and across ranks, disciplines, and campus units bring new perspectives to conventions and assumptions about teaching and learning and give rise to new questions and new modes of analysis (Giroux, 1999). The Scholarship of Teaching and Learning Program at Indiana University aspires to a model of collaborative problem-solving that engages multiple points of authority to foster faculty talents and administrative resources toward the common institutional goal of enhanced student learning.

Boyer's (1990) idea of a new scholarship of teaching and learning caught hold at Indiana among a small group of faculty, senior administrators, and staff members who, like most of their colleagues, were committed to both the teaching and research missions of the university. They saw potential in this new scholarship for bridging teaching and research and for addressing common faculty teaching concerns through the familiar intellectual lens of research. In small groups like those sponsored by the Carnegie Academy for the Scholarship of Teaching and Learning, faculty members discussed the literature on teaching and the place of teaching in higher education. Three things became apparent through their discussions. First, substantial "pedagogical content knowledge" and some experience with formal study of teaching and learning resided with group members and others on campus (Shulman, 1986). Second, questions remained about teaching and learning, especially contextualized questions addressing specific courses, student populations, disciplinary challenges, and teaching methods. Third, faculty members needed help investigating such questions in what was, for most, a new field with a new literature, new methods, and new audiences. The advance thinking done by these groups to identify collective strengths and weaknesses became an important precedent for the future, diversified nature of the scholarship of teaching and learning at Indiana University.

One of the key partnerships that formed to support these emerging faculty interests was

A key partnership to support faculty interests was between the vice chancellor for academic affairs and the vice president for research.

between the vice chancellor for academic affairs and dean of the faculties, the primary sponsor of the initiative, and the vice president for research and dean of the university graduate school. These two offices provided the crucial staffing and resources to support faculty inquiry into how to enhance student learning. Together these offices established the principles of governance, inclusiveness, and accountability by which the initiative functions. They organized annual seed grants to facilitate project development, workshops and other opportunities for skill and community building, and a series of colloquia designed to showcase projects by local and visiting scholars. Attendance at these colloquia provides one measure of their success. Between fall 1999 and spring 2003, attendance at 44 major events totaled 2,839, for an average annual attendance of 709 people. Tenure-track faculty members represented 35 percent of that total, nontenure ranks 28 percent, students 21 percent (nearly all graduate students), staff members 11 percent, and visitors and others 5 percent. Over those years, presenters at the colloquia came from 19 departments in the College of Arts and Sciences and from 5 professional schools.

Other campus units have also proved to be valuable partners in the scholarship of teaching and learning. A few examples suggest the scale of the staffing and resources that have been allocated in support. The University Libraries designates a librarian to assist faculty members in research reviews and provides online bibliographies and reserve readings. Instructional Support Services contributes essential human and material resources, including day-to-day leadership, coordination, and research development; instructional consulting; logistical and secretarial support; technology and website support; publications and graphics support; and video production. As a final example, the Committee for the Protection of Human Subjects has entered into an important, ongoing discussion with the faculty and administration about ways to facilitate ethical classroom research. As a result, several models for scholarship of teaching and learning research protocols have developed, procedures necessary for obtaining committee approval have been streamlined, and projects now move quickly and successfully through proper channels.

The initiative has always had faculty leadership and ownership (Cross & Stedman, 1996; Hutchings, 1993). A large advisory council to the program includes award-winning professors, academic deans, and scholars of teaching from all ranks. In addition, small ad hoc committees collaborate with the program director on specific projects. For example, in 2003, a working group attended the AAHE Summer Academy to draft a plan that would further institutionalize the scholarship of teaching and learning at the local level and position Indiana University for national leadership (Sept, Robinson, Nelson, & Schlegel, 2003). Key campus stakeholders, including deans, faculty members of all ranks, and graduate students, revised the plan during a half-day planning retreat. One year later, many components of the plan had been accomplished: the appointment of a steering committee, an award to a department for a study of and leadership in teaching and learning, active consideration of a doctoral curriculum in the scholarship of teaching and learning, a successful proposal for our leadership of a cluster of campuses in the Campus Program, and the first moves toward an international society with its home at Indiana. This level of organizational goal setting and achievement is a testament to the power of faculty dedication supported by administrative resources.

As a guiding principle, the program facilitates the efforts of faculty members to reposition themselves vis-à-vis scholarly work on teaching and to support their movement from private study to public scholarship (Shulman, 2000). The program invites novice participation but maintains an orientation toward scholarly rigor, expansion of knowledge, and publication of new findings. It assumes that some, and perhaps many, individuals will move from being "consumers" who apply the literature of teaching and learning to their own classes (scholarly

teachers) to also becoming "producers" of that literature (scholars of teaching and learning). From its initial audience of tenure-track professors, the program extended its services and grants to non-tenure-track faculty members after the first two years. And after the program began outreach to graduate students, their attendance at the campus wide colloquia steadily rose from 16 percent in the first year to 28 percent (215 people) in the fourth year. These latter two groups also increasingly pursue their own course portfolio writing, grant applications, and other scholarly activities.

Consistent with the scholarship of teaching and learning's principle of evidence-based argumentation, the 2002 retreat participants endorsed a "coordinated, multi-scale" assessment of the program. This assessment, both descriptive and evaluative, combines a survey of scholarly activity (publications and presentations) on teaching and learning, quantitative measures of participation in the program, and a qualitative study of the faculty experience with the scholarship of teaching and learning (motivation, involvement, networks, campus climate, and hopes for the future).

All of the Indiana University Scholarship of Teaching and Learning Program's policies and practices benefit from the diversity of its participants and depend on their engagement for its success. Indeed, campus involvement continues to grow. In the fourth year, 35 percent of colloquia attendance consisted of first-time participants, with 29 percent of that portion being tenure-track professors. As the program matures, newly urgent questions emerge about the evaluation of this scholarship, appropriate expectations for productivity, variability of accepted methods and models among the disciplines, and campus structures that will aid genuine and self-sustaining scholarship. As is

---

The Committee for the Protection of Human Subjects is discussing with faculty and administrators ways to facilitate ethical classroom research.

---

its habit, the scholarship of teaching and learning constituency at Indiana University will no doubt address these issues among its characteristically broad base of authority.

References

Boyer, E. L. (1990). *Scholarship reconsidered: Priorities of the professoriate.* Menlo Park, CA: The Carnegie Foundation for the Advancement of Teaching.

Cross, K. P., & Steadman, M. H. (1996). *Classroom research: Implementing the scholarship of teaching.* San Francisco: Jossey-Bass.

Giroux, H. A. (1999). Cultural studies as public pedagogy: Making the pedagogical more political. *Encyclopedia of philosophy of education.* Retrieved May 27, 2003, from http://www.vusst.hr/ENCY-CLOPAEDIA/cultural_studies.htm.

Hutchings, P. (1993). *Using cases to improve college teaching: A guide to more reflective practice.* Washington, DC: American Association for Higher Education.

Sept, J., Robinson, J.M. Nelson, C. & Schlegel, W. *Draft proposal for scholarship of teaching and learning institutionalization and leadership.* Indiana University. Retrieved May 30, 2003, from http://www.indiana.edu/~sotl/download/02_AAHE _sum_acad.doc

Shulman, L. S. (1986). Those who understand: Knowledge growth in teaching. *Educational Researcher, 15*(2), 4-14.

Walker, G. (2003). *Strategies for aggressive and creative cooperation.* Opening plenary address at CASTL Colloquium on the Scholarship of Teaching and Learning: Collaborating for Change, Washington, D.C.

Contact and URLs

Jennifer Meta Robinson
Director, Campus Consulting Services
Indiana University Bloomington
jenmetar@indiana.edu

For information about a variety of resources and activities regarding the scholarship of teaching and learning, see http://www.indiana.edu/~sotl/whatis.html#org>

For more information on Indiana University's Hesburgh award, see http://www.indiana.edu/~sotl/download/030214_hesburghprop.doc

For more information on the scholarship of teaching and learning at Indiana University Bloomington, see http://www.indiana.edu/~sotl

Indiana University Bloomington
Bloomington, IN
Doctoral/Research Extensive
http://www.indiana.edu/

Valuing the Scholarship of Teaching and Learning in Promotion and Tenure Reviews

Cheryl McConnell
Rockhurst University

Although many institutional policies and structures must be in place to support the scholarship of teaching and learning, no policy is more important than the inclusion of the work in promotion and tenure decisions. As Rockhurst University faced this challenge, we were successful in securing early promotion and tenure review committee support for the scholarship of teaching and learning.

In fall 1998, Rockhurst University began discussions about and found significant support for exploring the CASTL initiative. In the second year, a Campus Inquiry Group began meeting to explore the field, discuss ways to make the scholarship public, and begin projects in the scholarship of teaching and learning. The discussions quickly centered on foundational distinctions between "scholarly teaching" and the "scholarship of teaching and learning" and whether the latter would count for promotion and tenure decisions at Rockhurst University.

As the academic year progressed, the primary issue facing the group was how to articulate to the broader university community what it had learned in its meetings and how to recommend that the scholarship of teaching and learning be rewarded in promotion and tenure deci-

sions. Rockhurst's Promotion and Tenure Committee holds a reasonably broad definition of scholarship, being open to much of Boyer's model in *Scholarship Reconsidered: Priorities of the Professoriate* (Boyer, 1990). To maintain scholarship standards, this university-level committee has historically encouraged individual academic departments to submit statements that explain and give examples of acceptable scholarship within their discipline. The committee members review the statements and either accept them as reasonable examples that meet their conditions for scholarship or return the statements noting their concerns and their inability to apply the statement to promotion and tenure decisions.

The Campus Inquiry Group decided to develop a statement about the scholarship of teaching and learning, provide examples of the work, and submit their statement to the university promotion and tenure committee, the president, and the academic deans. The statement was drafted by a committee member, edited by the committee, and submitted to the committee near the end of the academic year. The committee, which found the statement to be a powerful argument for the support of the scholarship of teaching and learning at Rockhurst University, accepted the statement to be applied to all future promotion and tenure decisions. Essential elements of the statement are described below.

Forming a Statement to the Promotion and Tenure Committee

The Campus Inquiry Group created its own definition of scholarship that used some language from an earlier definition by Hutchings and Shulman (1999).

> We think that professional, "scholarly teaching" should be one of the important goals for faculty at Rockhurst University, and that it should be factored into hiring, tenure, and promotion decisions. We recommend this statement about scholarly teaching by Hutchings and Shulman as a useful definition: 'All faculty members have an obligation to teach well, to engage students, and to foster important forms of student learning—not that this is easily done. Such teaching is a good fully sufficient unto itself. When it entails, as well, certain practices of classroom assessment and evidence gathering, when it is informed not only by the latest ideas in the field but by current ideas about teaching the field, when it invites peer collaboration and review, then that teaching might rightly be called scholarly, or reflective, or informed. While the scholarship of teaching and learning incorporates elements of scholarly teaching, it is also different. The difference traces to these basic elements: the scholarship of teaching and learning is public, open to critique and evaluation, and in a form that others can build on. A fourth attribute, implied by the other three, is that the scholarship of teaching and learning involves question-asking, inquiry, and investigation – particularly around issues of student learning' (Hutchings & Shulman, 1999, p. 13).

Rockhurst's Carnegie Seminar group would add that an informed, working knowledge of how students learn is a key aspect of such scholarship. Knowledge about how students learn does not have to be on the level of expertise formed by discipline or graduate training on matters of learning theory (i.e., educational psychology). Still, someone engaged in the scholarship of teaching and learning, we believe, has to follow and understand theories, models, perspectives, and when appropriate, draw on the research methods available to scholars about learning.

Faculty engaged in research and scholarly activities — "the work of intellectual life" at Rockhurst University—should have a choice of all the scholarships identified by Ernest Boyer (1990): the scholarship of discovery, integration, application, and teaching. No one form of research and scholarly activity should take precedence over another, and faculty obviously should not have to be involved in all types of scholarship. The seminar faculty members recommended that research and scholarly activities be broadly defined to allow for the greatest latitude of intellectual involvement. They also recommended that all forms of scholarly activity by faculty meet the same high standards. http://cte.rockhurst.edu/

Reflections

Three essential factors contributed to our success in securing support for the scholarship of teaching and learning in our policies regarding promotion and tenure: a group process, administrative support, and sustained progress.

Campus Inquiry Group Process

Interested volunteers who constituted the Campus Inquiry Group included department and division chairs, a wide representation of academic disciplines, and a high number of experienced, respected faculty members. The group was administratively supported through Rockhurst's Center for Teaching Excellence, and the center's director gave time and energy to organize meetings, communicate with participants, and summarize discussions. The full statement to the promotion and tenure committee intentionally used language specific to our culture, attempted to anticipate concerns, and provided examples of scholarship of teaching and learning from respected Rockhurst University faculty. For example, the statement included familiar references and language from the Boyer model of scholarship, which is used and discussed at the university. Additionally, the statement proactively addressed potential concerns about the rigor of this scholarship, how it differs from scholarly teaching, and how this scholarship is an option for faculty rather than a replacement for discipline-based scholarship.

Administrative Support

Although the university president and deans were supportive of the CASTL initiative, they were not the leaders of the effort to include the scholarship of teaching and learning in promotion and tenure decisions. Administrative support was shown through formal and informal encouragement of scholarship of teaching and learning projects, in faculty performance reviews, and through appointments to the university's promotion and tenure committee. In the year following the initial campus conversations, appointments to the committee included faculty who were committed to quality teaching, had high standards for themselves and others in the classroom, had a broad view of acceptable scholarship, and had a history of producing quality, mission-based scholarship. In the year following the statement's adoption, Rockhurst's national Carnegie Scholar was appointed as chair of the promotion and tenure committee to enable the committee to identify and support quality initiatives in the scholarship of teaching and learning.

Sustaining Progress

Achieving success in including the scholarship of teaching and learning in promotion and tenure decisions is an essential step in supporting the larger initiative, but it is not sufficient. At Rockhurst University, our efforts have been successful because we have had multiple champions over time, including senior faculty members, the academic vice president, our faculty member who is a national Carnegie Scholar, the director of the Center for Teaching Excellence, and all academic deans. We have benefited greatly from a continuing connection to the national CASTL initiative, and we have brought many national scholars to campus through hosting regional conferences and institutes on this scholarship. Our faculty members have been inspired by seeing quality

---

Research and scholarly activities are broadly defined to allow for the greatest latitude of intellectual involvement and to meet the same high standards.

---

examples of the scholarship of teaching and learning in fields closely related to their own disciplines.

We find it essential to continue to communicate the distinction between scholarly teaching and the scholarship of teaching and learning. As time passes, new faculty members enter the university and experienced faculty move to different phases of their scholarly careers. Therefore, the language and definitions need to be included in university orientation programs, in Center for Teaching Excellence programs, and in formal faculty roles and responsibilities statements. In many important ways, having the scholarship of teaching and learning count for promotion and tenure decisions is an essential first step in a long journey of institutional support and alignment.

References

Boyer, E. L. (1990). *Scholarship reconsidered: Priorities of the professoriate.* Menlo Park, CA: The Carnegie Foundation for the Advancement of Teaching.

Hutchings, P., & Shulman, L. S. (1999). Teaching among the scholarships. *Change, 31*(5), 10-15.

Contact and URLs:

Cheryl McConnell
Associate Professor of Accounting
Rockhurst University
cheryl.mcconnell@rockhurst.edu

For the entire statement regarding promotion and tenure, see Rockhurst University's Center for Teaching Excellence website, http://cte.rockhurst.edu/

For more information on Rockhurst's conferences and institutes, see http://cte.rockhurst.edu/sotl/cluster.htm

Rockhurst University
Kansas City, MO
Master's I
http://www.rockhurst.edu/

Changing Policies and Procedures Related to Appointment, Promotion, and Tenure

Charlotte Ravaioli and Lansdale D. Shaffmaster
Keystone College

In 1998 when Keystone College received approval from the Pennsylvania Department of Education to offer baccalaureate degrees, the transformation from a two-year to a four-year college provided an opportunity to revise and update policies and procedures related to promotion and tenure. The addition of upper division courses necessitated a review of faculty qualifications and criteria for appointment, promotion, and tenure, elements that had not been revised since 1980. In the past, evaluation of faculty members had been primarily informal and unsystematic. The three major categories for evaluating faculty members were teaching, professional development, and service.

Beginnings

In 1999, the college joined the Carnegie Academy Campus Program by initiating a series of conversations related to the scholarship of teaching and learning. More than half of the faculty participated in these conversations, which fostered an atmosphere and a vocabulary that were very helpful as faculty began considering changes to time-honored traditions.

In summer 2001, the dean of the college formed a Committee on the Future of the Professoriate, composed of the senior faculty from each of the five academic divisions of the college. This committee was charged with the task of redefining the characteristics of faculty for each of the academic ranks. As our discussions developed, it became apparent that the criteria we were describing needed to apply to individuals in widely varying fields, from culinary arts to information technology to the fine arts. Qualifications for entry level and advancement in rank would vary greatly across divisions.

It was immediately evident that each academic division would need to determine the qualifications required for its faculty. The committee developed a framework of qualifications that could serve to establish some uniformity and equity across the college while allowing flexibility within divisions. Excellence in teaching, always the hallmark at Keystone, has not changed. Changes have been made primarily in requirements for professional development. Because most faculty at Keystone focused almost exclusively on teaching, campus conversations related to the scholarship of teaching and learning were very helpful in examining the different forms of scholarship that contribute to professional development. The essential component of professional development came to be evidence of scholarship.

Establishing the need for a terminal degree and identifying the appropriate degree for each academic area became necessary. The new criteria for rank were presented to the Faculty Senate in December 2001. Faculty raised questions, identified issues, and made suggestions. The draft version was revised, and in May 2002 the faculty approved the new criteria in principle. They requested that the dean work with representatives of the faculty to identify the policies and procedures that would accompany the criteria. This request coincided with the invitation to the 2002 AAHE Summer Academy. We had a project!

Summer Project

Our project team included broad representation from each academic division, the Faculty Development Committee, the Faculty Affairs Committee, and the Rank and Tenure Committee. The team, headed by the dean, also included non-tenured faculty, a division chairperson, early-career faculty, and seasoned faculty. The team's task at the 2002 AAHE Summer Academy was to flesh out the details of the new criteria in terms of policies, procedures, and timelines. These plans were presented to the faculty senate in fall 2002 and follow-

---

New plans added the Professional Development Plan and Peer Review.

---

ing minor revisions were approved for implementation with new faculty.

New Policies and Procedures
The new policies and procedures involve three basic changes:

1. Regarding the type of information used for faculty evaluation, the new plans added the Professional Development Plan and Peer Review.

2. Regarding committee structure, the new plans changed the composition of the College Promotion and Tenure Committee and the organization of Division Promotion and Tenure Committees.

3. Regarding timelines for faculty evaluation, the new plans based annual evaluation of faculty on an academic year rather than a calendar year.

The new policies also involve more extensive mentoring and evaluation of new faculty during the first three years of their appointment along with an extensive third-year review. New faculty members are required to develop and maintain professional portfolios that document their teaching, professional development, and service. Instead of application for promotion and tenure being considered by only one college committee with input from the division chair and a faculty advocate, faculty will be evaluated within each division, and those recommendations for promotion and tenure will be forwarded to the College Promotion and Tenure Committee.

The new procedures require greater participation by division faculty in providing information for both formative and summative evaluation of faculty. The College Promotion and Tenure Committee, with representatives from each division, will work with the Division Promotion and Tenure Committees to ensure equity and parity across the college. Policies, procedures, and timelines for newly appointed faculty are in place. They are still being developed for promotion to the ranks of associate professor and full professor, for the granting of tenure, and for post-tenure review.

Another significant change involves the schedule for faculty evaluations. The project team recommended that the faculty evaluation cycle be based on an academic year rather than a calendar year, as has been the tradition. This change will greatly facilitate collection and reporting of data. It was approved and immediately implemented.

Milestones

These new policies and procedures are the result of synergy created by several significant events that have occurred over the past few years. Conversations related to the scholarship of teaching and learning had much to do with changing faculty attitudes related to the importance of scholarly work. Establishing the Committee of the Future of the Professoriate, a group of senior faculty representing each academic division, proved to have sufficient credibility with the faculty to propose needed changes. The intensive work experience at the AAHE Summer Academy established a unified cohort of individuals who could disseminate the new policies and procedures to various campus constituencies.

An important part of the strategy for change was to investigate policies at similar colleges and to discover how faculty members at other schools are awarded promotion and tenure. The challenge was to select the ideas with the best fit for Keystone's mission. The results indicate a shift in faculty perspective on evaluation for the purposes of promotion and tenure. Generally, there will be more emphasis on formative evaluation and its relationship to professional development. The purposes of summative evaluations are more related to long-term institutional needs.

Summary

The success of this endeavor is primarily the result of faculty involvement in each step of the process. Although changing policies and procedures related to faculty evaluation for promotion and tenure is fraught with danger, these dangers were anticipated, expected, and planned for. The entire process included input from all faculty members, sometimes as a whole, but mostly from representatives who shared the work-in-progress with their constituents and regularly collected input and feedback. When changes were presented to the faculty, extensive discussion was encouraged, and all suggestions were considered.

The concerns of faculty who have been employed at the college for many years relate primarily to fairness in the application of higher expectations and standards. Changes to the policies under which they have been working must include assurance that their qualifications and contributions are still valued. The princi-

---

The practice most helpful in managing change is outcomes assessment.

---

ple that is most helpful in managing this change is outcomes assessment. Faculty will now be required to provide evidence of teaching effectiveness, evidence of professional development, and evidence of service. Professional portfolios are requirements for new faculty, but some veteran faculty will also use them. Each academic division is developing categories of evidence that will be appropriate for the courses faculty will be teaching and the co-curricular activities they support. During the 2003-2004 academic year, each division will establish its Promotion and Tenure Committee and elect a representative to the new College Promotion and Tenure Committee. These committees will work together to develop the new policies and procedures for promotion to the ranks of associate and full professor. We will use the same kinds of activities that worked so well for the first steps of this project and expect that the process will work equally well.

Contacts

Charlotte Ravaioli
Vice President of Academic Affairs and
    Dean of the College
Keystone College
charlotte.ravaioli@keystone.edu

Lansdale D. Shaffmaster
Professor, Division of Social and Behavioral
    Sciences
Keystone College
lan.shaffmaster@keystone.edu

**Keystone College
La Plume, PA
Associate's
http://www.keystone.edu/**

Promotion and Tenure Track Record

Constance J. Post
Iowa State University

"Not everything that counts can be counted, and not everything that can be counted counts."[1]

When Iowa State University issued a new promotion and tenure document in 1999,[2] it distinguished itself as one of the largest U.S. public universities to have embarked on a major revision of promotion and tenure policies in the last decade. Chiefly responding to local conditions but also to Boyer's *Scholarship Reconsidered* (Boyer, 1990), the document sought to embody the diversity of Iowa State's many colleges by evaluating a candidate's total scholarship in teaching, research/creative activities, and extension/professional practice. Under the new triad of discovery, learning, and engagement at Iowa State, research/creative activities typically qualify as discovery, teaching as learning, and extension/professional practice as engagement but by no means is this exclusively so. There can be discovery, for instance, not only in the scholarship of research/creative activities but also in the scholarship of teaching and the scholarship of extension/professional practice.[3] In all areas of scholarship, a faculty member's position responsibility statement plays a key role.[4]

Negotiated at the point of hire or at the new hire's appointment date and usually signed by both the faculty member and department chair, the position responsibility statement varies considerably in length, content, introduction, and frequency of revision. The document may be a few sentences, a few paragraphs, or even a few pages long, depending on what the department requires. Variety also governs the content, which may be customized or generic. Colleges with standard-issue statements include business, which stipulates that beginning assistant professors teach in the Saturday MBA program. Even one-size-fits-all statements may undergo some modification, especially in departments that do not expect faculty, new hires or otherwise, to devote equal amounts of time to research/creative activities, teaching, and extension/professional practice. To ensure that the new hire's responsibilities are placed within the context of the department's mission, a departmental preamble may serve as an introduction for the position responsibility statement. Finally, the statement must be broad enough so that it does not need to be rewritten every year, yet specific enough so that it is a useful document for understanding a faculty member's responsibilities.

Assessing the impact of the new document on Iowa State's promotion and tenure track four years later reveals mixed results, especially about what counts toward tenure and promotion and therefore should be included in the record. For some faculty, the new promotion and tenure document receives high praise for honoring what in the past did not count at all or, at least, not for much. Others fault the document for valuing matters that they do not believe will improve Iowa State's National Research Council rankings or contribute to its standing as a Carnegie Doctoral Extensive University. Many, however, believe that Iowa State can best achieve its strategic plan as a land-grant university by continuing to emphasize research while also widening the scope of what counts toward promotion and tenure. We will continue to make sure that teaching, creative activities, and extension/professional practice show up on the radar screen along with research.

Aside from a few idiosyncratic responses, most differences of opinion fall along college or departmental lines, underscoring the multitude of disciplinary cultures at Iowa State. At the same time, these cultures occasionally yield surprising similarities. One of Iowa State's oldest colleges, Agriculture, and one of its newest, Design, acknowledge that although the promotion and tenure document is new for the university, it has not wrought radical change in their own practices. In the College of Agriculture, where half of the 16 departments are jointly administered with other colleges, a faculty member in the Department of Agriculture and Biosystems Engineering, for example, will be evaluated for promotion and tenure both by the faculty of the College of

Agriculture and the College of Engineering. The primary department (the department with the majority percentage of the faculty member's appointment) holds sway in any promotion and tenure decision, but letters of evaluation submitted by the secondary department and any centers or institutes with which the faculty member is affiliated are also carefully considered. What the new promotion and tenure document facilitates is a much stronger interface between the primary and secondary departments, and it does so when National Research Council rankings for the first time will include three areas of the College of Agriculture.[5]

Although Design, like Agriculture, views the new standards for establishing a promotion and tenure record in its college as little changed, it welcomes the university-wide acceptance of the principles underpinning the new document. The college particularly prizes the document because it allows candidates to be evaluated on their whole scholarly life, putting it much more in line with how faculty members imagine their careers. Creating a sculpture or preparing a catalog for an art exhibit counts, rather than just a research article on Moore or Matisse. Not included in the National Research Council rankings, the College of Design is pursuing a cluster of joint appointments, junior and senior, as a way of growing the spirit of interdisciplinary work in the college and ensuring that such work will be recognized and rewarded.

The new promotion and tenure document also reflects the integrative goals of several departments in the College of Veterinary Medicine, the College of Family and Consumer Sciences, and Library Services. In the Department of Veterinary Pathology, professors combine professional practice, teaching, research, and service, with the percentage devoted to each based upon departmental need. Candidates for promotion and tenure are evaluated in all four areas. The Department of Food Science and Human Nutrition similarly finds that the new document makes for a very different record by giving the department permission to take into account all that the person has done, not just the number of research articles and federal grant dollars, for example, but also the scholarship of teaching that might include founding a journal of food science education. In Library Services, this means that professional practice, such as organizing workshops, leading training sessions, and engaging in technology transfer, now receives the credit it deserves.

The rub is how much. Although a professor's responsibilities may be divided among teaching, research/creative activities, and extension/professional practice, consideration for promotion from assistant to associate professor continues to rest almost exclusively on the scholarship of research/creative activities. According to the Chair of Health and Human Performance, new professors are informed at the point of hire that their tenure case will be made primarily on the basis of research, even if the position responsibility statement allocates 45 percent of the candidate's time to teaching, 45 percent to research, and 10 percent to service. In some disciplines, the expectation of x number of dollars in grant support is also a fundamental factor for promotion to associate professor. These practices vary not only from college to college but also within a college, especially Iowa State's largest, the College of Liberal Arts and Sciences.

Where the new document has exerted the greatest impact on promotion and tenure, in departments that emphasize research, is in the move from associate to full professor. A chem-

ical engineering professor may achieve the rank of full professor by developing software that has been widely adopted; likewise, a professor in the College of Business may be promoted from associate to full by writing a textbook that goes beyond a second edition. For promotion to this rank, the scholarship of teaching must extend beyond the local and is often gauged on the basis of published research. Although old ways of verifying scholarship rest on the number of articles in the best journals or books published by the best presses, pedagogy journals in a particular discipline are rarely top-tiered. That such journals are emerging suggests that many disciplines are beginning to grant greater importance to teaching, and this augurs well for those who seek such venues as the outcome of their scholarship of teaching.

In brief, the promotion and tenure record based on the new document has met with greatest acceptance in departments and colleges that have an integrated mission. Some helped to shape the document; all attest to its importance as a means to recruit and retain excellent faculty. Resistance to the new document from departments or areas of departments that valorize research persists, although flexibility has gained an important foothold for those seeking promotion from associate to full in many cases. Perhaps the most outstanding achievement of the new promotion and tenure document has been to widen the conversation about teaching to the point that even research-heavy departments are unlikely to grant tenure to someone with a poor teaching record. The broader conversation about teaching at Iowa State has also sparked a lively, ongoing debate about the role of peer review.[6]

By legitimizing the discussion of teaching and viewing it as a vital part of the totality of scholarship, the new document mandates a new metaphor. Instead of separate silos in which discovery, learning, and engagement remain neatly compartmentalized, the promotion and tenure record amassed by a candidate today more closely resembles overlapping circles. Making visible the totality of scholarship does not mean, however, that all circles will have the same circumference or overlap to the same degree. In repudiating the one-size-fits-all model, Iowa State stands at the forefront of change in promotion and tenure practices at public universities. As provost Benjamin Allen has noted, "the change carries with it special challenges, especially the way we evaluate the totality of scholarship that now counts." Although more counts and counts in more ways than ever before, the process of judging how it counts, Allen has said, "continues to evolve."

Acknowledgements

In preparing this chapter, I owe a great debt to Susan Carlson, associate provost, as well as to the following: Benjamin Allen, provost; Claire Andreasen, chair, Department of Veterinary Pathology; Mark Englebrecht, dean, College of Design; Charles Glatz, chair, Department of Chemical Engineering; Labh Hira, dean, College of Business; Eric Hoiberg, associate dean, College of Agriculture; Olivia Madison, dean, Library Services; Neil Nakadate, university professor of English; Peter Rabideau, former dean, College of Liberal Arts and Sciences; Jerry Thomas, chair, Department of Health and Human Performance; Faye Whitaker, associate provost during the development of the new promotion and tenure document; Pamela White, interim dean, College of Family and Consumer Sciences; and Michael Whiteford, interim dean, College of Liberal Arts and Sciences.

Endnotes

1 Attributed to Albert Einstein (Calaprice, 2000, p. 318).

2 In 1998, the document http://www.provost.iastate.edu/handbook/99toc.html was initially approved by the Iowa State Faculty Senate on March 24 and by the General Faculty on May 1. The revised document was approved by the Faculty Senate Executive Board on September 1, the Faculty Senate on October 13, the University Administration on November 12, and the Board of Regents on December 3.

3 Learning, likewise, may include the scholarship of research/creative activities and the scholarship of extension/professional practice, just as engagement may include the scholarship of research/creative activities and the scholarship of teaching.

4 A measure of the acceptance of this document for candidates considered for tenure and promotion since 1999 is demonstrated by the declining number of faculty choosing to be evaluated on the basis of the old document: of 69 dossiers reviewed in 2000, 39 adhered to the new document, and 32 to the old; of 76 dossiers in 2001, 57 adhered to the new document, and 19 to the old; of 65 dossiers in 2002, 50 adhered to the new document, and 15 to the old; and of 80 dossiers in 2003, 78 adhered to the new document, and only 2 to the old (data supplied by the Office of the Provost). As of 2003, candidates for promotion and tenure must be reviewed under the new document.

5 These are plant sciences, animal sciences, and agricultural economics. Given the importance placed on graduate education by the National Research Council, the scholarship of teaching and of research will receive more attention than ever before in addition to the scholarship of outreach that the college already emphasizes.

6 Peer review was included in a survey of current practices in the documentation of teaching at Iowa State conducted in Spring 2003 by the Office of the Provost and a faculty senate task force chaired by Jack Girton, 2003-2004 Faculty Senate President. Although practices vary among the groups surveyed, which included deans, associate and assistant deans, chairs of college promotion and tenure committees, department chairs, and chairs of department promotion and tenure committees, respondents stated that they rely on a formal or informal process of peer evaluation at the local level and only a few indicated that they do not conduct any peer evaluation of teaching at all. Unsurprisingly, the evaluation of teaching responsibilities depends more heavily on an international or national reputation for promotion to full professor than for promotion to associate professor.

Contact

Constance J. Post
Associate Professor of English
Iowa State University
cjpost@iastate.edu

**Iowa State University
Ames, IA
Doctoral/Research Extensive
http://www.iastate.edu/**

References

Boyer, E. L. (1990). *Scholarship reconsidered: Priorities of the professoriate.* Menlo Park, CA: The Carnegie Foundation for the Advancement of Teaching.

Calaprice, A. (2000). *The expanded quotable Einstein.* Princeton, NJ: Princeton University Press.

INTRODUCTION TO SECTION FOUR
Documenting and Assessing Impact

Ellen L. Wert
Teacher Education Accreditation Council

Interesting projects, exciting collegial collaboration, new areas of inquiry, innovative approaches to teaching—the actual work of the scholarship of teaching and learning should lead to something, giving us information and insights that can guide our actions. At the end of the day, we have to ask ourselves hard questions. What difference has this work made? For whom? Are we satisfied with these outcomes? Knowing what we know now, what is the next course of action? Do we know enough about the results of our work to make decisions and invest resources? Do we know enough about the effects of our efforts to provide information to those to whom we are accountable as they make decisions?

The seven chapters in this section focus on documenting and assessing the impact of campus efforts to support and use the scholarship of teaching and learning. Individually, they describe specific aspects of the process. Together, they explore reasons for asking those hard questions at the institutional level and provide ways of collecting and using the answers.

Three Basic Questions

The chapters in this section address three basic questions about documenting and assessing the impact of scholarship of teaching and learning efforts: Why document and assess the impact of our efforts? What forms might this documentation and assessment take? How do we use the data we gather?

Why document and assess the impact of our efforts?

In the first chapter, a well-known scholar of higher education and evaluator of countless projects and programs, Daryl Smith, comments on the "mapping progress" exercise completed by colleges and universities in the Campus Program. Through this instrument, AAHE encouraged each campus in the program to "map" its journey toward institutional support of the scholarship of teaching and learning and to use what is learned in the process of self-analysis to plan future efforts. In her chapter, Smith observes that the mapping progress instrument focuses campus leaders on factors that are critical to effecting positive change regarding the scholarship of teaching and learning: its centrality, leadership for the effort, integration into the work and culture of the campus, resources to support the

> ## The actual work of the scholarship of teaching and learning should give us information and insights that can guide our actions.

initiatives, signs of success, the effectiveness of strategies used, and strategies for sustaining change.

The next chapter offers a snapshot of how the mapping progress exercise led to further self-assessment at one campus. Sharon Lewis and her colleagues at Oxford College of Emory University explain the process and benefits of self-assessment prompted by the mapping progress exercise. Faculty members developed an assessment plan that led them to fully understand the role and effects of their scholarship of teaching and learning initiative and to design and take action accordingly. In offering a "how to" on self-assessment, the authors also make clear the benefits of starting the evaluative process early—with the project planning.

What forms might this documentation and assessment take?

The next three essays in the section focus on specific forms of assessment that campuses use to understand the effect of their scholarship of teaching and learning initiatives, portfolios in particular. A team of authors led by Elizabeth Barkley and Mike McHargue describes Foothill College's comprehensive plan to develop and integrate student, faculty, and institutional portfolios. This portfolio system provides information that is broad and deep and reveals both strengths and weaknesses. An important point in Foothill's plan is the decision to create a unit to coordinate the effort and communicate the results.

The next two chapters, while explaining more about particular ways to capture data, offer a glimpse into the initial missteps and important insights and discoveries that are so common as institutions start to develop and use assessment. In writing about capturing the effects on student learning of scholarship of teaching and learning initiatives at Western Washington University, Carmen Werder raises important questions about how and when to try to determine what students have learned, and how to get at the "heart and mind" learning colleges and universities hope to foster. Matthew Kaplan describes efforts at the University of Michigan to guide and support faculty in documenting teaching and student learning through course portfolios. The experience of these campuses reminds us that assessment is hard work, and much of it is new to faculty and administrators alike. Yet the benefits are worth the effort. Moreover, it is never too late to start—or start over.

How do we use the data we gather?

The last two chapters in the section discuss the use of assessment results to broaden participation in the scholarship of teaching and learning and deepen institutional support for that participation. Talya Bauer of Portland State University shares ideas about documenting and communicating information about the products of faculty members' scholarship of teaching; sharing the results with both internal and external audiences can lead to new understanding about scholarship and how it is evaluated and valued. Finally, a team from Illinois

State University, led by Kathleen McKinney, explains the various uses of data to show impact, and offers ideas about gathering data in multiple forms to understand the impact of the scholarship of teaching and learning.

Common Themes

The importance of understanding and building on the culture of the institution when developing an assessment process or system is a common theme throughout the chapters. What are the prevailing habits, attitudes, and values? What approach to assessment works best within that context? Similarly, can existing systems, structures, and incentives (internal and external) be used as a scaffold for assessment?

Another common theme is the importance of clarity: thinking ahead about the questions to ask, the information to gather, and the ways to communicate results. Likewise, communication about the process of and reasons for assessment is critical in getting and keeping colleagues on board.

The chapters highlight the effectiveness of assessment in distinguishing scholarship of teaching and learning from other campus initiatives through solid information about results. The assessment process reveals the

scholarship of teaching and learning as an integrating force, a means to connect disparate improvement projects, to connect faculty members who might have been working toward similar goals but in isolation, and to connect internal institutional goals with external expectations.

Another common message is the importance of understanding failure as well as success. Assessment results can yield insights about why something works—or does not—and give leaders and participants new ideas for next steps—and, importantly, the motivation to continue taking steps.

Most of all, in working through these three questions, the chapter authors show us that neat, familiar terms such as student learning, assessment plan, indicators, outcomes, portfolios, results, and data have significant implications for how we think about our roles and our work and how we continue to learn about teaching and learning. These terms are useful tools in the service of probing deeply into our work and the difference it makes for students, faculty, and institutions.

Contact

Ellen Wert
Teacher Education Accreditation
    Council
ewert444@yahoo.com

> The assessment process reveals the scholarship of teaching and learning as an integrating force.

Mapping Progress

Daryl G. Smith
Claremont Graduate University

Campuses today are full of initiatives addressing significant imperatives for needed institutional change. In complex institutions of all sizes, these efforts can generate long lists of activities requiring significant time and effort. Moreover, if the efforts are intended, as many of these are, to alter the culture, the norms, and the focus of institutional attention, it becomes urgent to ask: What difference are all the efforts making? Will they be sustainable without such concerted effort in the future? Where are we in moving forward? And, what issues are getting in the way of progress?

In the Campus Program, AAHE and Carnegie developed the Mapping Progress instrument to help participating campuses track their work and results over time. This mapping progress effort by AAHE through the CASTL program reflects an important strategy for using what we are learning about institutional change and organizational learning to help focus and frame institutional action and reflection. At its core, there is an assumption that change which is embedded deeply and broadly in the institution over time is likely to be sustainable. The mapping process looks at ways to describe where the teaching and learning efforts are

located. For example, in reading each of the completed campus reports, one gets a clear sense of the progress on embedding the scholarship of teaching and learning effort deeply and broadly into the work of the institution.

An overarching question for scholarship of teaching and learning efforts (and all improvement efforts) is, "What are the core characteristics of change that will lead to the likelihood of sustainable and manageable efforts?" The mapping protocol developed for the Campus Program reflects key elements of change in terms of breadth and depth, and it creates the opportunity for an institution to mark where it is in the change effort and to locate the elements of that change. The mapping protocol can be organized according to several key dimensions of change: centrality, leadership, integration, resources, signs of success, reflection, and strategy.

Centrality

Centrality assumes that the change is a core activity of the institution. Although many mission statements have become so generic as to be useless, the mapping process asks institutions to link their efforts to the mission by using actual statements or by clarifying how the CASTL effort can be directly linked to the academic culture of the institution. In the completed reports, for example, the research institutions are often careful to link the efforts to the research agenda of the institution and disciplines. The comprehensive institutions generally underscore the significant role of teaching and the professional and academic competencies involved in scholars as educators.

Leadership

Leadership is key to any institutional change. Leadership, however, does not just mean senior administrative leadership. In higher education, particularly in academic matters, leadership needs to be both broad and deep over time. Although initial change may rely on the passion and effort of a few, the mapping reports from campuses reflect the degree to which leadership spreads throughout departments and individual faculty.

Integration

Although integration might be a reflection of centrality, the mapping process suggests that integration be thought of systematically. To what else is the scholarship of teaching and learning connected? Whereas isolated initiatives can be mounted or might even be sustained (particularly with outside funding), linking the effort to other institutional efforts such as diversity, technology, program review, and research grants is more likely to embed the effort even more deeply into institutional life.

Resources

When we think of resources, we often think of money. The mapping document, however, makes eminently clear that resources extend beyond budgetary allocations—as important as these may be. Space, time, expertise, technology, and infrastructure are all resources that make sustained change more likely. Through the intentional uses of committee time, availability of financial resources, increasing faculty expertise on the scholarship of teaching and learning, making good use of technology for communication and sharing purposes, resources assist in facilitating the extension of change both broadly and deeply.

Signs of Success

Although mapping institutional dimensions is critical for thinking about the depth and breadth of change, it is also important to ask, "How do we know the change is taking place?" Some campuses have already indicated changes in the descriptions of what counts for tenure. In this example, changes in tenure review can be seen as both an indicator of success for the initiative and also as a means for deepening the cultural change required. What counts as scholarship surely is an indicator of success. Broad scale faculty participation would also count. Scholarly products related to teaching and learning are very direct indicators of the

Centrality assumes that the change is a core activity of the institution.

> Space, time, expertise, technology, and infra-structure are all resources that make sustained change more likely.

use of the scholarship of teaching and learning. Their frequency and location would suggest how broad and deep the change has been made.

Reflection

Writing a report to an outside audience, as the mapping progress protocol requires, can give an institution bragging rights. What becomes important, however, is the degree to which the information provided has been used by the institution. What meaning does the leadership give to the information provided? What barriers to change have been identified? Where is the information shared and communicated? Is the effort truly extending throughout the institution so that it makes a difference to students and to faculty? Making sense of the activities and efforts, discussing these interpretations, and sharing information become key components of change and thus a key element in the mapping process.

Strategy

Finally, developing strategies for modifications, dealing with obstacles, and keeping the effort moving create additional opportunities to learn from the process and to make alterations in strategy. The reports include times and ways in which campuses have learned what will work and what will not and have made modifications as appropriate.

Change in higher education is neither linear nor in the hands of a few. Indeed, change in the culture for teaching and learning requires broad engagement and sustained effort. The mapping process creates the possibility of bringing coherence to what could otherwise be isolated pieces, intentionality to what might otherwise seem random, a sense of collaboration and community to participants without requiring everyone to occupy the same space and time, and a sense of importance to an effort that otherwise might be seen as just one more institutional initiative in a laundry list of initiatives occurring on most campuses. Because its scale and scope are quite manageable, the mapping progress report creates the potential to communicate and share the results of these efforts.

Contact and URL

Daryl G. Smith
Professor of Education and Psychology
Claremont Graduate University
daryl.smith@cgu.edu

For more information on the Mapping Progress Reports, see
http://www.aahe.org/projects/campus_program/report_forms/

Why Do Self-Assessment?

Sharon Lewis, Ken Carter, and Heather Patrick
Oxford College of Emory University

One difficulty in many new programs is a lack of evidence for their effectiveness. Although there are no shortages of good ideas in academia, without documentation that a new initiative is effective, the program has only the appeal of novelty or the initial enthusiasm of participants to carry it forward.

As we discovered at Oxford College, assessing the impact is integral to a successful scholarship of teaching and learning program. Besides yielding important data, the process of assessment led us to use time and resources more effectively. Designing the evaluation pushed us to articulate our goals and start with a deep understanding of the program's context. In assessing the impact of our scholarship of teaching and learning efforts, we inventoried resources and determined levels of involvement. Charting the number and nature of faculty, staff, and student involvement over time provided our campus with a measure of the institutional impact of our scholarship of teaching and learning initiatives. Having solid information about effectiveness helped us leverage additional funding. Assessment also led us to share best practices with other institutions, create new initiatives, and modify exist-

ing programs. Finally, because evaluation yielded important feedback, it has helped all involved maintain momentum toward the program goals and build enthusiasm for new initiatives.

Six Important Steps in Self-Assessment

At first, assessment may appear to be either dreadfully simple or dauntingly thorny. Finding the balance between thinking "We'll know we are successful because we'll *feel* successful" and "We have to measure *everything*!" takes the same careful planning that goes into the creation of any new program. At Oxford College, we achieved that balance by following six steps of self-assessment.

1. Develop an assessment plan.

Rather than jumping right into implementation of the scholarship of teaching and learning program, we first sketched an assessment plan as part of the larger planning for the scholarship of teaching and learning initiatives. Establishing an assessment plan takes time, patience, and a clear understanding of program goals and objectives. We involved key administrators, faculty, staff, and students in deciding the assessment's beginning point, indicators, and methods, as well as strategies for getting the institution on board for both the scholarship of teaching and learning and the assessment process.

2. Understand the context for the scholarship of teaching and learning effort.

To be successful, a scholarship of teaching and learning initiative should be woven into the culture of the institution. We appraised how this scholarship would fit within the context of both Oxford's mission and existing initiatives. Our reflection helped us articulate exactly how this scholarship fits with our college values as expressed in our mission statements about achieving excellence in undergraduate education and our practice of holding administrators, faculty, and staff responsible for creating a learning community.

3. Establish a baseline.

Our next step was to choose a beginning point, the time at which we would begin to assess different indicators. By establishing a baseline, we have a complete picture of the state of our campus before, during, and after new scholarship of teaching and learning initiatives.

Assessing the baseline was necessary to chart our goals and identify steps for action. Also, taking this accounting early in the program brought to light hidden strengths and resources. We were able to know from the start, for example, what funds and resources were available and what outside funding might be necessary. Likewise, we knew which departments or individual faculty members were already engaged in similar processes or programs, which departments were already involved and supportive of scholarship of teaching and learning initiatives, and where we needed to concentrate outreach efforts.

Our baseline description of the context for the program also made clear that, for us, scholarship of teaching and learning was a culmination of many of the seemingly isolated efforts we were currently undertaking; we could show that it would serve as the connection among several disparate projects.

4. Identify key indicators.

Because there are so many possible outcomes to measure, we needed to decide exactly which indicators of successful change we would evaluate. We carefully chose outcome measures to track and focused on key behaviors the program was designed to change.

Certainly the main goal of any scholarship of teaching and learning initiative is to improve the practice of teaching and student learning through scholarly inquiry. Alone, this is a slow-changing, complex indicator of success. Who decides if teaching has improved? How do we know that student learning has improved by the use of the scholarship of teaching and learning? Because of the difficulty of evaluating these goals, intermediate outcomes—outcomes that, if met, are very likely to lead to meeting the main goal—are more appropriate to assess, and most of the intermediate outcomes assume that participation and active engagement in the scholarly inquiry into teaching will lead to improved teaching and student learning.

In choosing our indicators, we focused on what was meaningful to faculty, students, and administrators; measurable; objective; and easily assessed. We also made a commitment to stick with the initial assessment plan and not add additional indicators later, so that we would assess things for which we had baseline data and could track progress made over time. In our assessment, we tracked data in three broad areas: resources, involvement, and par-

> Having solid information
> about effectiveness
> helped us leverage
> additional funding.

ticipation and attitudes. We felt that if we saw changes in these areas, we would see a lasting impact of the scholarship of teaching and learning on our campus and, along with that, an improvement in teaching and learning.

Resources. We examined all resources directed toward the scholarship of teaching and learning before our program began and then tracked them throughout our efforts. These resources included support staff time, release time for the coordinator of our program, money to support our teaching resource library, infrastructure support, money for programs, and money to travel to conferences and workshops. We also tracked the effectiveness of incentives for faculty, staff, and students, such as stipends for individual scholarly research, inclusion of the scholarship of teaching and learning into tenure and promotion guidelines, release time, food at meetings, teaching awards, and even formal, public recognition. We also tracked which incentives were tied to a particular initiative to understand what rewards were more meaningful for whom, and when (for example having food available at meetings vs. paying individuals for participating in the meetings). Our understanding of effective incentives led us to modify our guidelines for evaluation of faculty for promotion, tenure, and salary increases to include the scholarship of teaching and learning in how we assess teaching and scholarly development.

Involvement. We looked at involvement in three ways: the avenues of involvement that were available, the number of people involved in scholarship of teaching and learning projects, and the pervasiveness of involvement (both in terms of numbers and attitudes).

Before we began implementation, we mapped the avenues of involvement—the ways in which faculty, staff, and students could be involved in the scholarship of teaching and learning, such as seminars, workshops, and guest lectures that provided training, and then, over time, tracked increases in the opportunities.

Participation and attitude. We also tracked participation. High attendance at these events could signal that the initiative may be a success, but it is important to correlate the outcome of this measure with the other measures. Low attendance, for example, may simply signal a need for greater publicity or possibly different incentives.

We also evaluated the pervasiveness of participation in our scholarship of teaching and learning effort. As we counted the number of participants, we tracked the different departments and programs they represented. Likewise, we tracked familiarity with and attitudes toward the scholarship of teaching and learning. Knowing where this scholarship was gaining acceptance helped us gauge and understand success, tap into new and existing resources, and initiate new policies and practices, such as changes in promotion and tenure guidelines.

5. Keep an up-to-date record of production.
The culmination of sufficient resources, adequate involvement, and positive attitudes should be the production of scholarly research.

We found that the most objective and easiest way to track production of the scholarship of teaching and learning is to count the numbers of projects, presentations, and papers that our faculty produced.

6. Use the results.

We shared the results of our campus-wide self-assessment with the people directly involved in the work as well as the broader scholarly community. Showcasing the impact of the scholarship of teaching and learning to others at one's own campus gives everyone a reason to listen, as they see how individual actions can be woven into institutional change. Others can be encouraged to participate through seeing signs of improved student work that resulted from prior research and through seeing the possibility of publications stemming from future work.

Scholarship of teaching and learning initiatives should lead to a community that not only has a culture of evidence regarding effective teaching, but also one that produces better teaching and promotes better learning in our students. A well-designed and executed process of self-assessment can help foster these results. At Oxford College, the process of self-assessment has helped us identify the strengths and weaknesses in our scholarship of teaching and learning programs as well as to chart future goals and directions as we move into the next phase of the Campus Program. We have built assessment into all of our new program initiatives, worked to ensure that it is viewed by faculty as routine inquiry, and will continue to rely on it to provide us with evidence in the future that our efforts are effective. Through self-assessment of our ongoing initiatives in the scholarship of teaching and learning, we have found common ground as educators and have become a more self-reflective community of teacher-scholars.

Contacts

Sharon Lewis
Professor of Psychology
Oxford College of Emory University
slewis@learnlink.emory.edu

Ken Carter
Associate Professor of Psychology
Oxford College of Emory University
kcart01@emory.edu

Heather Patrick
Assistant Professor of Chemistry
Oxford College of Emory University
hpatri2@emory.edu

**Oxford College of Emory University
Oxford, GA
Associate of Arts College within a
Doctoral/Research Extensive University
http://www.emory.edu/OXFORD/**

Making Learning Visible: Using Electronic Portfolios Across the Institution

Elizabeth Barkley, Mike McHargue, Karen Gillette,
William Patterson, and Charlotte Thunen
Foothill College

As demands increase for institutional reporting of learning outcomes, colleges are searching for ways to gather effectively and efficiently the evidence necessary to make learning more visible. The critical issue is how to document and make learning visible in a way that honors the complexity of the teaching and learning process, that is supported by multiple stakeholders, and that is readily understood and useful to a variety of audiences. Because electronic portfolios have emerged as a promising documentation tool to aid in this endeavor, Foothill College began in 1999 to create an integrated system of electronic portfolios to make learning more visible at the course, student, and institutional levels.

Portfolios are powerful tools: they can include multiple examples of work, be context rich, and offer a look at development over time. Electronic portfolios can be layered to include various ways to navigate through the information. They offer the reader direct contact with evidence. They can integrate interactivity, incorporate multimedia, contain large volumes of data, and be easily accessed and disseminated so that both individuals and institutions can build upon each other's work. The resources required for portfolio creation depend upon the portfolio's intent. For example, with templates, faculty course portfolios can be created with minimum resources. Complex institutional portfolios require more extensive resources.

Foothill College intends to use this integrated electronic portfolios system to make a direct impact on improving teaching and learning and to make learning more visible. Student portfolios provide a full picture of each student's accomplishments and progress, and students are able to use their portfolios to support their personal, educational, and career goals. The institutional portfolio provides faculty with a mechanism for capturing core-competency learning. The institutional portfolio, which presents the learning outcomes produced by the institution as a whole, is an effective, efficient mechanism for documenting and communicating institution-wide learning outcomes to the board of trustees, the college community, and accreditation agencies.

Internal forces that brought us to this point include extensive experience with using student portfolios and with developing faculty portfolios; a local model in the work of a faculty member whose course portfolio gained national attention and instilled local pride; and interest in developing portfolios. External factors also guided us. For example, the Western Association of Schools and Colleges, in moving toward a focus on learning outcomes, gives individual colleges the opportunity to define their own mode of self-study and then be evaluated against those standards.

Student Portfolios

In 2002, the academic senate began working with faculty and student leaders to develop student portfolios. These portfolios include evidence of learning, progress, and proficiency at the individual level. They incorporate records of accomplishments, such as a transcript of grades and proficiency scores, with a collection of material representing the student's academic and extra-curricular work. The student portfolios bridge a student's own personal academic and career goals with the faculty course portfolio's disciplinary learning goals and the institutional portfolio's core-competency goals.

For more than a decade, many Foothill faculty members have asked their students to collect their work in portfolios. Like most colleges, we began the work in the fine arts and expanded to the language arts. Although faculty mem-

> The integrated portfolios are a cutting-edge vehicle for cross-disciplinary, institution-wide communication.

bers in those disciplines continue to be most involved, other faculty members across the institution have already incorporated student portfolios into their teaching, learning, and evaluation. For example, departments in workforce development disciplines from dental hygiene to computer sciences have taken over the development of both course and student portfolios. Students collect samples of their work representing the two years that they spend earning an associates degree at Foothill. The evidence and artifacts are then presented and evaluated by a group of faculty and professionals in the field. Increasingly, these portfolios are being used for employment or transfer purposes after graduation.

Faculty Course Portfolios

Carnegie Scholar and Foothill faculty member Elizabeth Barkley introduced electronic course portfolios in 1999 through the example of a portfolio that documented her transformation of a general education music course. Using her work as a model, the executive committee of Foothill's Campus Program's Academy for the Scholarship of Teaching and Learning started guiding faculty to create course portfolios that document and improve teaching and learning at the course and programmatic level. Because of the ease of electronic dissemination, the course portfolios are helping faculty across disciplines to learn from each other. These portfolios are a major part of our promotion, tenure, rewards, and recognition process.

Institutional Portfolio

President Bernadine Fong and vice president William Patterson are leading a campus-wide effort to create an institutional electronic portfolio that moves beyond disciplinary and programmatic concerns. As one of sixteen community colleges in a League for Innovation for the Community College project, Foothill is creating an institutional portfolio that documents college-wide progress toward achieving broad learning outcomes. Titled *The 21st Century Learning Outcomes Project,* this portfolio tracks student achievement of core competencies in communication, creative/critical and analytical thinking, and community global consciousness at the institutional level. The institutional portfolio cross-references campus-wide faculty assessment of a course's role in developing these core-competencies with both individual and aggregated student achievement.

Work to Date: Documenting Learning; Using the Findings

Prompting our efforts to document learning at the student, department, and institutional level were two related questions: "What competencies should a Foothill College graduate have?" and "How do we assess the depth of mastery?" To address those questions, Foothill has defined "Five Cs" that represent the knowledge, skills, and attributes a graduate should document in a student portfolio and form our institution's core goals: communication computation creative/critical/analytical thinking, community/global consciousness and responsibility, and content/discipline curricula and activities.

At the departmental level, as part of program review self-study, faculty in all academic programs have completed an analysis of their degree requirements, documenting how the Five Cs are embedded in the curriculum. We are now evaluating courses in general educa-

tion, in transfer, and in workforce development programs to determine the activity level and the success level for each of those Cs for each class, tying expected outcomes to method and content. Faculty members are evaluating the activities and assessment to insure the core goals are being met. As a result of this process, faculty are restructuring program requirements and revising course outlines. For example, dental hygiene is beta-testing the use of portfolios to collect all important student evaluative materials. Student development and activities programs are also documenting the learning outcomes associated with participation in those services.

Coordinating the Portfolio Initiatives

Foothill formed the Learning Outcomes Assessment Network to develop the institutional portfolios. The Network coordinates with other campus groups documenting learning outcomes and leads or coordinates a range of activities.

◆ Moving beyond identification of outcomes to their documentation

◆ Marketing the benefits of portfolios and concept mapping to our college community; including identifying prospective faculty objections, especially regarding increased workload

◆ Creating portfolios of merit for recognition

◆ Establishing a faculty development course on portfolio review and increasing portfolio training for new faculty

◆ Developing a portfolios-across-the-curriculum program similar to those for writing and critical thinking

◆ Involving students more in those processes

◆ Displaying exemplary portfolios on our Web site and in our library, staff resource center, and campus center

Our Way of Gathering and Using Evidence

Developing and using portfolios is working well for us, but every college and university has its own experience, its own culture, and its own people. There are many ways to focus this process. Many of them can be found through the published work of other AAHE/Carnegie projects, through similar descriptions in this book, and through related reports in the League for Innovation's Learning Outcomes and Vanguard College programs.

The integrated portfolios are a cutting-edge vehicle for cross-disciplinary, institution-wide communication on improving teaching and learning. They also help Foothill define, document, and validate learning goals as well as provide the means for sharing evidence of progress toward achieving these goals. As pressure to make learning more visible increases, Foothill's approach, the integrated electronic portfolio system, offers a futures-oriented model for assessing learning at the course, student, and institutional level and for communicating this learning both internally and externally.

Contacts and URLs

Elizabeth Barkley
Music Department Chairman and Executive
    Director of the Performing Arts Alliance
Foothill College
barkleyelizabeth@foothill.edu

Karen Gillette
Librarian
Foothill College
gillettekaren@foothill.edu

Mike McHargue
Professional Development Coordinator,
    Emeritus
Foothill College
mcharguemike@foothill.edu

Bill Patterson
Vice President of Instruction and
    Institutional Research
Foothill College
pattersonbill@foothill.edu

Charlotte Thunen
Instruction Librarian
Foothill College
thunencharlotte@foothill.edu

For more information on the League for Innovation's Learning Outcomes and Vanguard Colleges programs, see
http://www.league.org/league/projects/pew/ and
http://www.league.org/league/projects/lcp/vanguard.htm

**Foothill College
Los Altos Hills. CA
Associate's
http://www.foothill.fhda.edu/index.shtml**

What Matters Over Time: Documenting Student Learning

Carmen Werder
Western Washington University

I wish that I could say that we had a master plan for assessing student learning when we began our affiliation with The Carnegie Academy for the Scholarship of Teaching and Learning. The truth is that we did not embark on this scholarship of teaching and learning voyage with the students securely on board. Of course, many of us understood and believed in the paradigm shift from teaching to learning as outlined by Barr and Tagg (1995), but did not foresee how student learning would move to the center of our scholarship of teaching and learning project.

We began our alliance with the Campus Program in 1998 primarily because it seemed like a good opportunity to support the faculty at our institution, which has had a long history of valuing teaching. Convening a core group of 15 faculty members who were known to be interested in teaching, we followed the protocol as outlined by CASTL, meeting mostly electronically to record our responses to questions posed.

Midway through the second year, however, a faculty member from our College of Education asked, "Where are the students?" We had to come to terms with the realization that we had neglected to secure a formal place for student voices in the work. Immediately, we considered how we might bring students into the conversation.

Considering our delayed entry into assessing student learning, what insights might we offer others considering how to assess student learning in the scholarship of teaching and learning? I believe that our process has led us to important questions about when and how to document student learning.

Evolution of Course Learning Outcomes

First we came up with a plan to use an existing adult and higher education leadership course for bringing students into the study with us. Students in this course became the pioneers in that curriculum which revolved around leadership and the role that students could play in leading institutional change.

Although the leadership course provided a crucial site for engaging students in the study of teaching and learning, it focused on the principles of leadership rather than on learning itself. In order to convene students representing a broader spectrum of our student body and to focus more squarely on outcomes that featured a study of the nexus between teaching and learning, we needed a scholarship of teaching and learning course. In 2000 at the AAHE Summer Academy, a team of students and faculty created such a course called "Organizing for Learning," a two-credit seminar designed to be co-facilitated by students and faculty. Inspired by a Peter Ewell article about the need to apply what we know about learning already (Ewell, 1997, p. 3) in order to effect institutional change, the course had objectives that focused on identifying an optimal learning environment and on organizing individually and institutionally to adjust to less than optimal environments.

For two years, we offered this course under a cross-disciplinary rubric (University 397) because we wanted the course to bring in students from across disciplines. Over the course of those two years, 137 students enrolled in the course, and during four of the six quarters, students participated in biweekly conversations with Carnegie faculty around common topics and readings. Course assessment measures such as short reflective papers, group demonstrations, and portfolio reflections provided evidence that the majority of students were achieving the course objectives.

Last year, in redesigning the class, we revised the desired outcomes, building in an expectation that students would participate in our new Teaching-Learning Academy, a campus-wide forum including faculty, students, administrators, and staff from across the university. The result was "Learning Reconsidered," a three-credit seminar with objectives that focus on students as active learners with ownership for their own education and with an understanding of how individual purposes for pursuing higher education relate to our institutional mission. The aim was to bring students more

squarely into the role of co-inquirers as we focused on the relationship between individual and institutional missions.

We have reinvented the course yet again! We discovered that, when students help create curriculum, things are ever on the move! Now an applied practicum through our Communication Department, the course has been redefined as "Communicating and Collaborating Across Power Differences." The overarching objective of the course continues to be studying and enhancing our own learning environment at Western. Specifically, we aim to understand power differentials in the academy, to develop a heightened sense of individual learning agency, and to gain strategies for communicating and collaborating across these differences in an effort to enhance our learning culture.

So, What is Missing?

Although we have confidence that the course artifacts represent key indicators of our project, we are coming to see a serious omission: long-term measures. As a current student course facilitator insists, if students cannot apply the insights gained from the learning seminar to other future contexts inside and outside the classroom, then what has really been accomplished? As AAHE Campus Program director Barbara Cambridge observes, "We want students to learn deeply, and we want to engage their hearts as well as their heads" (1998, 2). But how do we count the long-term head and heart effects of a course like this?

Our interest in pursuing long-term gains prompts ethical considerations. What right do we teachers have to keep on studying learning outcomes after students leave our classrooms?

> The best way we can continue to stay in touch with evolving learning is to invite all learners, but especially students, into these ongoing conversations.

Although most of us willingly embrace Lee Shulman's "pedagogical imperative" that we are obliged to inquire about the impact of our work on student learning (2000, vii), what are the appropriate boundaries and (time) limits of that inquiry? Is it right to count, for example, a former student's remark at a party a year after taking the course as one measure of his learning? A student course facilitator did, in fact, count a former student's comment at a party as a key measure of the course's success. If we believe that the best assessment and the best learning are authentic, then don't we need to study what students have applied from our courses in contexts beside the classroom?

One thing we have discovered is the need for both a bottom-up and top-down approach to studying how the scholarship of teaching and learning affects student learning. We cannot assess the learning objectives from our course in isolation because students have also participated in an institutional reform project concerning general education as part of their course work. How has their contribution to this institutional project affected their sense of self-efficacy? How might we measure that

change? And to what extent should we weight enhanced individual agency for learning over institutional change?

I also wonder about how to count the long-term effects on the students who have participated in the scholarship of teaching and learning course. How do we discern what influence the course might have exerted over their life and career choices? Again, there are ethical issues. When does the statute of limitations expire on any connection to their scholarship of teaching and learning experiences? In addition to the philosophical and ethical concerns, how do we harness the resources to do this kind of tracking?

Because the critical assessment questions seem to emerge over time, the best way to ensure that we are asking the right questions is to develop a scholarship of teaching and learning program that is designed to last over time. I would urge any institution working to assess the effect of scholarship of teaching and learning on student learning to consider first how to integrate longitudinal assessment measures into the plan. Because we did not begin with this vision, it is much more challenging trying to incorporate it now. No matter what the learning outcomes, I recommend adding the modifier "over time" to reflect this ongoing need to keep assessing questions based on the answers received.

Need for Authentic Dialogue

We have learned (and are still learning) to pay close attention to what students tell us. In our Teaching-Learning Academy, which is a laboratory for studying teaching and learning, students play a prominent role as co-inquirers. As Barbara Walvoord and her coauthors suggest in *In the Long Run,* their study of faculty in selected writing-across-the-curriculum programs, it is not so much the specific techniques that we should count but whether or not faculty members continue to have the conversations. The same could be said of the scholarship of teaching and learning. It is not so much about having a fixed set of objectives. Rather it is about ongoing discussion and reinvention of those outcomes over time. The only way we can continue to stay in touch with evolving learning is to invite all learners, but especially students, into these ongoing conversations.

References

Barr, R.B. and Tagg, J. (November/December 1995) From teaching to learning—A new paradigm for undergraduate education. *Change, 27* (6), 12-25.

Cambridge, Barbara. Architecture for change: Information as foundation, Foreword. *Proceedings from the 1998 AAHE Assessment Conference.* Washington, D.C.: American Association for Higher Education.

Ewell, Peter T. (December 1997) Organizing for learning: A new imperative. *AAHE Bulletin. 50* (4), 3-6.

Shulman, Lee. (2002) Foreword to *Ethics of inquiry: Issues in the scholarship of teaching and learning,* Pat Hutchings, ed. Menlo Park, CA: The Carnegie Foundation for the Advancement of Teaching.

Walvoord, B. E., Hunt, L. L., Dowling Jr., H. F., and McMahon, J. D., (1997) *In the long run: A study of faculty in three writing-across-the curriculum programs.* Urbana, IL: National Council of Teachers of English.

Contact and URL

Carmen Werder
Director, Teaching - Learning Academy
Western Washington University
carmen.werder@wwu.edu

For more information on Western Washington University's Teaching-Learning Academy, see http://pandora.cii.wwu.edu/vpue/tla.htm

Western Washington University
Bellingham, WA
Master's I
http://www.wwu.edu/home.shtml

The Long and Winding Road: Using Course Portfolios to Document the Scholarship of Interdisciplinary Teaching and Learning

Matthew Kaplan
University of Michigan

At first glance, the portfolio initiative is quite straightforward. Begun in 1999, the Interdisciplinary Faculty Associates program at the University of Michigan integrates assessment of student learning outcomes and the scholarship of teaching and learning. The program was conceived and designed by the university's Center for Research on Learning and Teaching as a way to promote interdisciplinary teaching on the undergraduate level. The program came about after a campus-wide conference on interdisciplinary teaching revealed significant faculty interest in expanded opportunities to team teach across departments, schools, and colleges.

> The course portfolio provides the space necessary to describe and reflect on the design and impact of the complex activity that is interdisciplinary teaching.

Faculty teams selected to participate in the Associates Program receive $10,000 grants to develop undergraduate interdisciplinary team-taught courses; promote the scholarship of interdisciplinary teaching and learning; participate in a monthly faculty development seminar to discuss issues interdisciplinary integration, team teaching, challenges and lessons learned; and develop course portfolios to document the genesis, design, execution, and impact of their courses.

This work, and the project overall, fit well with institutional priorities: the university has a long tradition of fostering faculty work that crosses disciplinary boundaries, particularly through research centers, programs, and informal networks. Indeed, in its most recent self study for re-accreditation, the university focused on advancing collaborative, integrative, and interdisciplinary research and learning. The Faculty Associates Program addresses two related needs. The first is to encourage students, especially undergraduates, to seek out these cross-disciplinary opportunities. The second is to provide institutional incentives to faculty who undertake interdisciplinary teaching, especially in concert with colleagues from other units, while also lowering administrative barriers.

Our plan was to have the associates program support the university's goal of expanding the options for integrative teaching and learning and document the impact of this interdisciplinary learning. The plan was also to document faculty experiences about their challenges and success, both administrative and pedagogical, in developing and teaching these courses and to improve interdisciplinary education.

Integrating Course Portfolios into the Associates Program

The simplicity of this project description masks the complexity of working with faculty to document the impact of their courses in a portfolio. By tracing the development of the associates program, I will share lessons we have learned, enabling others to learn from our experiences. For, as difficult as it was to get started, we believe that the course portfolio is worthwhile.

Beyond the hard lessons we have learned over the last three years about encouraging faculty to write course portfolios, the portfolios themselves provide a rich set of insights into inter-disciplinary teaching. We have gathered faculty perspectives on undertaking interdisciplinary team teaching. We are just beginning to see evidence of student learning in these course portfolios, and we hope to get better at this.

Our initial rationale for including the course portfolio within the associates program was both national and local. Nationally, the university was interested in becoming involved in the AAHE and Carnegie initiatives to promote the scholarship of teaching and learning through campus academies. Interdisciplinarity, as a central feature of the university's campus culture, was an obvious choice as a focus for our cam-

pus academy. Because the Center for Research on Learning and Teaching had previously coordinated the university's participation in AAHE's earlier Peer Review Project, it also made sense for us to organize this new initiative.

Locally, despite a clear institutional commitment, we had heard of the many administrative barriers to interdisciplinary team teaching, including skeptical curriculum committees and questions of covering reduced teaching loads. The portfolios would be a place for faculty to document and share with colleagues how they developed and listed their courses and what obstacles they faced along the way. Moreover, interdisciplinary teaching is a complex activity, especially when done in a faculty team. The course portfolio provides the space necessary to describe and reflect on the design and impact of this type of teaching. Such documentation would become what Pat Hutchings (1998) calls "an aid to memory":

> Most of us have the hope and expectation that we will teach the course better the next time, having learned from the current experience. And toward that end, we're sure that we'll remember, next year at this point in the course, what worked and didn't....But, somehow, time passes, and the details slip away. (p.17)

Beyond their value to individual faculty teams, we hoped that an accumulated set of portfolios would result in a collective memory from which we could distill best practices and lessons learned for the campus.

Stage I: Genre Pioneers

In 1999, the course portfolio was a new genre. The 1998 AAHE monograph on the topic had only recently appeared, and although there was a clear sense of overarching parallels to a research project, there was as yet no established structure for the course portfolio. Appealing to the creativity and independence of our faculty, we portrayed this situation as a unique opportunity: they could help invent the genre, especially at our university with respect to interdisciplinarity. To help them succeed, we gave each participant a copy of the monograph, built discussions of the portfolio into our monthly meetings, and invited a nationally known expert on course portfolios, Daniel Bernstein,[1] to talk to the group about the rationale and potential benefits of the course portfolio.

Although the faculty reacted positively at first, both substantive and logistical issues soon arose. Some participants felt that this type of writing was an example of academic surveillance, an unwanted institutional intrusion into their academic freedom. Others expressed confusion about exactly what we wanted from them, including basic issues such as exactly what to include and how long it should be. For example, several faculty participants were taken aback by a single reference in one of the readings to a portfolio that was 200 pages long.

In the end, we received two portfolios, one from a team of junior faculty who were quite enthusiastic about their course and wanted to make sure there was a clear record of what they and their students had accomplished. We also worked with another team of senior faculty who considered themselves good campus citizens and did not want to back out of their commitment. A colleague conducted a series of interviews with the faculty, which she then wrote up. Based on the findings, it was obvious to us that we needed a new procedure if we were serious about the portfolios.

Stage II: Structure, Structure, Structure

In planning for the second year of the program, we went back to basic faculty development principles. What became obvious is that faculty, like students, need a clear structure in order to successfully complete a writing project on an unfamiliar topic (teaching and learning) using a format they had never encountered in their own disciplines (the course portfolio). We developed guidelines for the portfolio (including a page limit and due date) and structured the monthly seminar around the portfolio. Topics included setting goals for student learning, teaching methods appropriate for interdisciplinary teaching, and reflections on what would constitute evidence of learning. We were, in effect, attempting to align the goals, methods, and outcomes of the seminar just as we would advise faculty to do in their own courses.

The guidance and structure lowered resistance. We received portfolios from three of the four projects in both the second and third years of the program. Encouraged, this past year, we added requirements for including samples of student work along with discussions of student learning.

Stage III: Moving from the Margins to the Center

One problem with our current model of a monthly seminar and a course portfolio due at the end of the academic year is that it, in effect, marginalizes the portfolio. The conversations we have are relevant to the various sections of the portfolio, but they take place months before the actual writing. When we review the contents of the portfolio at the end of the seminar, faculty participants react as if they will be starting from scratch.

reflected on the mismatch of our meth- ! desired outcomes, we realized that our experiences with the Peer Review of Teaching project offered a possible solution in helping us reframe the relationship between the seminar and the portfolio. In the peer review project, portfolio writing is broken down into three parts, each with a process. For each section of the portfolio—goals, methods, and student learning—faculty write a draft memo, have a group meeting to give each other feedback, and then revise their memos based on the feedback. By the end of the process, the only tasks remaining are writing an introduction and conclusion and collecting appendix material for each section, tasks that are quite manageable and not time consuming.

Our plan for the associates program, then, is to move the portfolio writing process into the monthly seminar, so that faculty participants write their portfolios over the course of the year. We can then alternate between meetings devoted to readings and discussions relevant to interdisciplinarity and meetings focused on draft memos of portfolio sections. In addition to facilitating the portfolio writing process, this approach should also lead to a richer conversation among the faculty. Discussions among faculty in the peer review project are informed by details of practice already spelled out in writing. The resulting exchange reflects a deep understanding of colleagues' goals and constraints.

Faculty members gain a great deal by teaching with each other and doing so outside of their disciplinary comfort zone. In the coming years, we will learn more from the portfolios about the impact of this type of teaching on student learning so that we can share insights on a variety of levels both on campus and nationally.

Endnote

1 Bernstein, a psychologist and Carnegie Scholar, has written a course portfolio of his own, has written about the course portfolio, and directed the Peer Review of Teaching project http://www.unl.edu/peerrev Funded by The Pew Charitable Trusts, the project supported five universities, including the University of Michigan, to experiment with course portfolios as a mechanism of peer review.

Contact and URLs

Matt Kaplan
Associate Director and Instructional
   Consultant, Center for Research on Learning
   and Teaching
University of Michigan
mlkaplan@umich.edu

To link to the Center for Research on Learning and Teaching at the University of Michigan, visit http://www.crlt.umich.edu/index.html

The Interdisciplinary Faculty Associates grants program is located at http://www.crlt.umich.edu/grants/ifagrant.html

For more information on the Peer Review of Teaching project, see http://www.unl.edu/peerrev

University of Michigan
Ann Arbor, MI
Doctoral/Research Extensive
http://www.umich.edu/

Documenting the Scholarship of Teaching and Learning: Celebrating Successes and Understanding Impact

Talya Bauer
Portland State University

Between 1994 and 1996, Portland State University expanded the definition of scholarship used to assess and reward faculty. Since then, Portland State University has developed a deep commitment to community-based learning and research. The University's motto, "Let Knowledge Serve the City," is displayed proudly on a main skybridge for all to see. As our provost, Mary Kay Tetreault (2002), has said,

> The faculty at Portland State University are committed to community engagement in a variety of ways- be it the city, the Northwest, or the world. By sharing their peer-reviewed research with colleagues locally and around the world, they affirm our belief that change, be it in the classroom or beyond, is scholarly work. (p. 1)

As the university began to integrate its focus on community-based research into the promotion and tenure process, an informal discussion group began to meet to discuss this different form of scholarship. The group members' research questions and projects were focused on an issue central to the campus community: ways to improve and understand teaching.

When university administrators saw the need to support the new forms of scholarship that developed from community-based research, this and other informal discussion groups were structured more formally as campus resources. The members became research teams of faculty members and students. Research groups focused on teaching and learning were supported through the university's Center for Academic Excellence as funds became available from a grant from AAHE and The Carnegie Foundation for the Advancement of Teaching.

What began as a small group of faculty peers is now the Scholarship of Teaching and Research Team. In the five years that STRT has formally been part of Portland State University, numerous faculty members, students, and community partners have participated in research on teaching and learning.

As the Scholarship of Teaching and Research Team enterprise, we have to ask ourselves questions such as "What is the effect of this commitment of resources—time, people, and money?" and "What is the effect of this research on the campus culture?"

> Based on data, we will target specific groups, strengthen the value and reward system, increase collaboration, connect people to national initiatives, and develop more processes to apply the results of this scholarly work.

From the outset, we believed that it is important to keep track of the team in terms of projects, presentations, and papers. Currently we are tracking the outcomes of the projects begun over the last three years by compiling data on the number of works-in-progress, presentations, publications, and grants that have resulted from projects.

The results from documenting the numbers and also collecting follow-up information about the projects are encouraging. For example, an idea that started life as an team project for the campus was developed into an article accepted in the *Journal of Management Education*. Reflections of faculty in the team projects are another source of evidence. As faculty members Ann Fulton and Reza Peigahi have noted in *Our Voices*, "The program strengthens the quality of [University] scholarship by connecting professors who enjoy sharing ideas and critiquing one another with the goal of improvement." (p. 15)

Indeed, one important lesson we have learned from tracking the progress of the projects is that, in scholarship, community matters. Having a sense of shared community and a place to brainstorm ideas, get honest feedback, work in a larger group, go to writing retreats, have deadlines, and be accountable is special. We foster the sense of community by celebrating the work of the Scholarship of Teaching and Research Team on campus and beyond. We publicly announce the rate of production of the Team, and we share information about the projects with our campus community.

For the past three years, part of the celebration of success on campus has been an end-of-year publication entitled *Our Voices: The Scholarship of Teaching Resource Team*. Each group writes a summary of its project as well as a personal reflection on the process. When we disseminate *Our Voices* campus-wide, the response is positive. Students, faculty members, and deans alike comment about the projects and individuals summarized in the pages. Of course, the campus public relations and development offices find the publication very useful in their work. In addition, we send copies of the book to other campuses and to organizations such as AAHE.

Although this publication is an important way to celebrate our successes and challenges throughout each year, it is critical to helping our colleagues and friends of the university understand the scholarship of teaching and learning. By deepening and spreading this understanding, we have been able to contribute to an extraordinary shift in the institutional notion of what constitutes scholarship and what benefits accrue from it.

As Judith Ramaley (2000) has noted, innovative academic projects often must function within a double standard of proof that requires a higher standard for new projects than for those representing the status quo. The scholarship of teaching and learning is seen as an innovation, and even on a campus with a formally expanded definition of scholarship, the notion of what constitutes academic "research" is slow to change. In the past year, especially, we have seen greater understanding that the scholarship of teaching and learning is valid as authentic research. As faculty member Yves Labissiere noted in his *Our Voices* reflection on 2002-2003, "Indeed, I strongly believe that this year's STRT has given credibility to the scholarship of teaching, in general, throughout [the University]" (p. 22).

But to date, the strongest evidence of the impact of the scholarship of teaching and learning is its role, with other expanded forms of scholarship, in helping the university better identify and manage the intellectual assets of the institution (Rueter and Bauer, in press). With my colleague John Rueter, I have been engaged in research on the effects of the university's 1996 expanded definition of scholarship. Our interviews of faculty and staff and our analysis of records and policy documents have yielded an understanding of what can happen when an institution's leadership consistently encourages faculty to approach teaching, learning, community engagement, research, and strategic planning — all from a scholarly perspective. The university's support of structures that encourage multiple forms of scholarly work—among them the Scholarship of Teaching and Research Team—has resulted in a cultural shift in attitudes about scholarship. That cultural shift has enabled meaningful changes in promotion and tenure guidelines, an increase in the range of acceptable products that can be used as evidence of scholarship, and external recognition of campus efforts and progress.

I believe that we are asking the right questions and trying to keep track of what scholarship of teaching and learning is produced and how it is used. But we will also keep our eye on how thinking about and studying teaching and learning—and then making that scholarship public—contributes to the institution as a whole.

References

Our voices: The scholarship of teaching resource team, Third Annual: 2002-2003. (2003). Portland, OR: Center for Academic Excellence, Portland State University.

Ramaley, J.A. (2000). Embracing civic responsibility. *AAHE Bulletin, 52*(7), 9.

Rueter, J., & Bauer, T. N. (in press). *Examining the expanded definition of scholarship to identify and manage university assets: A campus study of Portland State University.* Portland, OR: Portland State University.

Tetreault M. and Ketcheson, K. (2002). Creating a shared understanding of institutional knowledge through an electronic institutional portfolio. *Metropolitan Universities, 13*(3), 40-49.

... we will target specific groups, strengthen the value and reward system, increase collaboration, connect people to national initiatives, and develop more processes.

Contact and URLs

Talya Bauer
Associate Professor of Business Administration
Portland State University
talyab@sba.pdx.edu

For more information on faculty development and
support programs focused on teaching, learning,
and scholarship, as well as the Scholarship of
Teaching Research Team (STRT), see
http://www.cae.pdx.edu/fdprg03.html#strt

The Center for Academic Excellence at Portland
State University is located at
http://www.oaa.pdx.edu/CAE/

Portland State University
Portland, OR
Doctoral/Research Intensive
http://www.pdx.edu/

Using Data to Support and Enhance the Scholarship of Teaching and Learning

Kathleen McKinney, James Broadbear, Deborah Gentry,
Patricia Klass, Sharon Naylor, and Nicky Virgil
Illinois State University

Illinois State University has been involved in the scholarship of teaching and learning for decades, primarily through the efforts of individual faculty members. After joining the CASTL Campus Program in 1998, however, our efforts became more structured. Institutional efforts to support scholarship of teaching and learning stem from our belief in the practical use of such work to improve learning. We had reached a point in our work on campus, however, where it was clear that we needed additional information if we were to increase the impact of this work. Though we had listened to faculty and staff members talk about scholarship of teaching and learning in discussion sessions and focus groups over the years, we needed more detailed data on the status of this scholarly work on campus to help make decisions about how to further support and use scholarship of teaching and learning. We believed such data would help us target various groups, design new services, lobby various powerbrokers, share knowledge, and increase the impact of this work on student learning at the course, department, college, institutional, and cross-institutional levels.

Thus, as part of our 2002 AAHE Summer Academy project, we designed a multi-method, longitudinal study to gather such data. Our goal was to describe the current status of scholarship of teaching and learning on campus and to assess any changes in status at the time of a follow-up study. At the Summer Academy, we identified outcomes to measure change over time. These included a meaningful increase in the number of scholarship of teaching and learning presentations, publications, and grant applications by our faculty, staff, and students; an increase in products that involve teams or represent multiple disciplines; an increase in regional and national involvement in and recognition of this kind of scholarly work by our faculty, staff, and students; and an increase in the number of departments that reward the scholarly work on teaching and learning under scholarship. In addition, it is expected that, as indicated in required scholarship of teaching and learning grant reports, we would find a positive impact on some aspect of student learning or development in the person or team's class or program studied.

Gathering Existing Data

We decided to make use of both existing and new data in order in order to examine the status of the scholarship of teaching and learning on our campus. We identified a variety of types of existing data to review and summarize. These included the report of thesis and dissertation titles from the Graduate School, the annual report of the Research and Sponsored Programs Office, grant reports from the Center for the Advancement of Teaching, department/college faculty productivity reports, college and department promotion and tenure guidelines, and information on scholarship of teaching and learning faculty positions from department chairpersons. Obtaining some of this data was more difficult than we had anticipated. Though all data are for a one-year period, the exact time frame varies by such factors as calendar year or fiscal year. Thus, keeping in mind that these data are incomplete, descriptive, and without comparison data or groups, we have reached the following tentative conclusions.

Findings

Using the existing data, we discovered that only a handful of theses and dissertations in one year related to the scholarship of teaching and learning. Despite using a broad definition of scholarship of teaching and learning, few external grants, one internal-college level small grant, and five small grants awarded through the teaching center appear to be scholarship of teaching and learning in one academic year.

The scholarship of teaching and learning is alive and well on our campus, but in limited ways.

For a combination of four of our seven colleges for which we had data, faculty reported 35 presentations and 30 publications concerning the scholarship of teaching and learning in the past year. A review of 43 percent of the department/school promotion and tenure guidelines revealed that presentations and publications about teaching and learning in the discipline are not specifically mentioned. Related behaviors such as conducting classroom research or outcomes such as successful competitive grants related to teaching are usually listed under teaching. Finally, out of 700 tenure-line faculty positions, we currently have devoted to the scholarship of teaching and learning one university-level position and two positions within academic departments. Two additional positions in departments are seen as primarily based on the scholarship of teaching and learning.

These descriptive secondary data give us a tentative picture of the status of some scholarship of teaching and learning work and products on campus, but the image is partial and somewhat unfocused. As we suspected, the scholarship of teaching and learning is alive and well on our campus, but in limited ways. A small core of faculty members applies for internal grants, presents, and publishes such work. Graduate students are generally not engaged in this scholarship. External grants are uncommon. The status of the scholarship of teaching and learning in our reward structure is ambiguous.

More Data

We developed a self-administered questionnaire to assess definitions of, involvement in, rewards and value for, and attitudes toward the scholarship of teaching and learning. We obtained Institutional Review Board approval for the study and selected a 30 percent random sample of tenured, tenure-track, nontenure-track, and lab school faculty, as well as professional staff (N=545). The questionnaire was placed on a password protected web site. All those selected for the sample were sent a cover letter via campus mail explaining the study, its purposes, related ethical issues, and information on how to complete the questionnaire. A reminder letter was sent two weeks later. With an overall response rate of 21 percent, the final sample of 115 individuals consisted of 49 percent tenured and tenure-line faculty, 34 percent nontenure-track faculty, and 17 percent lab-school and professional staff. The mean number of years respondents had been involved in college-level teaching in some way was 10 years. Distribution of faculty by rank in the sample was very similar to the distribution in the population. Respondents came from a wide range of departments and units, including 30 out of 37 academic departments or schools and 21 units.

Findings

The data lead to a number of conclusions. We must view these with caution, however, as the low response rate may have resulted in response biases. Between 30 and 34 percent of these respondents are aware of the Illinois State's CASTL definition of the scholarship of teaching and learning, have done this kind of scholarly work, have collaborated with colleagues on such work, have presented this work, and have published the work. Thus, these results indicate that this work is fairly common on our campus. Generally, tenured and tenure-track faculty members report higher frequencies on these variables than nontenure-track faculty and staff.

Two-thirds of the participants gave definitions of the scholarship of teaching and learning similar to the campus CASTL definition, and two-thirds indicate they have used this scholarly work to improve teaching or learning. A few examples of how respondents reported using scholarship of teaching and learning literature or their own scholarship of teaching and learning work include adding more active learning assignments, more field work, and more problem-based learning; obtaining and using feedback from students; improving or increasing group work, Web-based support, and classroom participation; decreasing lecture and increasing interactive strategies; altering the physical learning environment or the syllabus; offering better supports for critical thinking and student engagement; and using grading rubrics.

Respondents reported benefits of scholarship of teaching and learning for teaching and learning and agreed with a variety of positive statements about it. Participants were neutral, however, about whether this work is valued and used at various levels on campus. In addition, 94 percent indicated that the impact of conducting scholarship of teaching and learning on their career would be neutral (48 percent) or negative (46 percent). Generally, participants who were aware of the University's CASTL definition had more favorable attitudes toward the work with two exceptions. They agreed less often that there is adequate funding for scholarship of teaching and learning, and they felt the impact of doing this scholarship on their careers was more negative than did those not aware of the campus definition. Finally, the most common responses as to how the university can promote the scholarship of teaching and learning fell in the category of funding, especially grants.

The tentative picture we see from this quantitative data is a rosy one in terms of most participant attitudes. In addition, about one-third of the respondents have actively engaged in the scholarship of teaching and learning. The results also show significantly greater awareness of and involvement in this scholarship by tenured and tenure-line faculty than by those in other groups. Finally, we see a hint of the impact of our CASTL involvement in that significantly greater percentages of those aware of our CASTL definition are involved in the work and these participants have more positive attitudes toward it than those not aware of that definition.

Using the Data: Acting on the Results

What are the implications of the results of this first wave of results of our larger study on promoting, rewarding, and using the scholarship of teaching and learning on our campus? First, the data confirm the importance of many activities that we have already initiated, including establishing a small grant program requiring teams; offering campus discussions about the values and rewards of the scholarship of teaching and learning; connecting grants to strategic plan values; creating various scholarly communities such as research circles and email groups; and promoting this scholarly

work at the department level, such as visiting departments to discuss it and providing a support by discipline-specific web pages.

These data also indicate that we need to do more, including targeting specific groups to use scholarship of teaching and learning, such as nontenure track faculty, professional staff, and students; strengthening the value and reward structure for this scholarly work on campus; increasing collaboration on scholarship of teaching and learning; connecting more people to national initiatives; and developing more processes to apply the results of this work. We are considering and developing ways to implement these additional ideas, and we will collect data for phase two of this study of the status of the scholarship of teaching and learning on our campus in 2006.

The tentative picture is a rosy one in terms of most participant attitudes.

Contacts and URLs

Kathleen McKinney
Professor of Sociology
Illinois State University
kmckinne@ilstu.edu

James Broadbear
Associate Professor of Health Sciences
Illinois State University
jtbroad@ilstu.edu

Deborah Gentry
Associate Dean, College of Applied Science
    and Technology
Illinois State University
dgentry@ilstu.edu

Patricia Klass
Acting Department Chairperson,
    Educational Administration and
    Foundations
Illinois State University
phklass@ilstu.edu

Sharon Naylor
Associate Professor, Milner Library
Illinois State University
sknaylor@ilstu.edu

Nicky Virgil
Graduate Student (Psychology)
Illinois State University
njvirgi@ilstu.edu

For more information on institutional efforts to support the scholarship of teaching and learning at Illinois State, see http://www.cat.ilstu.edu/sotl/index.shtml

For more information on Illinois State's multi-method, longitudinal study, see http://www.cat.ilstu.edu/pdf/sotlonlinequest.pdf

Illinois State University
Normal, IL
Doctoral/Research Intensive
http://www.ilstu.edu/

INTRODUCTION TO SECTION FIVE
Learning Along the Way

Marcia Babb and Richard Gale
The Carnegie Foundation for the Advancement of Teaching

Sections One through Four of this book describe changes in infrastructure, collaboration, policies, and impact; they focus on discrete accomplishments and challenges within a campus effort to support the scholarship of teaching and learning. In this section, we offer another way to think about the progress of institutionalizing the scholarship of teaching and learning at the campus level; through eight examples we highlight lessons gleaned from the journey, learning that has happened along the way.

The journey motif permeates this section because the scholarship of teaching and learning — in the classroom, on a campus, within a discipline — is always an expedition into student learning and because every inquiry happens in the context of a particular terrain. It has been said that position determines landscape, that where you stand influences what you see, and as Adrienne Rich says in her poem *Planetarium,* "what we see we see, and seeing is changing" (Rich, 1971). This is certainly true for teachers and students in the classroom, and for campuses committed to the scholarship of teaching and learning. With this in mind, authors in this section consider current perspectives, paths traveled, and future directions

— what they have now that they didn't have before, why the change has been important, what they know now that they didn't know when they started, what the most important milestones were on the journey, and what's next. These questions proved well suited to both a process-oriented analysis of campus accomplishments and a product-oriented account of the work.

These campuses and disciplinary societies have instructive stories to tell: lessons about launching the scholarship of teaching and learning, insights into sustaining germinal and ongoing initiatives, responses to the issue of faculty recognition, and innovative approaches to spreading the word and "going public." In their essay, Mary Beaudry and Alease Bruce at the University of Massachusetts Lowell assert that the key to a successful scholarship of teaching and learning campus initiative can be found in four simple words that communicate four complex ideas: "initiate, support, reward, and disseminate." We were so taken with this approach that we have applied it to describing how the work represented in these chapters has promoted the scholarship of teaching and learning.

Beginning such campus-level efforts in the scholarship of teaching and learning is never easy. Even with the high profile of Boyer's four scholarships and the importance of recognizing teaching as a form of scholarship, initiation of this work within a campus culture often begins slowly and intermittently before gaining momentum. Despite differences in institutional type and mandate, and varieties of place and purpose, the journeys of this section often began with the same few steps. Starting a pedagogical conversation with other faculty was often the most important. Whether through the CASTL Campus Conversations or through other institutional structures (such as dedicated workshops and faculty forums), articulation of the value and nature of the scholarship of teaching and learning and the development of a common language to do so figured prominently. Morehead State University, Southwest Missouri State University, and Indiana University-Purdue University Indianapolis (IUPUI) all elected to use Campus Conversations for initial stocktaking, while the University of Portland and the American Sociological Association focused their efforts on workshops. This definitional stage created awareness and visibility of teaching as a profession, raised the profile of teaching excellence, and encouraged faculty and administrators to think about the observation, investigation, and documentation of classroom work. The conversations have worked so well to maintain vis-ibility and momentum at Southwest Missouri State that there are often up to six "conversations" each year. At the National Communication Association, staff members receive numerous campus requests for disciplinary scholarship of teaching and learning events. Finally, also important to the instigation of campus-level work was acknowledging and honoring local cultural norms — finding the right entry point, aligning with established goals and processes, taking into account existing initiatives, and linking to infrastructures.

As with any journey, success comes not only from strong beginnings, but also from sustained support. Support for the scholarship of teaching and learning came from many quarters and took many forms. Indeed, this category seemed to be the most substantial across our examples. This should not be surprising, for as every faculty member knows, it is one thing to suggest or even mandate an initiative to improve student learning and quite another to provide the kind of scaffolding that will allow it to happen. Of no particular surprise too was the realization that starting is inseparable from supporting; often there needed to be a commitment to support an initiative before even the most rudimentary efforts could begin. Notre Dame, for example, used grants of $5,000 per study to raise the profile of and help spark interest in this kind of scholarly work.

Once the scholarship of teaching took hold, the lessons came quickly. Campuses soon understood that for faculty to do this work they needed connections to like-minded others. This often took the form of reflective cross-disciplinary exchanges and collaborative research groups with common questions, as so notably evidenced in the University of Massachusetts Lowell's account. On some campuses, like Malaspina University-College, this scholarship

> Four simple words communicate four complex ideas: initiate, support, reward, and disseminate.

was facilitated through a teaching and learning center. Others, like the University of Portland, developed leadership teams to act as focal points for initiatives and mentoring, building a critical mass of committed teachers and a shared concept of this kind of scholarly work. Still others, like IUPUI, developed programmatic and cross-campus faculty learning communities.

Some campuses broke new ground in the area of faculty support. Notre Dame established a collective approach to seeking approval from the Institutional Review Board, thus streamlining what has become, on some campuses, a discouraging and baroque process. IUPUI developed support networks for lecturers, who often bear the lion's share of teaching responsibilities without sufficient assistance or recognition. Throughout these examples, support was often synonymous with resources (defined not only as time and funding but also introduction to scholarly literatures), the sharing of innovative methodologies, peer and mentor advice, and assistance with accountability. The larger goal of building support on campuses was to develop relationships among individuals, programs, disciplines, and concepts that would internalize active participation in the scholarship of teaching and learning and keep ideas and initiatives current. Moreover, if one landmark of this journey stood above the rest, it was that the scholarship of teaching and learning required faculty leadership and ownership, with strong administrative support. Morehead State University provides the clearest example — it was vital that faculty be at the center, asking their own questions, developing their own inquiries, and guiding changes in the reward process.

Indeed, the issue of faculty recognition of and reward for the scholarship of teaching and

learning has been a leitmotif of the CASTL Program. In a way, all of the above-mentioned support mechanisms represent informal and formal reward structures, because support of innovative work is often provided as a response to perceived value. At another level, reward becomes a milestone on the road to integrating the scholarship of teaching and learning into campus cultures through retention, tenure, and promotion documents and procedures. Recognition of this scholarship as scholarship, on campuses and in disciplinary societies, led to the establishment of systems of accountability, acceptance within committee structures, and eventually incorporation into faculty handbooks (an important step at Southwest Missouri State) and mission statements (as at the University of Portland). Reward can also be seen in the placement of scholarship of teaching and learning proponents, as spokespersons for the campus at large, on key hiring committees and in policy positions. Admittedly, this aspect is the least developed on many campuses, because organizing principles and institutional cultures change slowly. Yet as these authors indicate, the movement to recognize the scholarship of teaching and learning is strong, and progress has been made on many fronts. Perhaps the most encouraging part of this story is the way that reward and appreciation have so often followed dissemination.

Often we think of dissemination in terms of traditional outlets such as books, journals, and monographs; these are certainly a part of disseminating the scholarship of teaching and learning. At the University of Massachusetts Lowell, for example, a conscious effort was made to structure projects that would "lend themselves to easy conversion into publishable articles." But authors in this section make it clear that there are other ways of thinking about what K. Patricia Cross has called, in conversations at the Carnegie Foundation, "the pedagogies of dissemination." Carla Howery and Sherwyn Morreale point out that the disciplines are in many ways the most important venues for "going public" with the scholarship of teaching and learning, a position charted by Carnegie senior scholar Mary Taylor Huber and contributors to *Disciplinary Styles in the Scholarship of Teaching and Learning*. Howery and Morreale also champion teaching and learning workshops as an outlet for involvement, and in all of the examples included here, campus events figure prominently as public venues for scholarly work. Likewise, involvement of various campus constituencies, informal distribution of teaching and learning resources, teaching circles and faculty networks, and center-sponsored casual conversations about teaching all constitute dissemination strategies. These kinds of opportunities help to develop strong local communities and rich environments where this kind of work can thrive and propagate. If it is true that all politics is local, perhaps it is also true that all scholarship begins at home.

And home is perhaps a fitting place to end this introduction. Fitting, because it is important to see the scholarship of teaching and learning as a local phenomenon, something that begins in the classroom, benefits the student, and enriches the practice of teaching. Also, because the scholarship of teaching and learning holds a particular position on each campus and in each discipline, there is, as Southwest Missouri State demonstrates, no one-size-fits-all approach. This variety should be encouraging to campuses, for the journeys described confirm that there are no simple answers. The process by which the scholarship of teaching and learning begins and travels on a campus, according to Morehead State University's authors, is "cyclical and recursive rather than sequential." Nancy Randall of Malaspina University-College notes that what is required is a "delicate balance between pressure and support," with both serving to establish landmarks and beacons for the scholarship of teaching and learning.

The scholarship of teaching and learning is profoundly valuable work, and it requires nurturing within a hospitable environment. Not all campus cultures are ready for or interested in the efforts necessary to succeed, but in this section we have provided selected landmarks for those considering the journey and a series of beacons for help along the way. All of these authors stress the ongoing efforts, of their campuses and societies, to value and prize existing endeavors, expand the support for this work, encourage new initiatives, and broadcast the lessons of the scholarship of teaching and learning. These eight stories represent not destinations but milestones, markers of progress, learning along the way. As such they are, like the scholarship of teaching and learning itself, not definitive answers but recurring questions springing from a core inquiry.

Contacts

Marcia Babb
Program Associate
The Carnegie Foundation for the
Advancement of Teaching
babb@carnegiefoundation.org

Richard Gale
Senior Scholar
The Carnegie Foundation for the
Advancement of Teaching
gale@carnegiefoundation.org

Navigating the Scholarship of Teaching and Learning

Nancy Randall
Malaspina University-College

Watching fishing boats navigate from Pilot Bay to Entrance Island lighthouse, I reflect on our institutional discoveries at Malaspina University-College as we have encouraged the scholarship of teaching and learning. What landmarks guide our journey and which beacons enable us to move forward? My reflections occur as I participate in a Blue Pencil Retreat at a waterfront lodge on Gabriola Island, off Vancouver Island. With an editor's assistance, faculty members prepare scholarly work for public sharing and critique. A First Nations writer and faculty member, portraying the power of healing through writing, revises a script for students. A nursing educator, striving to communicate how our understanding of spirit and soul helps us support those with terminal illness, considers ways to share these conceptions with health science colleagues and students. A faculty developer prepares this chapter for publication. The diverse questions being investigated demonstrate the wide-ranging but often subtle impact that the incorporation of the scholarship of teaching and learning has on our institution.

Malaspina's engagement with the scholarship of teaching and learning is framed by two questions: "How do we keep teaching and learning at the heart of what we do?" and "How do we begin to foster a culture of inquiry in which the scholarship of teaching and learning flourishes?" Key elements include the delicate balance between pressure and support in navigating change initiatives, collaborative relationships that internalize participation, and developmental processes and time needed for integrating the scholarship of teaching and learning.

How do we provide meaningful institutional support as disciplinary scholars choose to become fluent with the often alien scholarly literature on teaching and learning? Our initiatives provide catalysts for investigations of teaching and learning questions. However, facilitating institutional change requires balancing meaningful support with delicate pressure (Sagor, 1992). Pressure is often viewed as a negative factor; however, it is also a positive and critical element in furthering change. It may range from a gentle nudge, to encourage a new faculty member's participation in teaching and learning sessions, to shared leadership, through a cross-institutional design team, that engenders greater ownership of improvement initiatives.

Both institutional pressure and support are external motivators. To encourage sustainability, engagement with the scholarship of teaching and learning must become internalized. This may occur when professional relationships, through collegial communities of practice, begin to form through the volition of the educators themselves. Encouraging and facilitating professional networks and relationships is key to our continued implementation (Fullan, 2001).

Knowing what works in an institution in terms of change initiatives is critical, and the process must be contextualized. At Malaspina, administrative directives for change will likely be resisted whereas an organic movement with strong administrative support works well. Therefore, time is needed for percolating the ideas related to the scholarship of teaching and learning, with differing types of support required over time. On our campus, after three years of support and pressure, discussions related to the nature of scholarly activity are becoming a natural element of institutional operations.

Further supporting this work is our partnership with the University of Portland in the CASTL Campus Program. Our cluster focus, "Supporting Scholarly Work at Learning-Centered Universities," includes developing descriptions of a continuum of growth toward the scholarship of teaching and learning (see Appendix). We encourage faculty members to move along this continuum from an initial phase of focusing on growth in one's teaching to a second phase of investing energy in scholarly teaching. Those who elect to develop the scholarship of teaching and learning move to phase three, with its focus on public engagement.

Raising the profile of teaching may seem ironic in an institution with a primarily teaching and learning mission, but the examination of assumptions about effective practices requires a venue. Three years ago, we initiated Teaching

> # Beginning with existing strength enables an appreciation rather than a deficit model of change.

Matters sessions, which focus on questions that faculty members bring from their practice. We have maintained these sessions as we recognize the importance of providing arenas of inquiry in which faculty from across the disciplines may explore teaching and learning dilemmas. To support reflective and cross-disciplinary exchanges, we fund Reading Circles centered on a selected text. Faculty members commit to participating in a series of seminars in which they share leadership. We quickly learned, however, that gentle pressure is also required, as participation dwindles unless we ensure ongoing, dynamic facilitation. Reading Circles are now flourishing, with faculty investigating a range of scholarly teaching and learning literature. Participants are asking questions such as what "engagement in learning" means, what "engagement in teaching" looks like, and what it means to be a "successful student." From these cross-disciplinary conversations, faculty members begin to consider how they might investigate these questions in their practice, and thus embark on the scholarship of teaching and learning.

Collaborative Inquiries that occur at the intersection of faculty and student learning form a growing focus for recent initiatives. Students act as key collaborators with the teaching, learning, and research nexus emphasized. In our Center for Digital Humanities Innovation, a key mandate is research into pedagogical concerns associated with computing in the humanities. Our history students are developing their understanding of disciplinary scholarship through contributions to The Homeroom, an online gateway for information about the history of education and schools in British Columbia. The Canadian Letters and Images Project, an online archive of Canadian war history, enables our students to work with faculty to process and analyze primary data. In the Applied Environmental Research Laboratory, students are co-investigators in regional environmental studies and present their scholarship at disciplinary conferences.

Because most scholarly presentations occur off campus in discipline-specific conferences and publications, we decided to honor and learn from scholarly work within our educational community in a more public way. Therefore, we implemented a series of Scholarship Seminars, based on Boyer's framework of scholarship (1990) and featuring a wide range of faculty scholarship. Fostering the scholarship of teaching and learning is important; however, we believe that we need to equally honor the scholarships of engagement, integration, and discovery. For faculty undertaking all forms of scholarship, the Blue Pencil Retreat provides support and pressure within a devel-

---

Encouraging and facilitating professional networks and relationships is key to our continued implementation.

---

opmental progression, fostering collegial relationships and facilitating public sharing of scholarship.

Beginning with existing strengths enables an appreciative rather than a deficit model of change. This approach was emphasized in completing the Mapping Progress Report, which was a critical element in our change process. In creating infrastructure to support the scholarship of teaching and learning, we were able to recognize and build on existing resource centers already in successful operation.

As we plan for the future, beacons provide evidence of increasing institutional synergies that cross and combine, enabling the scholarship of teaching and learning to flourish. These synergies continue. Our research officer and our faculty developer collaboratively planned the Scholarship Seminars and the Blue Pencil Retreat to ensure the greatest impact from combined initiatives. Another beacon is the work of a cross-institutional design team shaping a teaching and learning center. The team, comprised of key teaching and learning resource people, has recommended institutional principles for teaching and learning that provide a cohesive grounding for future developments. One principle encourages the fostering of a culture of inquiry that supports all types of scholarship, including the scholarship of teaching and learning. The design team has also recommended an ongoing collaborative cluster of institutional development resources (such as the library, human resources, educational technology, and research officer) that will be coordinated through the Teaching and Learning Center. The beacon guiding us is that powerful synergy noted by Zahorski (2002), and in describing our change process we hope that our learning may guide others embarking on similar journeys.

References

Boyer, E. L. (1990). *Scholarship reconsidered: Priorities of the professoriate.* San Francisco: Jossey-Bass.

Fullan, M. (2001). *Leading in a culture of change.* San Francisco: Jossey-Bass.

Sagor, R. D. (1992). Three principals who make a difference. *Educational Leadership, 49*(5), 13-18.

University of Portland. (2003). *Statement on scholarly teaching.*
http://www.up.edu/up_sub.asp?ctnt=1074&mnu=40&chl=310&lvl=2

Weston, C., & McAlpine, L. (2001). Making explicit the development toward the scholarship of teaching. In C. Kreber (Ed.), *Scholarship revisited: Perspectives on the scholarship of teaching* (pp. 88-97). San Francisco: Jossey-Bass.

Zahorski, K. J. (2002). Nurturing scholarship through holistic faculty development: A synergistic approach. In K. J. Zahorski (Ed.), *Scholarship in the postmodern era: New venues, new values, new visions.* San Francisco: Jossey-Bass.

Contact and URLs

Nancy Randall
Faculty of Education Professor and Faculty
    Development Coordinator
Malaspina University-College
randall@mala.bc.ca

For more information on Malaspina's Reading Circles, see http://web.mala.bc.ca/research/circles_files/frame.htm

For more information on the Center for Digital Humanities Innovation, see http://cdhi.mala.bc.ca/

For more information on The Homeroom, The Canadian Letters and Images Project, and the Applied Environmental Research Laboratory, see http://www.mala.bc.ca/Homeroom/, http://www.mala.bc.ca/history/letters/, and http://web.mala.bc.ca/research/aerl/aerl_files/frame.htm, respectively.

**Malaspina University-College
Nanaimo, British Columbia, Canada
Baccalaureate College-Liberal Arts
http://www.mala.ca/index.asp**

Appendix

Continuum of Growth Toward the Scholarship of Teaching and Learning

We have developed a rubric on the continuum of growth toward the scholarship of teaching and learning. Each institution will benchmark its current position on that continuum and define its desired position. These statements are intended to be descriptive rather than prescriptive and are intended to assist in identifying developmental stages toward the scholarship of teaching and learning. As in any developmental process, it is expected that individuals will simultaneously demonstrate elements in two or three stages of this continuum. It is also understood that individuals will not likely demonstrate equal strengths in all areas. It is intended that individuals would provide evidence to document their progress, and by documenting overall patterns, this continuum may assist individuals in fostering further growth. Our goal is that all faculty members at Malaspina will attain Phase Two, Scholarly Teaching. This expectation is consistent with institutional missions that focus on student learning.

Stage	Phase One: Growth in effective teaching	Phase Two: Growth in scholarly teaching	StageThree: Growth in the scholarship of teaching and learning
Description	Develop personal knowledge about their own teaching and student learning disciplines	Develop and exchange knowledge about scholarly teaching and learning within, across, and beyond the discipline and institution	Develop scholarly knowledge about teaching and learning that has significance and impact
Engagement with students' learning	Exhibit curiosity about their students, student learning, and learning environments	Identify issues and inquiries related to some aspect of student learning	Collaborate with students in investigating teaching and learning issues
Inquiries into teaching and learning issues	◆ Engage in institutional teaching development activities ◆ Implement teaching innovations ◆ Intentionally evaluate own teaching for improvement ◆ Read about teaching and learning ◆ Demonstrate validity of teaching knowledge through assessment by students, peers, and administrators	◆ Engage colleagues within and across disciplines and make explicit their pedagogical content knowledge ◆ Develop, plan, and implement strategies designed to address and enhance student learning ◆ Document the outcomes of their strategies using methodology aligned with their problem or consistent with their discipline ◆ Demonstrate growth in understanding the complexity of teaching and learning	◆ Draw on literature and research on teaching and learning to inform institution and field ◆ Carry out scholarly investigations of teaching and learning using an approach to inquiry consistent with understanding teaching and learning
Making public and learning from critique	◆ Understand and apply principles underlying teaching and learning decisions ◆ Reflect on teaching practices	◆ Reflect upon and share with others ideas, designs, strategies, and outcomes of their work ◆ Mentor other teachers and provide leadership within the discipline or institution ◆ Consistently and continually build upon their work and the work of others through an iterative process	◆ Make public scholarship on teaching and learning through presentations or publishing ◆ Obtain funding for research on teaching and learning ◆ Mentor others in doing research on teaching and learning ◆ Demonstrate comprehensive knowledge of the research on teaching and learning

Adapted from Weston and McAlpine (2001) and University of Portland (2003).

Embedding the Scholarship of Teaching and Learning Through Cross-Campus Collaboration

Barbara Mae Gayle and Marlene Moore
University of Portland

The lessons learned over the past four years at the University of Portland demonstrate that faculty members can spearhead a movement that integrates the scholarship of teaching and learning into campus life without a formal structure such as a center for teaching and learning. As part of the Campus Program, faculty formed the Carnegie Conversations Committee as a grassroots effort to provide the necessary leadership to enhance teaching and learning on campus. Because the initiative was aligned with Portland's vision of becoming a "premier Catholic teaching university," it received the backing of the administration. Faculty support, however, required a different approach. Faced with demands for an accreditation self-study and the development of a campus assessment program, faculty members were understandably hesitant to take on additional responsibilities. However, by linking the scholarship of teaching and learning with the self-study, the committee demonstrated that faculty could investigate their classroom practice while serving the needs of the campus as a whole.

Several planning decisions enhanced the committee's ability to successfully engage faculty in discussions about the scholarship of teaching and learning. Meetings were designed so that no prepreparation from faculty attendees was required, and hands-on workshops were engineered to engage faculty both as learners and experts. The committee relied on campus expertise to help lead meetings and worked hard to create a collegial atmosphere for discussion by including time to socialize over wine and cheese. An interdisciplinary team identified common problems in enhancing teaching across campus. The group designed opening exercises that encouraged faculty to mingle with individuals they did not yet know, making it easier to cross disciplinary lines. The resulting series of co-sponsored events attracted engineering, nursing, education, business, humanities, social science, and science faculty to any given meeting. The greatest evidence of success was attendance at events; although voluntary, more than 80 percent of the faculty attended one or more of the meetings, motivated by a desire to be part of the community and the realization that the topics could make their jobs easier and more enjoyable. These interdisciplinary meetings laid a foundation for partnerships that would involve the entire faculty in a campus-wide exploration of teaching and learning, including, within two years,

> Interdisciplinary meetings laid a foundation for a campus-wide exploration of teaching and learning.

the unanimous approval of a redesigned General Education Program.

The committee learned that by cultivating partnerships with other committees and campus leaders, they were able to subtly and intentionally embed the scholarship of teaching and learning into university initiatives. These collaborations also spread the workload among members of several committees; it was easier to plan campus-wide forums that were innovative and creative when the assessment committee, the core evaluation team, or the general education assessment program group was also involved in the conceptualization and implementation of the meetings. One such forum resulted in students becoming more active intellectual partners in the learning process, through meetings that addressed issues about teaching practices, critiqued the core curriculum, and discussed the self-study documents.

Infusing the scholarship of teaching and learning into campus initiatives required the majority of faculty members to participate in some sort of scholarship of teaching and learning project at the individual, university, or multi-institutional level. The committee recognized that broadening the scope of the scholarship of teaching and learning to include projects at all three levels made it easier to help faculty transcend the idea that the work was too time consuming. For example, to promote individual

scholarship of teaching and learning projects, the university committee charged with increasing assessment of student learning invited the Conversations Committee to work with them. During an institution-wide Faculty Development Day sponsored by both committees, faculty chose one thing they wanted to know about student learning. These individual projects helped faculty reflect on their teaching as they planned their course objectives, consider how to enact their learning goals, and examine the linkages between teaching and learning. At the university level, a partnership between the Conversations Committee and the Core Evaluation Team helped University of Portland faculty understand what students were learning in the old core curriculum. During the process, faculty worked collaboratively to identify best teaching practices, plan a cycle for review of their courses, and develop a process for evaluating, disseminating, and incorporating their assessment results into their courses. Another partnership involved Portland faculty in a multi-institutional scholarship of teaching and learning project, Senior Presentations as Indicators of Institutional Effectiveness. Portland's innovative approach to assessing seniors' ability to equitably and dispassionately articulate differing perspectives on an issue of societal importance was compared with senior capstone presentations at Willamette and Pacific Universities. The result was a project that could have impact beyond the three campuses involved.

Although the committee was created outside the existing governance structure, it has worked through established channels to institutionalize change. One of the founding members served as chair of the Committee on Teaching and Research and led an effort that resulted in descriptors of "excellent teachers." These descriptors were adopted by the College of Arts and Science and used as part of the formal faculty evaluation process. Most recently, Portland has partnered with Malaspina University-College as cluster co-leaders in the CASTL Campus Program. Together, we have developed a rubric on the continuum of growth toward the scholarship of teaching (p. 185 in this book), and each institution will define its current and desired position on that continuum. This move toward a community fully engaged with the scholarship of teaching and learning is the best way to achieve the liberal education goals so central to the mission of learning-centered universities. The University of Portland continues to build upon the cross-disciplinary spirit of cooperation that has successfully integrated the scholarship of teaching and learning into our campus life.

Contacts and URLs

Barbara Mae Gayle
Associate Dean for Curriculum, College of
    Arts and Sciences
University of Portland
gayle@up.edu

Marlene Moore
Dean, College of Arts and Sciences and
    Professor of Biology
University of Portland
moore@up.edu

For more information on University of Portland's funded work on the scholarship of teaching and learning, see
http://lewis.up.edu/cas/hewlett/

For more information on the University of Portland's assessment policies, plans, and general education program, see
http://lewis.up.edu/cas/genprogram/index.htm

University of Portland
Portland, OR
Master's I
http://www.up.edu/

An Ongoing Journey

Lawrence S. Albert, Michael R. Moore, and Kathryn C. Mincey
Morehead State University

In his absurdist one-act play "Zoo Story," Edward Albee writes, "Sometimes a person has to go a very long distance out of his way to come back a short distance correctly." Recently, American institutions of higher education seem to be orienteering their way back to their central mission: teaching and learning. The CASTL Campus Program encouraged Morehead State University to raise awareness of and commitment to the scholarship of teaching and learning. These initial campus conversations evolved into an extended conversation on the scholarship of teaching and learning that has influenced Morehead State's goals, initiatives, and resource allocation. We have learned five major lessons: administrative and leadership support are essential, visibility is vital, perception of tangible benefits is helpful, one initiative in an institution causes ripple effects (systemic change), and transformation in academic culture takes time and patience.

Administrative and Leadership Support

We have learned the crucial need for continuous reinforcement of the importance of the scholarship of teaching and learning through a commitment of funding, resources, and staffing by the president, provost, chairs, and faculty leadership. Without a commitment to the improvement of teaching and learning on the part of senior administrators, Morehead State would not have developed and sustained interest in new programs or entered the Campus Conversations. These ongoing conversations among faculty, administrators, staff, and students, with key faculty members and recipients of past teaching awards serving in active and advisory roles, have helped to foster trust in a process that is not "top-down."

Visibility

The establishment of a physical presence and outdoor signage for the Center for Teaching and Learning has provided not only the necessary space and resources for operations, but also credibility. The Center has a workplace with communications, computing, and printing support, a meeting room for the advisory board and staff members, and a staff work room. The director, staff, and student workers promote the value of teaching and learning by providing faculty development opportunities within the scholarship of teaching and learning, supporting faculty engagement in scholarly teaching, and providing faculty with mentoring. In addition, the Center houses a library of reading and video materials and maintains a website with links to teaching and learning resources.

Tangible Benefits

The Center's proliferation of resources, workshops, and professional development opportunities gradually convinced a growing number of participants that they could tangibly benefit from Center activities and events. Recent support included sponsoring a team to begin Morehead State's participation in the AAHE/Carnegie cluster on the mentoring of new scholars. Another visible benefit is collaboration in research between students and faculty. Students present this collaborative research in honors program venues on and off campus, as well as at the Governor's Poster Session, a statewide forum. These collaborations reinforce the concept of the university not merely as a purveyor of information, but as a "community of learners."

Ripple Effects

Our experience has also taught us that one initiative in an institution creates ripple effects in other parts of the institution, effecting systemic change. As a result of our campus conversations, we are moving toward a clearer understanding of the scholarship of teaching and learning. This understanding is beginning to convert catchphrases like "the importance of teaching" and "teaching institution" from vague slogans into affirmations of the value of teaching and learning as institutional priorities. Our 2001-2006 Strategic Plan defines the university as a "community of learners," and under the heading of "core values" it characterizes the institution as "an academic enterprise

committed to providing optimal opportunities for teaching and learning." We believe our early work with the scholarship of teaching and learning paved the way for placing these key phrases in our mission statement and that they are now given more than lip service. Comments of tenure and promotion committees (deans, chairs, and departmental committees) recorded in written promotion and tenure evaluations now reveal a broader understanding of scholarship that values the scholarship of teaching and learning. These evaluations typically cite critical components of a faculty member's portfolio, such as statements of philosophy, course materials, and selected publications, as evidence that the faculty member is approaching teaching in a scholarly fashion. Revised faculty evaluation plans used by department chairs and committees for tenure, promotion, and annual salary allocations contain a more clearly articulated emphasis on teaching in general and the scholarship of teaching and learning in particular. The College of Business Faculty Evaluation Plan now defines one of the "components of intellectual contribution" as "Applied Scholarship: The application, transfer and interpretation of knowledge to improve management practice and teaching," where it did not before. The plan also permits "instructional scholarship" to count as "professional achievement" where once it would have been discounted.

Despite this progress, inertia is still an institutional concern that extends beyond the physics department. In addition to being slow to change, the campus community also enjoys the mixed blessing of diverse philosophical viewpoints. We did not anticipate the degree of divergence in views, both on campus and across the nation, regarding the meaning and application of the scholarship of teaching and learning. Had we been aware of the vast differences in interpretation, we would have taken more time to define it clearly for ourselves. As it was, it took awhile to emerge, and it is still a fuzzy concept for many. For example, there is some debate about how rigorous methods must be. Some faculty members assert that, to have credibility, this scholarship must conform to the research standards of their academic discipline, whether scientific or humanistic. Others argue that the scholarship of teaching and learning can encompass "action research" that has a different purpose and a different set of standards. Disagreements on such points can be impediments to a campus-wide appreciation of the scholarship of teaching and learning, though in the long run they strengthen that appreciation by generating healthy conversations about the issues, thereby enabling us to move further ahead.

Another ripple effect has been increased efforts to emphasize and integrate technology into instruction. The campus-wide PT3 initiative (Preparing Tomorrow's Teachers to Use Technology), funded by a U.S. Department of Education grant, has engaged faculty in using information technology to create and deliver online courses and enhance traditional instruction. It has done so within a scholarship of teaching and learning framework that encourages faculty not simply to utilize technology but to reflect upon its use in relation to student learning. One of the many examples of this kind of work is a faculty member in Biology and Environmental Sciences. This faculty member created a project-based learning activity involving Internet research and website

Visibility is vital.

creation and then went on to assess the effectiveness of his approach and report his results online.

A second issue that affects the process of transformation is the lack of permanence in any change that occurs in a culture where members are continuously replaced because of retirement and resignation. In a given year, the institution might lose a significant number of faculty or a small number of key faculty who appreciate the scholarship of teaching and learning, requiring us to start again, defining and promoting the work with new hires. A similar problem can occur when department chairs, deans, and key members of committees rotate in or out of their positions of responsibility. Consequently, as our campus conversation evolved, we discovered that the scholarship of teaching and learning had not permeated the campus culture in neat stages. Our attempts at integration had been cyclical and recursive, rather than sequential.

To continue our progress, we have included an emphasis on the scholarship of teaching and learning in our annual new faculty orientation and our distance learning training. A link to new faculty orientation events is available at the start of the academic year on the website of the Center for Teaching and Learning, while distance learning training opportunities are posted throughout the academic year. We will continue faculty support for major projects that can have visible impact, and we expect mentored and other interested faculty to take advantage of the Center to implement their scholarship of teaching and learning projects through the Center's faculty development grant program. We will publicize and celebrate these projects as a way of affirming the value of such work, and we will continue integrating the scholarship of teaching and learning into the faculty evaluation plans of all departments. All of this will take time, and it may require us to "go a very long distance out of [our] way to come back a short distance correctly." Our efforts to infuse the scholarship of teaching and learning into the institution's culture have reminded us that an organization is a symbolic entity that must be created and maintained through sustained discourse and activity. It is only through intentional and persistent discussion of the scholarship of teaching and learning that it will become part of the fabric.

Contact and URLs

Lawrence S. Albert
Professor of Speech Communications
    and Director of the Center for Teaching
    and Learning
Morehead State University
l.albert@moreheadstate.edu

Michael R. Moore
Provost
Morehead State University
m.moore@moreheadstate.edu

Kathryn C. Mincey
Associate Professor of English
Morehead State University
k.mincey@morehead-st.edu

For more information on the Center for Teaching and Learning's teaching and learning resources, see
http://www.moreheadstate.edu/units/ctl/

For more information on the University's distance learning opportunities, see
http://www.moreheadstate.edu/units/distance

For more information on the Center's faculty development grant program, see
http://www.moreheadstate.edu/units/ctl/fdg

Morehead State University
Morehead, KY
Master's I
http://www.morehead-st.edu/

What It Really Takes

Barbara E. Walvoord
University of Notre Dame

The scholarship of teaching and learning is an elegant, straightforward idea — faculty will inquire in their own classrooms about the learning of their students, engaging the keen eye, the curiosity, and the disciplined inquiry they ideally bring to all areas of scholarship. To succeed, however, any campus project must realistically plan for the amount of support that faculty will need if they are to conduct meaningful inquiry into student learning in their classrooms and departments. At the University of Notre Dame, the scholarship of teaching and learning project has supported 13 individual and team faculty research projects, as well as five projects from neighboring institutions. As CASTL project leaders launched our initiative and worked with other campuses (a small Protestant institution, an urban Catholic university, a state comprehensive university, and a theological seminary), we learned the importance of inviting faculty to answer their own questions, providing individual and team funding, giving methodological advice and assistance, facilitating networking with other faculty, and demonstrating examples of and attention to systems for accountability.

Successful projects begin with finding out where on your campus questions are being asked about student learning, how they are being addressed, and what difficulties stand in the way. At Notre Dame, our initial CASTL project meetings with several hundred administrators, faculty members, and department chairs revealed that the scholarship of teaching and learning was trying to happen, but the system wasn't always helping. Faculty and chairs frequently posed questions about their classrooms they felt they could not answer. For example, members of the College of Engineering were launching an extensive revision of the college's introductory course— would advances in student learning merit the extra cost? Chemistry professor Dennis Jacobs was exploring student retention and success — could the Office of Institutional Research provide supporting data in a timely fashion? An English Department faculty member was wondering what students really consider when end-of-semester evaluations ask how well "the instructor stimulates creative or analytical thinking"— could the system offer any support, advice, or methodology to address this question? Such questions, we learned, were arising all the time. Talking to faculty, chairs, and deans to identify questions already being posed is the most important first step, whether through a series of lunches and brown-bags, phone calls, appearances at department or college-level meetings, or emails.

Next, faculty members should be invited to explore their own questions (those which emerged from campus conversations, as well as those not yet uncovered). At Notre Dame, we offered grants of $5,000 per project, to be used in any way the faculty member wished. The money provided an occasion for the new effort, demonstrated the provost's support, and added the panache of getting a grant. For faculty from other institutions, we required the home institution to provide matching funds. We learned that money is important for both practical and symbolic purposes, but amounts can be modest.

As we publicized our grant program, we led not with the term "scholarship of teaching and learning" or with any other terminology that might seem like jargon to faculty. Instead, we asked faculty to articulate their own questions. Our mailed flier asked, "Do You Have Questions About Student Learning You Want to Answer?" It offered some examples: "Teaching method X is taking a lot of time; is it working as well as I hope it is?" and "Why are my students not getting this particular point, even though I've doubled the time I spend on it in lecture?" We also contacted potentially interested faculty members and chairs whose questions had emerged in our earlier conversations — a very important strategy. The application process is also a central part of the invita-

> **Money is important for both practical and symbolic purposes, but amounts can be modest.**

tion. The process must spur faculty members to think through their projects in a careful way, must not be too intimidating for those who need help with shaping a research question and design, and must reassure them that they need not have a perfect research project at the time of application.

Faculty who possess fine research expertise in their own fields may need to develop a very different set of investigative tools for the scholarship of teaching and learning. For this reason, a crucial element of support has been methodological advice, including assistance and guidance with research design, literature searches, gaining permission from the Human Subjects Research Committee, access to institutional data, interviewing, survey construction, statistical computation, and data analysis. At Notre Dame, the provost funded staff members (in the Office of Instructional Research and in the Teaching and Learning Center) who spent many hours working with faculty members on these tasks. We held individual consultations with each faculty member during the project at the beginning, midway, and throughout by request. These consultations were time-consuming but crucial to the success of the projects.

Networking and accountability are the final types of support. Regular meetings are important, even though faculty members are very busy. At Notre Dame, group meetings were held several times within the first couple of months and then twice a semester during the two years of each cohort's funded projects. To ensure that everyone could be included, we sometimes held duplicate meetings, on Tuesday and Wednesday afternoons, so that participants could attend one or the other. In the groups, faculty found support, shared expertise for their projects, and developed a sense of collegiality, always over coffee and cookies. Some meetings focused on methodology, including one on constructing questionnaires for students and composing rubrics to evaluate student work. As a result of this meeting, participants constructed 15- to 20-minute presentations on research design and, later, emerging findings. At another successful meeting, three chemists presented their data about observations of chemistry students' learning activities in laboratory. Other gatherings were devoted to progress reports, beginning with the most committed and energetic participants to model and set a tone for the rest. These meetings, as well as the scheduled individual consultations, helped keep faculty on track and leaders informed about their progress. We also facilitated accountability by asking faculty to provide a plan and timeline with their applications, which also included a letter from the department chair and relevant academic administrator supporting the project and asserting that the faculty member was being given time to conduct the research.

Boyer and those who followed him have emphasized the commonality of all types of scholarship within the life of the faculty member. The scholarship of discovery in disciplinary fields always requires a great deal of support, but faculty members need even more when they turn to the scholarship of teaching and learning. Providing that support is a crucial element for successful scholarship of teaching and learning projects. The five key elements — faculty answering their own questions, financial support, methodological advice and assistance, networking with others, and accountability — must work in tandem to support faculty as they move into a welcoming yet challenging area of scholarship. The institution

that provides such support can create a climate in which faculty members receive the encouragement and resources they need to address the questions about student learning that lie at the heart of scholarship.

Contact and URL

Barbara E. Walvoord
Coordinator of the North Central
   Accreditation Self-Study, Fellow of the
   Institute for Educational Initiatives, and
   Concurrent Professor of English
University of Notre Dame
Barbara.E.Walvoord.3@nd.edu

For more information on the University of Notre Dame's projects on the scholarship of teaching and learning, see
www.nd.edu/~kaneb/pages/sotl.shtml

University of Notre Dame
Notre Dame, IN
Doctoral/Research Extensive
http://www.nd.edu/

Gathering Support for Change

Kelly McNeilis, Richard Myers, and Timothy Knapp
Southwest Missouri State University

Creating cultural change and reforming institutional practices in a university require time, patience, and dialogue. They also require faculty input, administrative support, and a leadership group of faculty willing to advocate for change. At Southwest Missouri State University, faculty and administrators have made significant progress over the past three years in establishing structural, cultural, and policy support for the scholarship of teaching and learning using the CASTL Campus Program as a model and base.

The university has developed several key organizational supports, including a CASTL Task Force, consisting of faculty from all University colleges. This faculty core initiated change in the teaching environment by drawing together the interested and curious to establish a definition of the scholarship of teaching and learning for the university, conducting Campus Conversations to broaden faculty discussion of this scholarship, and implementing a New Faculty Network program to emphasize teaching and learning as part of the mentoring of new faculty. Perhaps the most significant result of a heightened awareness of the Carnegie Task Force initiative is a proposal before the Faculty Handbook Revision Committee to change the section on scholar-

ship in the Faculty Handbook to more accurately describe the scholarship of teaching and learning. The proposed changes are influencing departmental promotion and tenure policy statements. In addition, the task force initiative was enhanced with the recent establishment of an Academic Development Center, which has the scholarship of teaching and learning as a core function.

Four key elements have been useful in gathering support for change and in advancing the scholarship of teaching and learning at Southwest Missouri State University. First, the composition of the task force and periodic rotation of members have worked to our advantage in promoting change. To maintain continuity of ideas and goals, the task force has established a three-year rotation, with only two members rotating off the committee at a time. The current task force, an interdisciplinary group with a variety of experiences, includes teaching award winners, a teaching fellow, a department head, and other faculty. This combination of experienced and new members from across the university quickly established credibility and visibility for the task force, as well as support among faculty and administrators.

Second, academic affairs, the faculty administrative unit, provides a generous budget consistent with the needs of the task force. Funds are used to send delegates to national, state, and local meetings and to purchase materials for the conversations and the New Faculty Network. Third, the director of Southwest Missouri State's newly formed Academic Development Center has maintained a close working relationship with the task force, is a passionate advocate for the scholarship of teaching and learning, and has given the CASTL Campus Program another outlet to share its goals and initiatives. The synergy between the two groups allows for a broad range of effective scholarship of teaching and learning services. Finally, Campus Conversations — up to three sessions per semester — have worked well to maintain visibility and momentum for the goals of the initiative. Conversations revolve around contemporary topics that relate to enhanced learning in the classroom. Recent conversations engaged members of the faculty and administration at all levels in frank discussions about how the scholarship of teaching and learning should be recognized and rewarded at Southwest Missouri State University.

Several important lessons have emerged from task force efforts. One is that success comes through listening to faculty and taking their ideas seriously. Conversations with faculty in

---

Having a university-wide definition establishes a common conceptual base.

---

formal and informal settings provide perspectives and views about teaching and learning as scholarly activities. The first — and still current — definition of the scholarship of teaching and learning was generated by an enthusiastic group of 100 faculty on a Saturday morning in fall 2000. Having a university-wide definition establishes a common conceptual base, and it has become useful in proposing a definition of the scholarship of teaching and learning for the faculty handbook, which will be useful in faculty rewards, tenure, and promotion decisions. Faculty members participate freely and openly in CASTL-sponsored events because activities are supported by, rather than dictated by, the upper administration.

It is also clear that a one-size-fits-all approach to methods of inquiry does not work. Because faculty efforts to implement the scholarship of teaching and learning usually have a disciplinary focus, discussions often fall along disciplinary lines. Faculty members interested in classroom research are funded through competitive programs, with successful applicants encouraged to pursue scholarly projects that are framed within their expertise and to discuss their thoughts on teaching and learning within disciplinary practices. Common ground about the scholarship of teaching and learning is frequently the outcome of such serious discussions.

Mentoring new faculty in the area of teaching involves more than lectures about techniques and teaching strategies. At Southwest Missouri State, New Faculty Network groups provide forums to discuss teaching and learning issues. Experienced faculty facilitators who host the meetings establish clear guidelines for discussion topics. Facilitators, as mentors, recognize that new faculty have changing needs and interests, and thus make meetings flexible.

Participation is voluntary, and the number of new faculty involved is encouraging. Reports indicate that discussions are individually fulfilling and widely applicable.

Even with extensive efforts to host conversations and other events, not all faculty members choose this path for their scholarship efforts. However, many who enter higher education eventually come to value the benefits of coupling inquiry with teaching in ways that improve instruction and advance student learning. Discussing misperceptions about the scholarship of teaching and learning helps quell faculty concerns about conducting research on teaching and learning without training in educational research methods. And for those who do want to develop scholarship of teaching and learning projects, we provide opportunities for faculty to work in interdisciplinary teams so that they can approach questions about teaching and learning without fear of failure.

Southwest Missouri State University has accepted the challenge of institutionalizing and supporting the scholarship of teaching and learning by establishing organizations, promoting change that becomes the campus standard, and implementing new programs. Change has been slow but steady, with new and established faculty members coming to greater understanding and acceptance of the value of this scholarship. The practices and lessons learned at Southwest Missouri State University provide a foundation for faculty who want to become involved in the scholarship of teaching and learning.

Contacts and URL

Kelly McNeilis
Associate Dean, College of Arts and Letters
Southwest Missouri State University
ksm911f@smsu.edu

Richard L. Myers
Professor of Biology
Southwest Missouri State University
rlm967f@smsu.edu

Timothy Knapp
Professor of Sociology
Southwest Missouri State University
tdk986f@smsu.edu

For more information on the SMSU-Carnegie Initiative, see
http://www.smsu.edu/acadaff/Carnegie/

Southwest Missouri State University
Springfield, MO
Master's I
http://www.smsu.edu/

From Discussion to Action

Mary L. Beaudry and Alease S. Bruce
University of Massachusetts Lowell

Until the invitation to participate in CASTL arrived at the University of Massachusetts Lowell, many of us had no idea of the extent to which our faculty members were already engaged in reflective teaching. The 100-member, institution-wide Teaching and Learning Council that encourages and supports faculty explorations to improve teaching and student learning formed and funded a Carnegie Task Force to investigate faculty practice and promote the CASTL initiative. The Task Force constituted a unique entity to affirm the teaching efforts of faculty and raise the status of teaching on the campus. By treating teaching not just as an expectation but also as a professional area that could be examined and critiqued like discipline-based research, faculty would be exposed to additional venues for professional advancement.

In reflecting on how we were able to move from the discussion phase of the initiative to one of action and outcomes, we found that the formula that worked for us can be summarized as "initiate, support, reward, and disseminate." The initiated activities were supported by workshops, peer discussions, and Faculty Teaching Center and Council services. Faculty members who engaged in research projects were rewarded with stipends, small mementos,

and public recognition. Pilot project outcomes were showcased at campus-wide events, and research project samples were posted on our Carnegie website.

The Campus Program helped more faculty members approach their teaching as scholarship. Before the Carnegie initiative, the Council on Teaching and Learning, which began in the early 1990s, provided a few opportunities for faculty to talk about teaching. Once each semester, faculty gatherings called Conversation Dinners stimulated discussions about teaching. Summer workshops also provided a topic-driven venue. But neither allowed enough time for focused sharing about individual teaching experiences and dialogue about this kind of scholarship. The new Carnegie Task Force provided faculty members with the necessary forum.

The first year of the initiative was relatively easy. We gathered approximately 20 faculty members to serve as charter members of the task force and convened a yearlong series of conversations about teaching. At first, task force members shared success stories that progressed to problem solving strategies, which members discovered could work across disciplines. As the members became more comfort-

> The formula that worked for us can be summarized as "initiate, support, reward, and disseminate."

able with each other, some began to reveal teaching attempts that had failed, moving the discussion into inquiries about different types of teaching methods and their effectiveness. The cross-disciplinary makeup of the group provided richness to the conversation that faculty confessed did not occur at departmental levels.

The second year of the initiative involved transitioning the discussion into a campus project and developing and implementing an action plan. The two-stage plan for the task force involved identifying a research question and developing groups within the task force to study aspects of the question. After months of discussion, the task force identified a research question: "Which instructional practices motivate and/or enable students to learn in specific courses?" Interest groups were formed to examine a classroom practice and formulate research questions to assess the practice's impact on students in a specific course. Group members read and discussed journal articles, including articles on action research and assessment, and these readings provided grounding for their work. Once groups had decided on a particular instructional practice to examine, their readings became more focused according to pedagogical interest. For example, faculty who were already attempting

small group activities in their classrooms questioned whether empirical evidence showed that students learned any better or achieved better grades. Their readings — and ultimately their classroom research — centered on this issue.

A proportion of the task force budget was allocated to stipends for members engaged in this research. The task force decided that the studies should be developed in a style that would lend itself to easy conversion into publishable articles, and together they developed a set of proposal guidelines. Although most projects were research studies of classroom practices, some members considered developing case studies explicating classroom dilemmas. The collaborative development and refinement of proposal guidelines, an important step in the process, enabled the members to hone ideas for their action research projects or cases and to identify the necessary background research. To launch the projects, the task force held a workshop open to faculty across campus to encourage participation and provide a forum for clarification, discussion, and support.

To facilitate the research, the task force applied to the Institutional Review Board for approval of the Carnegie research projects. By prescreening and clustering the projects under the Carnegie Initiative, we facilitated a step in the research process that many faculty members had considered a hindrance. Each year, our group has filed a progress report with the Board and requested an extension rather than requiring the individual project investigators to apply and file separately. Task force co-chairs serve as the principal investigators and oversee the process. Together with members, they review and screen the research proposal applications.

Throughout the semester, the projects were supported by our monthly meetings and the background readings that related to the research areas. In addition, the task force found it helpful to bring in a consultant on educational research. Though adept at conducting research in their disciplines, many project investigators remained uncertain about the expectations of action research about teaching and feared making unfounded conclusions or inaccurate interpretations. Discussions with the consultant gave them more confidence as they began to collect and evaluate the data from their projects. The consultant also gave increased credibility to the pilot projects that were underway. As the year ended, seven of the ten initial pilot projects were completed.

The next significant aspect of the initiative was to recognize the researchers' projects. What began as a simple poster blossomed into presentations connected to two campus-wide events. Faculty at large became involved in the Carnegie discussion. In preparation for the presentations, the group agreed on common guidelines and critiqued each other's work. An Editorial Review Workshop provided an opportunity for the participants to think like assessors and critically give and receive feedback on their projects as potentially publishable articles. During the first year of the initiative, the task force surveyed the campus faculty about their teaching publications, and there will be a follow-up survey to determine whether the scholarship of teaching has increased on campus.

The Carnegie Task Force has been pleased with our initial progress and its impact on campus. Faculty who are interested in improving their teaching now have a better sense of ways the campus can serve them. The task force now sponsors summer and winter workshops, in collaboration with the Faculty Teaching Center and the Task Force on Faculty Enrichment, that focus on the Carnegie Initiative. On the Carnegie Task Force website, campus constituents can review sample products in the scholarship of teaching and learning. A core group of faculty is ready to mentor others interested in developing similar projects. Most recently, linking a major campus interest to our Carnegie question, we are exploring how technology can be used to enhance deep learning in order to involve more members of the campus in our Carnegie initiative.

The task force is now attempting to create another nucleus of faculty who will support each other in the design of scholarship of teaching and learning projects. The group of new researchers has remained small, and it has been difficult to maintain the interest of those members who have completed their projects. Next efforts will attempt to broaden the core of new faculty by establishing a number of campus-wide community teaching circles, using charter members of the task force as consultants or members. Having identified what has worked, the task force will continue to explore creative ways to involve even more faculty in our scholarship of teaching and learning mission.

Contacts and URL

Mary L. Beaudry
Director, Faculty Teaching Center
University of Massachusetts Lowell
Mary_Beaudry@uml.edu

Alease S. Bruce
Professor of Health and Clinical Sciences
University of Massachusetts Lowell
Alease_Bruce@uml.edu

For more information on pilot project outcomes,
see our Carnegie website,
http://www.uml.edu/centers/FTC/carnegie.html

University of Massachusetts Lowell
Lowell, MA
Doctoral/Research Intensive
http://www.uml.edu/

Scholarship at an Urban, Comprehensive University

Richard C. Turner

Indiana University-Purdue University Indianapolis

Ernest Boyer meant *Scholarship Reconsidered* to reorient faculty in their relationship to their institutions and in their sense of what constitutes valuable faculty work. Boyer did not just rename research as the scholarship of discovery; he also added a new dimension in suggesting faculty members have a responsibility to nurture the climate for inquiry on their campuses. Thus, successful scholarship of discovery would include scholars becoming more invested in their institutions alongside their clear and traditional allegiance to the invisible college of their disciplines (Boyer, 1990, p. 17). The added dimension for the scholarship of teaching was viewing teaching as an activity to be made public and presented for review by peers. Pursuit of any of the goals that Boyer outlines requires practitioners to maintain this complex sense of faculty work.

At Indiana University-Purdue University Indianapolis (IUPUI), pursuing the scholarship of teaching and learning involves maintaining a complex sense of faculty work and student success at an institution that is complex in its origins and structures and multifaceted in its institutional culture. Like many urban comprehensives (with predominantly commuter, first-generation students), these origins and a history of expanding missions

and expectations make it difficult to identify a reigning culture in any area or a clear sense of the university as a community. Approaching the many and complex issues surrounding the scholarship of teaching and learning at an institution that does not have a clearly defined teaching culture makes this work especially challenging.

A chain of related assumptions informs the steps taken toward developing a culture of teaching and learning at IUPUI. Perhaps the most elusive is the tendency of faculty members and students to form their identities outside of their university community — university values and missions shape only a small part of what defines or motivates them. Thus, within the academic community, work on the scholarship of teaching and learning must be aligned with already-existing campus, school, and department goals, missions, and priorities, such as retention, student success, or enhanced diversity. Approaches that require added work will fail to get the community's attention. Conversations need to focus on the ways in which such scholarship lies within the mainstream of faculty responsibilities.

IUPUI began its explicit engagements with the scholarship of teaching and learning in response to the AAHE Campus Conversations,

conversations that led to a shared, working definition of this scholarship and the appointment of a coordinator. Although the scholarship of teaching and learning at IUPUI lacks a sense of overall cohesion and uniformity, it is suggestive of how universities and colleges with multiple and emerging missions and expectations can still pursue effective work. Creating an awareness of the nature and the value of the scholarship of teaching and learning is a necessary early step in getting the academic community to accept it as a special and authentic form of faculty work. For all faculty members, IUPUI prepared a publication entitled *Conversations,* based on the work of the initial campus talks. In this publication, early participants in the scholarship of teaching and learning conversations developed a definition for this scholarship, an explanation of its implications, and some suggestions about future directions:

> The scholarship of teaching and learning addresses the intellectual work of the classroom, especially teaching and learning, as the focus of disciplinary-based inquiry, captures that work in appropriate formats for self-reflection or presentation to peers, and applies the results to practice. The scholarship of teaching and learning regards teaching as part of the collaborative inquiry undertaken by faculty and students that drives the intellectual work of an academic community. (Office of Professional Development, 1998, p. 2)

An informal group has revisited this definition to update it and capture recent innovations in teaching and leaning. The coordinator met with most of the IUPUI deans to acquaint them with the scholarship of teaching and learning, to discuss what might already approximate this scholarship, and to consider what activities they might want to promote with available resources. Most deans were willing to embrace the scholarship of teaching and learning as long as its products are recognizable and meet more traditional research criteria — publication in refereed journals, presentations at major conferences, evidence of impact at a national level, or successful grant applications. Keeping the scholarship of teaching and learning current in the minds of the academic community is central, as is continuing the conversations about how the scholarship of teaching and learning shapes and defines an institution. As such, workshops highlighting best practices offer recognition and a forum for people doing the scholarship of teaching and learning, and they demonstrate how teaching can be treated as a scholarly activity. Early presentations proved relatively easy to arrange because the campus had a number of faculty who had done outstanding and effective research on their teaching. One faculty member reported on the wide range of interventions he had made, acting at the behest of his department, in an introductory psychology course. A sociologist and

---

The scholarship of teaching and learning regards teaching as part of the collaborative inquiry undertaken by faculty and students that drives the intellectual work of an academic community.

---

an English composition instructor described the nature of the collaborations that had developed under the auspices of a Pew project. Faculty members in English, religious studies, and other disciplines presented the innovations they had made and the measures they had taken to capture the impact of those interventions. Although many faculty developers agree that offering workshops does not by itself effect much change, these events do enact part of the structure that must be built to locate the scholarship of teaching and learning at the center of a university's culture.

Another strategy for getting new people involved is the formation of research groups made up of people from across campus that support each other's inquiries and seek out collaborations where useful. These faculty learning communities provide an ongoing source of expertise and interest for those working on the scholarship of teaching and learning, and they have the flexibility to incorporate and initiate new members. Joining a community of peers is, after all, one of the major reasons many faculty turned to academic life. The School of Liberal Arts created a learning community of five to seven faculty members who received a stipend to work on individual or group activities, as well as to present what they have learned about the scholarship of teaching and learning to their colleagues in the school. That first cohort included a faculty member in French, who developed the use of writing as a primary learning strategy in an advanced French language course; a faculty member in English, who developed a plan for a textbook highlighting effective ESL strategies; and another faculty member in English, who assessed learning outcomes in face-to-face and online Shakespeare courses. A new cohort (with some overlap for continuity) is selected each year with the expectation that over a period of years the

School will have created a critical mass of faculty who have engaged with the scholarship of teaching and learning in significant and substantial ways, thus carrying what they know and do into all aspects of their work.

The hope is that faculty learning communities, especially as they incorporate the principles and practices of the scholarship of teaching and learning, will become a regular part of the University's culture. Another opportunity occurred through participation in a FIPSE dissemination grant that creates faculty learning communities focused on a theme or a project and organized according to the principles of the scholarship of teaching and learning. Some of this year's eight, topic-oriented communities will continue after this year; next year, 10 communities are planned. Another grant, from Lumina Foundation for Education, used faculty learning communities to structure an effort to increase the climate for diversity in classrooms.

Like many other universities, IUPUI covers sections of introductory classes with full-time, non-tenure-track lecturers, usually outstanding instructors who focus most of their work on teaching. The scholarship of teaching and learning offers an excellent framework for creating the environment and the encouragement for these gifted and experienced teachers to capture what they discover about teaching. Providing a widely accepted version of what constitutes this kind of scholarship, establishing that faculty work is a central and valued part of university life, and highlighting their achievements creates an atmosphere within which teaching captures attention and recognition. Although the main task for such efforts lies in finding support to provide the time for these teachers to reflect on and study their teaching successes, it is at least a start to create forums on campus and at regional and national meetings for the presentation of their work, to each other and to the university community at large. Short of significant new resources being developed for the support of teaching, campuses working to enhance the place of teaching can explore ways to reapportion faculty work to create at least some of the opportunities that lecturers need for professional growth. The scholarship of teaching and learning provides exactly the context and the structure to foster a welcoming and supportive network for lecturers.

The multiple forms of, and avenues to, the scholarship of teaching and learning at IUPUI keep both the advantages and the value of this work in the public consciousness of the academic community until it takes root in schools and departments. The campus's attempt to establish more rigorous documentation of teaching excellence, the increasing prominence of teaching awards, and expanding resources (journals and professional meetings) makes it easier for faculty to see how the scholarship of teaching and learning will help them meet their professional responsibilities. Continued pursuit of these programs and opportunities will build an increasingly prominent and effective profile at IUPUI and at similar universities, so that the scholarship of teaching and learning is a recognizable part of everyone's teaching culture.

Reference

Boyer, E. L. (1990). *Scholarship reconsidered: Priorities of the professoriate.* San Francisco: Jossey-Bass.

Office of Professional Development (October 1998). *Conversations.* Indianapolis, IN: IUPUI.

Contact and URLs

Richard C. Turner
Professor of English/Philanthropic Studies and Director of Administrative and Organizational Development
Indiana University-Purdue University Indianapolis
rturner@iupui.edu

For more information about IUPUI's work in the scholarship of teaching and learning, see http://www.iport.iupui.edu/teach/teach_efftea ch.asp

For information about IUPUI's work with faculty learning communities , see http://opd.iupui.edu/special/flc/

Indiana University-Purdue University Indianapolis
Indianapolis, IN
Doctoral/Research Intensive
http://www.iupui.edu/

Disciplinary and Campus Collaborations

Carla B. Howery
American Sociological Association

Sherwyn P. Morreale
National Communication Association

For faculty members' scholarship of teaching and learning to thrive at the campus level, it has to be accorded status and recognition nationally in the publications and conferences of professional organizations and disciplinary societies. Two social science societies exemplify CASTL's integrated model of educational innovation through their work with members to promote change on college and university campuses. The American Sociological Association and the National Communication Association approached this work differently but in equally effective ways as they helped set national and campus agendas for the scholarship of teaching and learning.

The American Sociological Association convened an invitational workshop of 60 sociology colleagues, each committed to synthesizing "what we know and what we need to know about teaching and learning in sociology" and to developing a research agenda for the scholarship of teaching and learning in the discipline. The workshop, which received coverage in the association newsletter, evidenced a critical mass of sociologists pursuing the scholarship of teaching and learning. Participants developed a set of actions to increase visibility and regard for this work within the field, including devoting a section of the association's journal *Teaching Sociology* to teaching and learning; dedicating thematic sessions at the annual meeting; featuring the scholarship of teaching and learning at the Association's Chair Conference; and including this kind of scholarly work in the efforts of the Association's consulting team, which undertakes program reviews and provides advice on assessment, learning styles, and teaching effectiveness in sociology. All of this activity clearly established that sociology has a body of knowledge and experienced faculty dedicated to the scholarship of teaching and learning.

The National Communication Association's primary goals were to create awareness and better understanding of the scholarship of teaching and learning and to encourage as many members as possible to join in the scholarly examination of communication education. The association promoted participation by linking the support and infrastructure of a national association to faculty engaged in the scholarship of teaching and learning on their campuses. The National Communication Association formed a leadership team consisting of representatives from all levels of the discipline and the association, including several journal editors, the chair of the association's Educational Policies Board, and faculty and administrators from campuses ranging from two-year colleges to research universities. Through their efforts, the association established a website of resources, scheduled panels at national and regional conventions, and conducted a national survey on the scholarship of teaching and learning in communication studies. The association also initiated communication-based campus symposia and designed campus-specific trainings and workshops focused on this work. The organization now features a series of programs and panels on the scholarship of teaching and learning at the annual national convention; devotes a special section to this scholarship in every issue of the monograph *Communication Education;* involves Carnegie Scholars as active leaders; serves as a core member in an AAHE/Carnegie cluster; and has contributed to a monograph on disciplinary styles in the scholarship of teaching and learning. In 2003, the association established a new national leadership team to systematically involve scholars who specialize in areas such as interpersonal, gender, and computer-mediated communication in the examination of teaching and learning.

Both the National Communication Association and the American Sociological Association have found that the key to successful disciplinary collaboration with campuses is discovering the right point of entry for the scholarship of teaching and learning on a given campus, with such access typically coming through key individuals, links to other initiatives, or special events. Often, the access begins with language: clarifying terms; honoring a campus's local

description of the scholarly examination of teaching; and finding common ground for a discussion of why the scholarship of teaching is important, where to begin, and how to pursue it.

The National Communication Association's "critical communication events," which foster change in relationships and organizations, illustrate how the national ambassadors from the disciplines have adapted their efforts to the cultures and values of various campuses. The events that launched successful collaborations on various campuses were quite different. At Howard University, the kick-off event was a formal plenary program, at which campus leaders highlighted the value of the scholarly examination of teaching and learning. At George Mason University, a program of national speakers was followed by several hours of working roundtable discussions among faculty and administrators. Finally, at Samford University, breakfast and luncheon meetings with selected administrative leaders marked a turning point for the valuing of the scholarship of teaching and learning. Though other campuses may require different types of events, all can benefit from a public connection on the campus between disciplinary work and institutional commitments.

One campus-based activity evolved directly from National Communication Association and American Sociological Association grant projects, funded by CASTL, in support of scholarship of teaching and learning activities. Interdisciplinary symposia on the scholarship of teaching and learning were convened on campuses. Typically, the symposia started with meetings of key campus administrators — college deans, faculty senate leaders, and teaching and learning center directors — addressing issues such as promotion and tenure policies and promoting hospitable campus climates for the scholarship and teaching and learning. Following these meetings, opportunities for interdisciplinary collaboration were explored in workshops focused on the meaning of the scholarship of teaching and learning and its importance to the academy and to the campus. Faculty and administrators engaged in discussions to determine how they could collaborate on their campus, tap into resources and support systems that were already in place (including other campus initiatives), and envision future needs.

The disciplinary societies for communication and sociology learned a great deal about successful campus collaboration. One important lesson we learned was that because representatives of academic associations and campus colleagues often differ significantly in how they think about and approach the scholarship of teaching and learning, collaboration has to be built on a new, common language. Moreover, because campuses can be vastly different, individual cultures, priorities, and values must be taken into account. The American Sociological Association and the National Communication Association have learned to be aware of not only the needs and goals of their disciplinary faculty but also the cultural norms and values of any given campus. Therefore, while the commitment of disciplinary devotees has been essential at the campus level, success in bringing national perspectives to an institution has been based on respectful interactions between the campus and scholarship of teaching and learning loyalists.

Contacts and URLs

Carla B. Howery
Deputy Executive Officer and Academic and
   Professional Affairs Program Director
American Sociological Association
howery@asanet.org

Sherwyn P. Morreale
Interim Director for External Affairs
National Communication Association
smorreale@natcom.org

For more information on the American Sociological Association's work on the scholarship of teaching and learning, see-
http://www.asanet.org/

For more information on the National Communication Association's website of resources, see
http://www.natcom.org/resources_links.htm
and for more information on Communication Education, see
http://www.natcom.org/pubs/CE/CE_des.htm

American Sociological Association
Washington, DC
13,000 members
http://www.asanet.org/

National Communication Association
Washington, DC
7,400 members
http://www.natcom.org/

Movement in the Scholarship of Teaching and Learning

Pat Hutchings
The Carnegie Foundation for the Advancement of Teaching

In educational reform circles, the word "movement" is often used casually or as a form of wish fulfillment, but as evidenced by this volume, the time has come when it seems to be the right word to describe the scholarship of teaching and learning. The individual campus reports assembled here constitute an impressive larger narrative, which, as described by the authors from Morehead State University, is about "institutions of higher education…orienteering their way back to their central mission: teaching and learning." While the details vary from campus to campus, the general contours of the shift are evident in accounts of new structures to support scholarly work on teaching and learning; policies that create incentives and rewards for such work; and lively, growing communities in which the pedagogical work of faculty is talked about, exchanged, and built upon. There has been, in short, a good deal of *movement,* and it is time — in the evolution of the scholarship of teaching and learning as a phenomenon and in this volume — to measure this movement, asking what has moved, how much, and in what directions. This conclusion offers three lenses for addressing these questions.

Individual Development

The first lens focuses on the experience of individual participants who become involved in the scholarship of teaching and learning. Their experience is often transformative, and as we see in the essays in this volume, when individuals are transformed, larger changes are likely to be unleashed.

More than a decade ago in *Change* magazine, Parker Palmer (1992) proposed that the improvement of teaching and learning calls for a "movement theory of change" (p. 10). His point was to emphasize the critical role of individual energies, passions, feelings of discontent, and purpose in changing the status quo. The stories in this volume are deliberately cast not as personal narratives but as reports about what campuses have done to support and advance the scholarship of teaching and learning. Still, between the lines of institutional reports we hear stories of individuals (including the authors of these reports) who became excited about this work and carried it forward for reasons that were often deeply personal. As one participant in the Carnegie/AAHE initiative stated in an earlier volume, "The wrong reason to do the scholarship of teaching is because it's now listed in the criteria for promotion and tenure." The right reason is to pursue "something that you really care about, something you're really interested in learning about, something that fascinates you" (Cerbin, p. 19).

In our rush to "systemic" reform and in acknowledging the importance of building the scholarship of teaching and learning into the sustaining economy and ecology of the campus — especially through the reward system — we should not overlook the transformative power of the scholarship of teaching and learning for individuals directly involved in the work. Be it in studying their own classes, collaborating with colleagues around crosscutting issues of teaching and learning, or helping to organize campus initiatives to support the work of others, faculty members are often reinvigorated in doing this work. As one faculty member at Maricopa Community College noted, the scholarship of teaching and learning is "a wonderful opportunity to become once again a learner, specifically to focus my learning on the topic of student learning."

This kind of personal engagement, though it may be difficult to scale up, is a powerful engine of change and "movement." Indeed, on many campuses, the scholarship of teaching and learning has taken hold because of the commitment of an initial, small group of activists whose energy and enthusiasm draw others in. At Middlesex Community College, for instance, it was a Carnegie Scholar and several colleagues who set things in motion, eventually creating a larger community of practice whose work continues to grow and evolve as "charter members now serve as mentors to the newer members." At The Citadel, activity began with a small group, which grew to include 25 percent of the fac-

ulty representing 13 of 15 academic departments. Involvement by students, as well, is often a powerful impetus for this kind of personal engagement by faculty. We see this evidenced through the seminar developed at Western Washington University.

In Carnegie and AAHE's own studies of how the scholarship of teaching and learning travels from site to site, we have been especially struck by the power of this kind of person-to-person impact. So many times, we have seen a scholar of teaching and learning move from an individual project to engagement with local colleagues or from leadership on campus to broader national leadership and involvement in initiatives undertaken through a scholarly society. The scholarship of teaching and learning is spinning webs of connection that have the potential to support changes at multiple levels.

The introduction to Section One captures this dynamic beautifully. "It is the people involved," Connie Cook writes, "both the leaders and those with whom they work, who ultimately shape a structure to fit an institution." To put the point a little differently, the scholarship of teaching and learning movement has progressed from the personal engagement of a small number of people to more structural manifestations that are noted throughout this

When individuals are transformed, larger changes are likely to be unleashed.

volume: promotion and tenure guidelines, new awards, revised policies for hiring, and resource allocation. In short, individual engagement is the necessary foundation for more systemic kinds of development and change.

Field Building

This brings us to a second lens for looking at the scholarship of teaching and learning: its development as a "field." The term, as it is used here, is not meant as a synonym for an academic discipline. Here, it signifies an arena, territory, or domain of action, and the various mechanisms that allow its work to go forward — for example, publication vehicles, national meetings, and professional organizations. Thus, in asking how the scholarship of teaching and learning movement has progressed, we can ask about the extent to which it has developed mechanisms for its own ongoing work and advancement.

Looking at the evidence in this volume, we see significant progress in this regard. Most notable, perhaps, are the number of lively communities — both formal and informal — that have formed around the scholarship of teaching and learning. Many campuses have established teaching academies or other structures that allow the local community to come together around significant questions about student learning. The Campus Clusters, to which some 90 campuses (including most represented in this volume) now belong, constitute broader multi-campus communities, typically organized around a theme (the first year experience) or an institutional type (research universities). There is even an International Society for the Scholarship of Teaching and Learning, housed at Indiana University Bloomington. These communities, large and small, on campus and beyond, national and international, create an essential condition for future work — a place for engaged individuals to find one another and be part of something larger. Importantly, these communities also allow for a shared language to develop.

A robust field also needs mechanisms to document and exchange its work, and again, it's possible to see progress. A number of campuses now sponsor journals (increasingly online) or have published special volumes featuring work done by local scholars of teaching and learning. Disciplinary and professional organizations have taken steps to support the exchange of work as well. The National Communication Association established a special section for the scholarship of teaching and learning in a long-standing disciplinary journal. The American Political Science Association recently established a new, special conference to bring together scholars whose work focuses on teaching. The American Sociological Association sponsored a special summer seminar to which faculty could apply.

These kinds of outlets are important in their own right, but they also serve as a context and a catalyst for a third element of field building — the development of shared standards for judging quality. Peer reviewed journals and other "scarce goods," such as awards (e.g., the University of Georgia System's Regents' Scholarship of Teaching and Learning Awards) force attention to issues of judgment and quality. As in other fields of work — be it the discipline of anthropology or the healthcare industry — questions of quality, of what is "good," will not be settled once and for all but must be the focus of ongoing deliberation and debate. Some of that debate has now begun around the scholarship of teaching and learning. Ethical standards for studying one's classroom, for instance, are a topic of discussion on many campuses (Hutchings, 2002), and faculty in some settings have worked with their colleagues and with Institutional Review Boards to develop guidelines appropriate to such work.

Knowledge Building

In his chapter on collaboration in the scholarship of teaching and learning, Darren Cambridge proposes that technology can play a key role in three ways, by "providing spaces through which to manage the transition from private to public, integrating multimedia for multivocal representations of practice, and offering tools for brokering knowledge." He thus underscores what for many will seem like the most important lens for examining the progress of the scholarship of teaching and learning movement — the generation of new knowledge. It is reasonable to ask, "What new knowledge has this movement produced?"

Again, the stories in this volume shed useful light. The University of Maryland reports on a project to make better use of digital images in history courses. At the University of Wyoming, an ambitious study of the climate for learning has resulted in a volume of essays entitled *Warming Up the Chill.* At Buffalo State College, data from interviews with faculty developing new approaches to diversity in the classroom "will inform the work of the [new] Buffalo State Equity and Diversity Council." The American Sociological Association, working with scholars of teaching and learning in that field, has undertaken a systematic review of "what we know and need to know about teaching and learning in sociology," creating a research agenda for future work.

This is not the place to try to capture the details

of any of these knowledge-building efforts, but the details are, in many ways, the point. The scholarship of teaching and learning is unlikely to result in neat bromides about what to do. As Craig Nelson has written, in the complex world of teaching and learning, "approximate and suggestive knowledge can be very helpful, and, indeed, may often be the only kind that is practical or possible" (2002, p. 1). Indeed, as a form of reflective practice, the scholarship of teaching and learning aims to preserve the particulars that, after all, largely define our classrooms. We don't teach students "in general" or a subject "in general." Rather, we teach *Moby Dick* to a group of English majors in a large lecture hall at a selective state university, or calculus to community college students preparing to transfer to a four-year engineering program. As Kenneth Eble observes in his 1988 classic study, *The Craft of Teaching,* "it is attention to particulars that brings any craft or art to a high degree of development" (p. 6). The scholarship of teaching and learning concentrates such attention and allows others to learn from it.

Knowledge about teaching and learning is not the only knowledge being built by this movement. What is apparent in many of the campus reports is a new vision of faculty development. This vision, as Nancy Randall from Malaspina University-College points out, is "not a deficit model" but rather builds on faculty's intellectual interest in what it means to understand their discipline or interdiscipline deeply and to bring novice learners to deeper understandings. "The potential suggested in using such discipline-based 'habits of mind' on questions in higher education rests at the center of the scholarship of teaching and learning," notes Jennifer Robinson, in her report from Indiana University Bloomington. Or, in the words of Tony Ciccone at the University of Wisconsin-Milwaukee, "The scholarship of teaching and learning perspective, which has challenged us to redefine the value of teaching improvement in terms of its effects on student learning, is gradually becoming the *lingua franca* of professional development."

At a CASTL gathering some time back, participants were discussing the progress of the scholarship of teaching and learning in their campus settings. There were plenty of success stories but also accounts of competing agendas, counter tensions, and back sliding. "On our campus," one participant noted, "the scholarship of teaching and learning has moved from a high visibility initiative to the back burner."

Ironically, one of my conclusions from reading the reports in this volume is that the back burner is perhaps not a bad place to be. If this work is to take permanent hold, it cannot be a stand-alone, add-on initiative. It must advance other work that the campus cares about. It must be built into the economy and ecology of the campus and faculty life.

There is, of course, a risk in this point of view. The risk is that the thing one cares about gets diluted and distorted as it is integrated into the larger culture. This, I take it, is what the Elon University essayists mean by "keeping falcons as falcons" — the challenge of institutionalizing the scholarship of teaching and learning and finding ways to make it broadly meaningful to the academic community, but also preserving its distinctive features and benefits. The scholarship of teaching and learning is not, after all, everything under the sun that's good for teaching. It is a particular set of habits, skills, and values that have not traditionally been present in most of academe — seeing teaching as substantive intellectual work, framing teaching problems as questions for system-

atic inquiry, seeking evidence about student learning, and sharing what is learned with others who can critique and build on the work. What the essays in this volume make clear is that these habits and values connect in powerful ways with broader interests, agendas, and needs in higher education today. It is these connections that help to create a movement.

This essay uses three lenses to examine the evolution of that movement thus far, but it seems appropriate to conclude by looking ahead as well. Several possible futures for the scholarship of teaching and learning present themselves.

First, the scholarship of teaching and learning might become a specialty within the disciplines, as it already is in fields such as chemistry and composition where there are long-standing, active communities of faculty doing research on classroom practice. This scenario has some distinct advantages. If this work is not for everyone, if it is indeed a specialty, it garners the much-needed prestige and reward that comes with scarce goods.

In a second scenario, the scholarship of teaching and learning evolves on the model of women's studies or area studies (Shulman, in press). Faculty interested in teaching and learning, who in their own department may be alone in that interest, find like-minded colleagues from other fields and come together to form a multidisciplinary center for the study of teaching and learning, joining forces, learning from one another, and building a domain of knowledge that eventually infuses their home disciplines.

It is possible to see movement in both of these directions in the reports in this volume. Both are important. But a third scenario strikes me as most promising *and* most consistent with the collection of essays included here. It is a scenario in which the scholarship of teaching and learning is infused into the ongoing work of the institution — not as a new requirement for promotion and tenure, a mechanism for accountability, or something that replaces other work, but as a new conception of teaching in which habits of reflection, inquiry, and exchange are built into the regular rhythms of campus life. This, I take it, is the truly "transformational" change that is described by Barbara Cambridge in the introduction to this volume. Getting there is a long-term proposition, but there's movement, certainly, in that direction.

References

Cerbin, W. (2000). Investigating student learning in a problem-based psychology course. In P. Hutchings (Ed.), *Opening lines: Approaches to the scholarship of teaching and learning* (pp. 11-22). Menlo Park, CA: The Carnegie Foundation for the Advancement of Teaching.

Eble, K. (1998). *The craft of teaching: A guide to mastering the professor's art* (2nd ed.). San Francisco: Jossey-Bass.

Milford, L., Nelson, J., & Kleinsasser, A. (Eds.). (2003). *Warming up the chill: Teaching against the structures.* Laramie, WY: University of Wyoming.

Nelson, C. E. (2000). How could I do scholarship of teaching & learning? Selected examples of several of the different genres of SOTL. [CD accompanying P. Hutchings (Ed.), *Opening lines: Approaches to the scholarship of teaching and learning,* Menlo Park, CA: The Carnegie Foundation for the Advancement of Teaching.]

Palmer, P. (1992, March/April). Divided no more: A movement approach to educational reform. *Change, 24,* 2: 10-17.

Shulman, L. S. (in press). Visions of the possible: Models for campus support of the scholarship of teaching and learning. In W. E. Becker & M. L. Andrews (Eds.), *The scholarship of teaching and learning: Contributions of research universities.* Bloomington, IN: Indiana University Press.

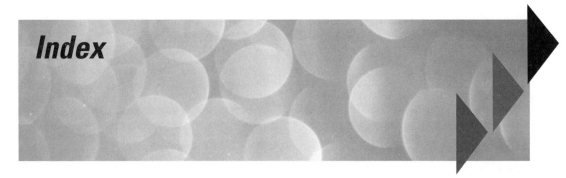

Index

Topics

Titles

Institutions, Organizations, and Initiatives

Other AAHE and Carnegie publications about
the scholarship of teaching and learning

Balancing Acts: The Scholarship of Teaching and Learning in Academic Careers

Four case studies feature scholars who have successfully integrated their scholarship of teaching and learning into academic careers: a chemist at the University of Michigan, a psychologist at the University of Nebraska, a mechanical engineer from Stanford University, and an American literature professor at Georgetown University. Mary Taylor Huber. American Association for Higher Education and The Carnegie Foundation for the Advancement of Teaching. 2004.

Disciplinary Styles in the Scholarship of Teaching and Learning

Scholars from ten disciplines describe the evolution of discourse about teaching and learning in their fields, the ways in which their discipline's style of discourse influences inquiry into teaching and learning, and the nature and role of intellectual exchange across disciplines around such inquiry. Mary Taylor Huber and Sherwyn P. Morreale. (Eds.) American Association for Higher Education and The Carnegie Foundation for the Advancement of Teaching with the National Communication Association. 2002.

Electronic Portfolios: Emerging Practices in Student, Faculty, and Institutional Learning

Chapters by 19 portfolio practitioners from a range of disciplines and institutions describe the generation of portfolios by students, faculty members, and institutions. The documentation of teaching and learning is central to electronic portfolios, a genre that offers a new way to share scholarly work. Barbara Cambridge (Ed.) American Association for Higher Education. 2001.

Ethics of Inquiry: Issues in the Scholarship of Teaching and Learning

Seven case studies by scholars of teaching and learning reflecting on ethical dimensions and dilemmas in their work. Topics include informed consent, the use of student work, impact on audiences and policy making, and response to campus and federal regulations on research with human subjects. Pat Hutchings (Ed.) The Carnegie Foundation for the Advancement of Teaching. 2002.

Opening Lines: Approaches to the Scholarship of Teaching and Learning.

Eight essays highlight the work of faculty members examining their teaching and their students' learning in ways that advance practice. Each case study documents a process of reflection and analysis, illustrating a wide range of methods for undertaking such work in different fields and diverse institutional contexts. Pat Hutchings (Ed.) The Carnegie Foundation for the Advancement of Teaching. 2000.

The Course Portfolio: How Faculty Can Examine Their Teaching to Advance Practice and Improve Student Learning

Nine case studies of faculty members who have developed course portfolios focus on purposes, processes, frustrations, and successes. The course portfolio is one of the new genres emerging as appropriate for generating, documenting, and assessing the scholarship of teaching and learning. A first essay by Lee Shulman and a list of additional resources begin and end the book. Pat Hutchings (Ed.) American Association for Higher Education. 1998.